Managing Corporate Culture, Innovation, and Intrapreneurship

Managing Corporate Culture, Innovation, and Intrapreneurship

HOWARD W. ODEN

QUORUM BOOKS
Westport, Connecticut • London

Library of Congress Cataloging-in-Publication Data

Oden, Howard W.
    Managing corporate culture, innovation, and intrapreneurship /
Howard W. Oden.
        p.   cm.
    Includes bibliographical references and index.
    ISBN 1–56720–047–8 (alk. paper)
    1. Corporate culture.   2. Organizational behavior.
    3. Organizational change.   4. Industrial productivity.
    5. Entrepreneurship.   6. Technological innovations—Management.
    I. Title.
    HD58.7.O324   1997
    658.4—dc21   96–54283

British Library Cataloguing in Publication Data is available.

Library of Congress Catalog Card Number: 96–54283
ISBN: 1–56720–047–8

First published in 1997

Quorum Books, 88 Post Road West, Westport, CT 06881
An imprint of Greenwood Publishing Group, Inc.

Printed in the United States of America

The paper used in this book complies with the
Permanent Paper Standard issued by the National
Information Standards Organization (Z39.48–1984).

10   9   8   7   6   5   4   3   2   1

Contents

Preface and Introduction

PURPOSE OF THE BOOK

American corporations can no longer compete in the global marketplace based on cheap labor and resources. To win in global competition they must develop new products (innovation) and new businesses (intrapreneurship) better and faster than their competition. This requires a special culture that is much different from the traditional culture of American businesses. To be most effective, these three essential elements for success (culture, innovation, and intrapreneurship) must be well matched and integrated. However, to date all three have not even been discussed in the same book, let alone integrated.

Intrapreneurship (developing new businesses from inside an existing corporation) cannot succeed without innovation (developing new products). Ninety percent of new businesses are based on new product development. Neither new product development nor new business development can be successful unless the company has the appropriate culture (values, beliefs, and management style). A book that discusses all three of these subjects in an integrated manner has been needed for a long time. It is the purpose of this book to fill this need.

CONTENTS OF THE BOOK

To achieve its purpose, this book will cover, in the following order, the development of corporate strategy and culture (Part I), the development of new products and businesses (Part II), and the extension of the corporate venturing process (Part III). What follows is a chapter-by-chapter synopsis of the book.

Chapter 1, ''Introducing the Corporate Innovation Process'': presents the fundamentals of the corporate innovation process, indicating that it is composed of two major parts: developing an innovative corporate culture and developing a corporate venturing (new product development/new business development) process. Corporate planning, both strategic and cultural, is needed to realize an effective corporate innovation process.

Part I: Developing an Innovative Corporate Culture

Part I covers those actions that a corporation must take to provide the proper environment for a successful corporate venturing process. The corporation must have an aggressive strategy, a culture that supports innovation and intrapreneurship, an organization and work force that will change as needed, and well structured and controlled processes, especially the venturing process.

Chapter 2, "Integrated Strategic Planning for Innovation": provides a detailed method for determining the nature and timing of new product developments. Since new product developments cannot be planned without also considering new market and new process developments, planning must be performed in an integrated manner.

Chapter 3, "Continuous Cultural Change and Improvement": provides the guidelines for organizing, planning, and implementing a culture needed to support innovation and intrapreneurship in the corporation. To provide assistance in a most difficult endeavor, the cultural implementation procedures are detailed and specific.

Chapter 4, "Changing Organizational Behavior and Structure": presents methods for changing the behavior of both managers and employees to support the innovative culture. The change in organization from the traditional organization to the learning organization is also described.

Chapter 5, "Reengineering Organizational and Venturing Processes": utilizes the concepts of reengineering to optimize all major organizational processes—and in particular the venturing process. The concept of integration, both in function and in time, is used extensively to optimize the venturing process.

Part II: The Corporate Venturing Process

The corporate venturing process is divided into three phases: *concept* development, *technical* development, and *business* development. In turn, the concept development phase is divided into two stages: idea generation and concept evaluation. The technical development phase is divided into three stages: preliminary design, prototype build and test, and final design and pilot production. The business development phase has only one stage: launching the new product.

The concept development phase is primarily concerned with the development and testing of product *ideas*—not hardware or even software. In the technical development phase, the hardware and software are developed, first as prototypes and then as final products. Business development is primarily concerned with ensuring the product is a success in the commercial world.

Chapter 6, "Idea Generation; Start Concept Development": shows the product development process starting with the generation of ideas for new products. Ideas are generated primarily through two processes: search and creative synthesis. Search sources and procedures are presented. Creative synthesis can be performed using a number of procedures. The most useful and popular are described, with detailed references to others.

Chapter 7, "Concept Evaluation; Finish Concept Development": reduces the number of ideas generated in the previous stage, before developing a more specific *product concept* for each idea retained. The product concepts are then tested by marketing, engineering, production, and others to determine whether they are viable or not. For the best product concept, justification for proceeding into technical development is prepared, consisting primarily of a business plan and a performance specification.

Chapter 8, "Start Technical Development; Preliminary Design and Review": The first action of technical development, if not already taken, is to form the venture team that will manage the venture through its entire life. The next step is to prepare the product design specification that will guide and coordinate all involved in the design. The product architecture (top-level design) follows. The preliminary design of the production process is also performed in this stage.

Chapter 9, "Prototype Build and Test; Final Design and Pilot Production": The next step is to build and test prototypes of the product and process. A number of different types of prototypes can and should be built and tested by engineering, marketing, and production. After successful test results, the final design of the product and production process is generated, and a pilot (limited) production of the final product using the final process is conducted.

Chapter 10, "Developing New Business: Launching the New Product": The new business development stage represents the high point to which every prior stage of the venturing process has been building—the full-scale market introduction of the new product. Before launching the product, the nature, scale, and timing of the launch must be determined. The pre-launch preparations by marketing, production, and engineering must also be completed. And finally, the organization and management procedures for launch must be determined.

Part III: Extensions of the Corporate Venturing Process

There are several vital concerns about the corporate venturing process that could not be readily included in Part II. These are: How can and should a company tailor the corporate venturing process to best fit its situation? How can and should a person behave in order to be successful in the corporate venturing process? These questions will be answered in Part III.

Chapter 11, "Customizing the Corporate Venturing Process": The corporate venturing process can and should be customized for differences in organization size, product type, and product development strategy. Information is provided to do this. Additionally, developing new services, which is considerably different from developing new goods, is discussed in detail.

Chapter 12, "Guidelines for Innovators and Intrapreneurs": provides the reader with information on how to win and prosper in the venturing process. Specific guidelines for interfacing with the parent organization, developing an intrapreneurial management style, and managing the venture team are provided. Also the intrapreneur must understand the sources of power, how to use it, and specific techniques for using power in the venturing process.

FEATURES OF THE BOOK

The following section gives a brief description of some of the features provided in the book to make it more useful.

Corporate Innovative Culture Emphasized

To win in global competition, American companies must develop new products (innovation) and new businesses (intrapreneurship) better and faster than their competition. This requires a new culture that is far different from the traditional culture of American business. The organizational culture will affect the number of new product ideas that are generated, the number of people with innovative and intrapreneurial talent who surface, and a host of other aspects that will determine the success (or failure) of any innovative effort. Creating the necessary culture is an important part of the innovative process, and we discuss it comprehensively, devoting one-third of our book to it.

The book does not dwell on generalities on how to develop an improved culture. Rather, it provides specific guidelines and procedures that can be easily followed. The four chapters of Part I go into this subject in detail and describe how strategic planning, cultural planning, organizational change, and process reengineering must be accomplished in parallel to achieve the innovative culture.

Extensive Integration of Corporate Innovation Process

Culture, Innovation, and Intrapreneurship Are Integrated

Intrapreneurship (developing new businesses from inside an existing corporation) cannot succeed without innovation (the development of new products). Most new businesses are based on new product development. Neither new product development nor new business development can be successful unless the company has the appropriate culture (values, beliefs, and management style). These three essential elements for success (culture, innovation, and intrapreneurship) must be well matched and integrated. There has been little effort to date to integrate these three essential features of a successful organization. This book discusses them extensively in an integrated manner.

Functional Integration

Various functional activities are involved in the venturing process, with (1) high-level management, (2) marketing, (3) engineering, and (4) production being the most involved. To ensure these functions are integrated, the book recommends that the appropriate functions be represented on an integrated venture team. These functional activities would then be performed by members of the venture team acting in an integrated fashion, with assistance from personnel in the functional department if necessary. It is neither intended nor desired that these activities be performed by a functional department operating independently. Additional integration methods are discussed in Chapter 5.

Optimized Corporate Venturing Process

Well-Structured Basic Process

We have structured the New Product/New Business Development Process into six natural stages corresponding to the six levels of product concept: (1) *idea* generation, (2) *concept* evaluation, (3) prototype *design*, (4) *prototype* build and test, (5) final *product* design and pilot production, and (6) *new business* development. Since these stages are defined by the levels of the product concept, they are easily recognized and understood. The basic structure is simple enough and obvious enough that it can be easily understood and remembered by all participants in the process.

Definitive Review at the End of Each Stage

At the end of each stage, high-level management must make a Go/No Go decision, with clearly defined requirements, before the development is allowed to proceed to the next stage. They do not allow the development to continue to the next stage until the necessary actions of the current stage have been satisfactorily completed. During the stage review process, high-level management will make the strategic-level product decisions, allocate resources to product development efforts, and provide direction and leadership to the venture team.

Flexibility to Meet Special Situations

Although there is a firm structure to our basic process, it has the ability to be flexible to meet the special requirements of the situation. Probably the most important flexibility concerns the ability to respond to the type of product development being pursued. Whether it is a good or service or whether it is a repositioned, improved, differentiated, diversified, or breakthrough product, the process can handle it. There must be sufficient flexibility within each stage to ensure we can respond to special situations effectively and efficiently. Actions required for special-type products and special situations are discussed in detail in Chapter 10.

Venture Team Composed of Core and Virtual Components

The *full* venture team is composed of two components: the *core* and the *virtual* venture team. The *core* venture team consists of three to ten members who are assigned *full-time* and make all venture decisions. The *virtual* venture team consists of an unlimited number of people who contribute to the venture on a *part-time* or *as-needed* basis. The core team is the permanent nucleus of the team, while the virtual team is the ever-changing outer layer.

Although virtual team members do not work full-time for the venture, they continuously report to and receive information from the venture and are made to feel they are definitely on the venture team. The virtual team provides an excellent mechanism to tap the expertise, information, and other resources of the parent organization and other activities.

Written in a Highly Readable and Practical Style

The book is written in highly readable and concise style. A lot of useful information is packed between the two covers. It is intended to be a hands-on, action-oriented, how-to guide for improving the output of the corporate venturing process—not a theoretical or technical treatise. Consequently, it is written in a very practical and nontechnical style so the practitioner can readily understand and use it.

A number of advanced techniques are incorporated directly into the corporate venturing process (Design for Manufacturability, Quality Function Deployment, product architecture, prototyping, perceptual mapping, and creative synthesis). To enable the reader to make the most use of these techniques, they are introduced and described where they are to be used. Where space is not available to completely describe the procedure, references are provided.

Chapter 1

Introducing the Corporate Innovation Process

Innovation has rapidly assumed a position of prominence in world competition. Today's marketplace is characterized by fast-paced and unremitting competition on a global scale. To compete in this environment, organizations need a level of innovation and intrapreneurship that was unheard of even a decade ago. As competition becomes more global and time-based, corporations must develop and deliver better new products in less time. The challenge for modern organizations is to revitalize themselves so they can successfully and continuously develop new products and new businesses. They must not only improve their procedures for new product and new business development, but must also improve their culture. It is not enough that a company have an effective innovation process; it must also have an innovative culture.

In this book, we will use the term **innovation** to mean the development of something new from its earliest beginning to it ultimate completion. **New product development** refers to the development of a *product*, either a good or service, from its initial idea until it becomes a commercial product available for public use. A **venture** is a product, market, or process development *project* that goes all the way from the initial idea to a commercial product, market, or process. A venture refers more to the development *project* than to the new product itself. The term is also more general in that it can refer to market and process development as well as product development. We will usually use "venture" in lieu of the more lengthy "new product development project." When we discuss the *venturing process* we are discussing the *development process* primarily for new products, but possibly for new markets and new processes as well. An **intrapreneur** is involved in the venturing process, that is, in developing a new business *inside* a corporation from its initial idea until it becomes a viable business. *Entre*preneurship differs from *intra*preneurship in that *entre*-

preneurship refers to a new business developed *outside* an existing business rather than *inside*. **Innovation** will be used as the more inclusive term that includes both **intrapreneurship**, **new product development**, and **venturing**.

The innovation process is extremely detailed and complex. If a company is going to be successful at innovation, it must have a model of the innovation process that everyone in the company knows and follows. In this way, the collective actions of everyone involved will be coordinated, even though the people involved may change with time. History indicates that one of the major causes of failure in new product developments is the lack of a valid model that everyone in the company can follow.

This book provides a time-tested, easy-to-follow model of the innovation process that organizations can use to become competent in new product development. The Corporate Innovation Process is made up of two processes: (1) the Innovative Culture Development Process and (2) the New Product Development (Venturing) Process. As we will learn, the Innovative Culture Development Process is a continuous process that never ends, whereas the Venturing process is a repetitive process that repeats for each new product. After defining the meaning of an innovative culture, we will provide an overview of its development in the first half of the chapter and then describe the development of the corporate venturing process in the second half of the chapter.

DEFINING AN INNOVATIVE CULTURE

For an enterprise to succeed in global competition, it must develop new products and new businesses in less time with higher quality than its competition. There is no question that the new product and new business development processes themselves must be highly effective and efficient. However, that alone will not ensure that a company's new products and new businesses will be competitive. The product and business development processes must be supported by an appropriate culture throughout the enterprise. A growing body of research indicates that the individual innovators and intrapreneurs must have an organization that supports, encourages, and fosters innovation for the company to succeed in the long run. In short, for an innovative company to succeed, it must have an innovative culture.

We do not take the position that innovation cannot occur without the proper culture. It has occurred in the past in an extremely hostile culture, and it will undoubtedly occur in such cultures in the future. However, the appropriate culture will enable innovations to occur faster and better. If all companies use the same product development procedures, the company with the better culture will win the competition. However, a company should not wait for its culture to be right before starting innovation. Not only might the wait be long, but a successfully completed innovation is one of the best actions for improving a company's innovative culture.

In the first half of the chapter, we will define an innovative culture, the culture a firm should have to excel at new product development. We will first look at corporate culture in general, then identify the characteristics of an innovative culture, and finally look at how an innovative culture is developed.

What Is Corporate Culture?

Every organization has its own culture. Organizational culture is similar to an individual's personality—an intangible, yet ever-present theme that provides meaning, direction, and the basis for action. Culture is the shared values, beliefs, expectations, and norms learned by becoming a part of and working in a company over time. Much as personality influences the behavior of an individual, shared values and beliefs within a company influence the pattern of activities, opinions, and actions within the firm. A company's culture influences how employees and managers approach problems, serve customers, deal with suppliers, react to competitors, and otherwise conduct activities now and in the future.

Corporate culture is an organization's basic values, beliefs, and assumptions about what the organization is all about, how its members should behave, and how it defines itself in relation to its external environment. A culture is an organization's reality; its culture shapes all that goes on within an organization. Culture represents the unwritten, informal norms that bind organization members together. A culture is reflected in an organization's philosophies, rules, norms, values, climate, symbols, heroes, and almost everything its member do. In summary, we will define **corporate culture** as *"the set of shared behaviors, artifacts, values, beliefs, and assumptions that a corporation develops as it learns to cope with the external and internal aspects of survival and success."*

We will define an *innovative culture* somewhat more practically and broadly. When we use the term innovative culture we are referring to the *total internal environment* that supports, or hinders, new product development throughout the total enterprise. An innovative culture includes anything and everything within the total internal environment of an organization that affects new product development. Success in new product development requires a supporting, innovative culture, one that strives for excellence and endeavors to win continuously by developing products and services that are unequaled in its marketplace.

Corporate culture can be pictured on two levels, as shown in Figure 1-1: the upper level is outwardly observable, but the lower level is hidden from view and resides in people's minds. The upper observable level includes observable phenomena such as artifacts, patterns of behavior, speech, formal laws, technical know-how, and the use and production of physical objects and products. The deeper, hidden level is located in the minds of the members of the organization. It includes the mental frameworks, ideas, beliefs, values, attitudes, assumptions, and ways of perceiving the environment. It contains the internal processes through which behavior is learned and the implicit (often unstated) rules through which behavior is governed.

These two levels of culture are easily distinguished, but nearly impossible to

Figure 1-1
Observable and Hidden Levels of Culture

OBSERVABLE LEVEL *Readily observable, but hard to interpret*	Behaviors and Artifacts	Includes anecdotes, art, ceremonies, heroes, habits, communications, jargon, language, management practices, myths, norms, physical arrangements, rituals, stories, symbols, and traditions
HIDDEN LEVEL *Not directly observable--can be inferred from how people justify what they do*	Values, Beliefs, and Assumptions	Includes assumptions, beliefs, cognitive processes, commitment, consensus, ethics, feelings, ideologies, mind-set, philosophy, principles, purpose, sentiments, thinking, understanding, values, vision, worldview

separate. In reality they are two parts of the same entity. The hidden level of culture usually can be inferred by observing the behavior of organizational members, especially those at the top. Each level reflects and reinforces the other. Each person inherently desires the two levels to be consistent and will instinctively modify his or her behavior and/or thoughts to make them consistent.

The hidden aspect of the culture is the substantive portion of the culture, the part that truly influences peoples' behavior. If managers focus only on the observable aspect of culture, they will not fully understand the human behavior they are trying to manage, which is controlled by employees' values and beliefs, the hidden aspect of culture.

Culture emerges in organizations because of the organization's need to deal with the **external** and **internal** aspects of survival and success. Organizations face options and influences as they face their customers, suppliers, regulators, and other entities in the external environment. To cope with the **external environment**, they must develop cultural solutions for adapting, including

- A sense of corporate purpose (mission)
- Corporate objectives and strategies for achieving the mission
- Lower-level objectives and strategies, focusing on product-market strategy
- Procedures for measuring and revising planned courses of action

To adapt to and integrate the **internal environment**, a firm must address the following issues:

- A sense of shared meaning (vision)
- Organization structure
- Developing and Managing Human Resources
- Designing and Managing Work Processes
- Continuously improving processes and people

In Chapters 2 through 5, we will discuss these aspects of an innovative culture in more detail.

What Is an Innovative Culture?

An answer to the simple question of "What is an innovative culture?" is neither simple nor short. In the following pages, we will try to give you an idea of the complexity and scope of an innovative culture by discussing some of its most significant characteristics.

1. Far-Sighted High-Level Strategic and Cultural Leadership. High-level leaders in innovative companies take the long-range view, looking down the road and striving to anticipate every contingency. They develop a mission and vision that are consistent, challenging, but realistic. They also develop strategic plans to achieve the mission and cultural plans to achieve the vision. Innovative leaders attract the voluntary commitment of followers to the company's mission and vision through example and assertive, convincing persuasion. Innovative high-level leaders take charge, make things happen, dream dreams, and then translate them into reality. They make decisions that serve long-term strategic and cultural purposes rather than making short-term politically expedient decisions.

2. Emphasis on Innovation, Intrapreneurship, and Achievement. The need to be innovative and the need to explore new approaches in the future are integral parts of the company's culture. All employees at all levels of the organization welcome new ideas and are extremely active in generating new approaches and new ways of doing things. There is a willingness to take risks and an eagerness to break new ground. People are hired for their creativity, talent, and diversity. Innovative people are held up as examples and appropriately recognized. Formal training sessions are used to help people free up their creative energies and become more innovative. The corporate growth plan includes a definition of the role of internally developed new products during the next five years.

3. Strong Customer Focus. Members of an innovative organization recognize that every company and every person are part of a long chain (actually many long chains) of customers and suppliers. Each company and person is a customer to its suppliers and a supplier to its customers. They understand both near-term and long-term customer needs and expectations and employ systematic processes for gathering customer needs and market information. They understand the linkages between the voice of the customer and marketing, design, and production. They measure customer satisfaction, compare the results relative to competitors, and use the information to evaluate and improve internal processes. Products are designed to satisfy the customer's needs rather than what the producer thinks they need or can best build.

4. Emphasis on Total Quality Management. In the innovative organization everyone—both managers and workers—are deeply involved in a continuous integrated effort to improve the quality of the firm's goods and services at every level. Continuously improving quality will maximize the customers' total satisfaction and minimize the firm's total costs. Total Quality Management is a total system approach that is an integral part of the firm's high-level strategy. It works horizontally across functions and departments, involving all employees, top to bottom, and extends backward and forward to include the supply chain and the customer chain.

5. *Flexible and Adaptable Organizations.* If hierarchy was central to traditional organization, the lack of hierarchy is central to the innovative organization. The innovative organization is much flatter, with fewer levels of managers. Most work will be horizontal (process) knowledge work performed by multidisciplinary teams. Rather than satisfying their immediate supervisor (vertical relationship), team members concentrate on satisfying the needs of the next person in the process (horizontal relationship). The composition and life of the project teams will be dynamic. Teams will be given considerable autonomy and will be expected to carry out the intent of the company's mission and vision. Networking will be used to hold the teams together and coordinate their actions. Project managers and network managers will replace most of the middle managers and functional staff in the traditional organization.

6. *High Levels of Collaboration, Teamwork, and Trust.* An act of collaboration is an act of shared innovation and/or shared discovery. It takes the collaborative efforts of people with different skills to create innovative solutions and innovative products. Current situations put a real premium on group processes, trust, and reaffirmation of what we believe. Companies succeed by tapping the talent and dedication of their people and by combining that talent and dedication in a team effort. The building of trust is emphasized. Politics, infighting, and departmental jealousies are minimized. Leaders work hard to earn their peoples' trust and to create conditions in which trust can flourish. There is widespread enthusiasm, a spirit of doing whatever it takes to achieve organizational success.

7. *Participative Management Style and Employee Empowerment.* Innovative organizations are taking the lead in implementing employee empowerment. Empowerment means giving power and is the natural extension of employee participation concepts such as quality circles and task teams. However, it is more than employee participation. It represents a high degree of involvement in which employees make decisions themselves and are responsible for their outcomes. The objective of empowerment is to tap the creative and intellectual energy of everybody in the company—not just those in the executive suite—and to provide everyone with the responsibility and resources to display real leadership within his/her own individual sphere of competence. The ultimate goal of empowerment is *self-management*, in which employees exercise complete responsibility and initiative, monitor their own work, and use managers and staff as teachers and facilitators.

8. *Emphasis on Human Resources.* In the current era, human resources—not financial and physical capital—are the organization's competitive edge, and innovative organizations maximize the output of highly educated workers. Human

resources management (HRM) evolves from a support function to a leadership function in the innovative organization. It develops policies and procedures to ensure that employees can perform multiple roles, improvise when necessary, and direct themselves toward continuous improvement of both product quality and customer service. HRM integrates human resource plans with the mission, vision, strategic plans, and cultural plans to fully address the needs and development of the entire work force.

9. *Continuous Learning, Change, and Improvement.* Everything, at all levels, at all times should be improving. People, processes, management practices, everything should improve continually; the best is never good enough. Everyone, including all managers and employees, takes responsibility for continuous improvement. To improve processes and systems, managers seek out root causes of problems. Performance improvement comes primarily from process and system improvement and not by improving people. Unending, proactive change is focused on broader systems. Both big breakthroughs and small increments of change are pursued.

10. *Effective Information, Communication, and Decision-Making Systems.* Survival in today's competitive business world makes the sharing of information throughout an innovative organization absolutely critical. A supply of accurate, consistent, and timely information across all functional areas facilitates a better organizational response to rapidly changing customer needs. Everyone is expected to "tell it like it is" and ask the questions necessary to find out how it is. Anyone who contributes an idea for a new product, service, or process can count on effective feedback about their idea that is accurate, specific, prompt, and appropriate. All ideas get a fair hearing by encouraging open creative discussions and preventing arbitrary interference, such as action being blocked by an employee's boss. Decisions are made at the lowest level at which the necessary information can be assembled.

11. *Emphasis on Process Management.* The purpose of process management is to manage those critical processes that cut across the whole enterprise, such as: new product development, quality, cost control, delivery, and the like. Process management involves aligning and coordinating all the operations necessary to deliver a product to a customer. The emphasis is on horizontal (cross-functional) systems and relationships rather than on vertical (hierarchical) systems and relationships. Management by process helps break down the functional (vertical) barriers that impede smooth-flowing collaborative work in the traditional organization. Processes are defined, owned and optimized—not negotiated across functional interfaces.

12. *Emphasis on Corporate Venturing Process.* There is one cross-functional process that is of especial interest to an innovative firm, the corporate venturing process. The corporate venturing process is organized into six natural stages corresponding to the six levels of product concept: (1) idea generation, (2) concept evaluation, (3) prototype design and review, (4) prototype build and test, (5) final product design and pilot production, and (6) new business development.

At the end of each stage, high-level management makes a Go/No Go decision, with clearly defined criteria, before the development is allowed to proceed to the next stage. The process is fully integrated across functions and across stages. There is a well-defined new product strategy in writing that identifies the strategic roles, screening criteria, and financial hurdles that new products must satisfy.

Who Needs an Innovative Culture? Why Is It Important?

With technological, geographic, and political barriers to business competition crumbling, there is now an enormously expanded buyer's market. Alvin and Heidi Toffler believe that all companies are faced with an "innovation imperative," which they describe as follows: "No existing market share is safe today, no product life indefinite. Not only in computers and clothing, but in everything from insurance policies to medical care to travel packages, competition tears away niches and whole chunks of established businesses with the weapon of innovation. Companies shrivel and die unless they can create an endless stream of new products."[1]

Developing an innovative culture is critical if innovation is to blossom within the organization. It's true that innovation can spring up in the most controlled environments, just as flowers can force their way through the cracks in a sidewalk. But for innovation to thrive, for it to be continuous and consistent, the organizational culture must encourage and nurture it.

Innovation is the product of *knowledge* (of customer needs, of market trends, of competitors' offerings, of distributors' concerns, of changing technologies) and *empowerment* (the combination of autonomy and responsibility). The culture in which innovation is most likely to flourish is one in which employees are encouraged to accumulate knowledge continually. It is a culture in which open communication is the norm, in which employees have easy and complete access to information. It is an environment in which all employees are empowered to act on their accumulated wisdom in order to generate continuous innovation.

It is clear that innovation blossoms in a favorable culture. When employees are given free access to information, when they are allowed and encouraged to enter into partnerships and learn with others inside and outside the organization, innovative ideas multiply. A company's most important innovations often spring from such partnerships—with other employees; with customers, suppliers, and distributors; even with the community in which the organization operates.

Company-to-company partnerships provide a sign of the interdependency that is developing as corporations move from the industrial to the modern society. The paradox of competing through cooperating is well illustrated by the 1991 announcement that archrivals IBM and Apple planned a joint venture to produce operating software compatible with the equipment of both companies.

DEVELOPING AN INNOVATIVE CULTURE

Need for Strategic and Cultural Planning for Innovation

If a company aspires to become an innovative organization, one of the first actions is to initiate long-range planning—both strategic and cultural. Becoming innovative is not something a firm can achieve on a short-term basis. Determining strategic and cultural goals, developing plans to achieve those goals, and implementing these plans comprise a long-term proposition that can be done well only with organized long-range planning.

Committing a company to the development of a specific product is an expensive commitment that should only be undertaken after extensive long-range planning. The new product will affect the operations of the company for some time to come; it is therefore prudent to perform the planning necessary to ensure the product decision was the right one.

The Need for Integrating Strategic and Cultural Planning

As noted in our definition of corporate culture, an organization's culture must enable it to deal with both the internal environment and the external environment. The internal aspects of culture are concerned with how the organization will operate internally and how members of the organization will deal with each other. They are normally spelled out in the *planned culture* (*vision, core values*, and *guiding principles*). The *external* aspects of an organization's culture expresses how it will operate with the elements in the external environment—competitors, customers, suppliers, and the like. The relationship of a firm with the elements in the external environment is primarily spelled out by the firm's *strategy* (*mission, strategic objectives*, and *strategic plans*).

If an organization is to be successful, these two important expressions of corporate guidance (strategy and planned culture) must be well matched and supportive (i.e., their development and implementation must be integrated). Normally the development of relations with the external environment (strategy) should come first. Although the organization lacks complete control over its internal environment (culture), it has even less control over the external environment (competitors, economy, technology, etc.). Therefore, the company must first adapt itself to the external environment by developing its strategy. Then it must develop a planned culture that is consistent with its strategy.

By understanding their organizations from a cultural viewpoint, high-level managers can and must strive to create a culture that facilitates rather than hinders achievement of the mission and strategic plans. The high-level managers' values, beliefs, and assumptions about how the organization should operate to adapt successfully to and serve the external environment form the basis for the development of the organization's culture. Employees, based on their experiences and understanding, adapt to the tone set by top managers. This inter-action between managers and employees, through time and learning, ultimately results in corporate culture.

Brief Description of Strategic Planning

To better understand how strategic planning and cultural planning can be better integrated, we need to understand better how each is performed. In the following paragraphs, we will give a very brief description of strategic planning that will be sufficient to compare it with cultural planning. A more complete description can be found in textbooks and professional books on strategic planning.

Outputs of Strategic Planning

In our discussion we will be primarily concerned with the three most impor-tant outputs of strategic planning: the organization's mission, strategic objec-tives, and strategic plans or strategies.

A **mission** states the basic purpose of the organization and its scope of op-erations. It specifies what a company intends to *do*, to *achieve*, in the *external* environment on a *one-time* basis. The mission statement should distinguish your business from others, making clear what is unique about what you do. It tells, from the customer's perspective, what you offer. It provides high-level guidance to coordinate the development and implementation of strategic plans outlining the long-range actions to be taken in the external environment. The mission is often written in terms of the general set of products and services the company provides and the markets and customers it serves.

Strategic Objectives are derived from the mission of the organization. They represent major milestones of the strategic plans in achieving the mission. These objectives are one-time goals that should be clear and measurable.

Strategic Plans or Strategies outline how strategic objectives will be achieved. Strategies can include positioning the firm for growth through new products or new markets, global expansion, technological innovation, quality performance, or cost-price leadership.

Process of Strategic Planning

As shown in Figure 1-2, the first step in strategic planning is to **Assess the Current Strategy** by examining the firm's strategic planning process, namely, the mission, strategic objectives, and strategic plans. Planners describe the cur-rent strategy and the strategy of the recent past and assess how successful they have been. Problems with current and past strategy will suggest changes for future strategy.

The second step is the **Internal Resource Analysis**, where the *strengths* and *weaknesses* of major functional areas within the organization are identified and

Figure 1-2
Strategic Planning Process

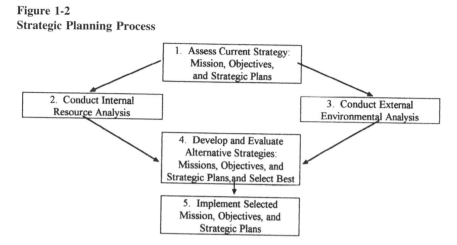

analyzed. The analysis provides strategic planners with an inventory of the organization skills and resources and its overall functional performance levels.

The third step is the **External Environmental Analysis** that begins with the analysis of the market and industry. Next, stakeholders are analyzed—particularly competitors, but also buyers, suppliers, owners and shareholders, government and regulatory agencies, and unions and employee groups. The environmental analysis should also examine other forces in the environment such as macroeconomic conditions and technological factors. The External Analysis provides planners with a number of *opportunities* they could pursue and a number of *threats* they must counter.

After conducting the Current Assessment, Internal Analysis, and External Analysis, strategic planners are ready for the fourth step to **Develop and Evaluate Alternative Strategies** for the future. Development of new strategies can be aided by conducting a **SWOT** (Strengths, Weaknesses, Opportunities, and Threats) analysis. A good strategy should match the company's strengths with opportunities in the environment while countering threats and weaknesses. Alternative strategies can be evaluated using the following criteria: (1) the strategy should exploit or create an advantage over the competition, (2) the strategy and its components should have consistent goal and policies, and (3) it should be capable of producing the intended results.

The most sophisticated and creative strategy will not benefit the organization unless the last step of **Implementation** is carried out effectively. Strategy implementation requires taking the appropriate action concerning a number of elements in the internal environment: organizational culture, organizational structure, leadership style, human resources, processes, and systems, particularly information and reward systems. Just as the strategy of the organization must be matched to elements of the external environment, it must also be matched to elements in the internal environment. Strategic planning and implementation is the subject of Chapter 2.

Brief Description of Cultural Planning

Outputs of Cultural Planning

A **vision** states what a company intends that its *internal* (cultural) environment should *be* or should *become* on a *continuing* basis. A vision is a picture of a preferred future state, a description of what the organization would be like some years from now. The vision provides an image of what the organization intends to be in the future, to provide the guidance for designing and managing the cultural changes that will be necessary to achieve those intentions. By providing a few broad concepts rather than a multitude of specific details, the vision can be easily remembered, allowing many levels of the organization to make decisions without the necessity of consulting with their superiors.

Core Values are the organization's essential and enduring tenets—a small set of general values—not to be compromised for financial gain or short-term expediency and not to be confused with specific cultural or operating practices, which are included in the guiding principles. Innovative companies tend to have only a few core values, usually between three and six. Indeed, we should expect this, for only a few values can be truly *core*—values so fundamental and deeply held that they will never change or be compromised.

Guiding Principles describe *how* the vision and core values will be achieved. They establish the professional standards for the work done inside the organization. They specify the relationship between people in the organization—on all levels. In short, they outline how all members of the organization will behave to achieve the core values, the vision, and the mission. The characteristics of an innovative culture discussed earlier in the chapter are examples of guiding principles that can be adopted.

Process of Cultural Planning

As shown in Figure 1-3, the first step in cultural planning is to identify and assess the current outputs of the firm's cultural planning, namely, the vision, core values, and guiding principles. Planners determine what the culture is now

Figure 1-3
Cultural Planning Process

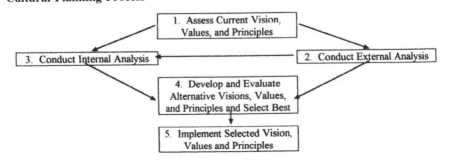

and what it has been in the recent past and assess how successful it has been. The best method for doing this is through a series of surveys.

The second step is the **External Analysis**, which primarily looks at the organization's strategy—its mission, strategic objectives, and strategic plans—to determine what type of organizational culture is required to support the organization's strategy. The strategy is presumed to be matched with the external environment. Certain parts of the *Strategic* External Environmental Analysis, such as the stakeholder analysis, may also be studied. It is not anticipated that a separate external environmental study will be conducted for cultural planning, since the primary external concern of cultural planners is to match the culture to the strategy.

The third step is the **Internal Analysis**, which compares the current culture with the culture that best supports the firm's strategy and determines how the major outputs of the organization (organizational structure, leadership style, human resources, processes, and systems, particularly information and reward systems) must change. It also assesses the organization's capability to make the required change. We need to determine the areas where the current culture is most divergent from the desired culture—these will be the focus of our implementation plans.

After conducting the Current Assessment, External Analysis, and Internal Analysis, cultural planners are ready for the fourth step, to **Develop and Evaluate Alternative Cultures**: Visions, Core Values, and Principles.

The most sophisticated and creative culture will not benefit the organization unless the last step of **Implementation** is carried out effectively. Implementing culture is even more difficult than implementing strategy. Culture implementation requires taking the appropriate action concerning a number of elements in the internal environment, namely, organizational structure, leadership style, human resources, processes, and systems, particularly information and reward systems. Detailed culture development and implementation is the subject of Chapter 3.

Relationship between Strategic Planning and Cultural Planning

We will discuss the relationship between strategic and cultural planning by first comparing the primary outputs from each (the mission and the vision) and then comparing the two planning processes.

Comparison of the Strategic and Cultural Planning Outputs

Before we compare the mission and vision, let us take another look at our definitions. As the reader is aware, there are almost as many definitions of mission and vision as there are authors writing about them. We're not saying that our definitions are necessarily the right ones, but only that they are the definitions that we will use here and throughout the book. Our definition of vision is somewhat different from most definitions, so we will go into considerable detail to make it clear.

A **mission** states what a company intends to *do*, to *achieve*, in the *external* environment on a *one-time* basis. The mission statement should distinguish your business from others, making clear what is unique about what you do. It tells, from the customer's perspective, what you offer. The mission statement is the guide for what strategic actions should be taken by the organization. The purpose of the mission is to provide a top-level long-range goal to coordinate the development and implementation of strategic plans, which outline long-range actions to be taken in the external environment.

A **vision** states what a company intends that its *internal* (cultural) environment should *be* or should *become* on a *continuing* basis. The vision is an enduring but living statement that provides firm cultural guidance, but can be modified if the environment changes. To coordinate the development and implementation of cultural plans, the vision provides an image of what the organization intends to be in the future. Visions themselves tend to be surprisingly simple. By providing a few broad concepts rather than a multitude of precise details, the vision becomes a memory tool allowing many levels of the organization to make decisions without the necessity of consulting with their superiors.

The vision plays a critical role in motivation. When the organization provides a clear sense of meaning that is widely shared and acceptable to its members, individuals can then find satisfying roles both in the organization and in society at large. Not only is a vision an idea or an image of a more desirable future for the organization, but the right vision is an idea so energizing that it in effect jump-starts the future by calling forth the skills, talents, and resources to make it happen. The vision is a signpost pointing the way for all who need to understand what the organization is and what it intends to be.

The mission and the vision should definitely be consistent and supportive, but they will not be exactly alike, since they serve two different purposes. A vision is really a dream created in our waking hours of how we would like the organization to be. It differs from a mission statement in that a mission statement is a statement of what business we are in and how we intend to succeed in that business. The mission statement names the game we are going to play. A vision is more a philosophy about how we are going to play the game. Mission statements tend to be longer, with more technical details, than vision statements. Vision statements should be simple enough and short enough that they can be easily understood and remembered by all hands in order to provide the motivating force that is needed.

Normally the mission should be developed first, with the vision of what the organization should be like to achieve the mission being developed second. Many organizations have experimented with developing an image of the future—their vision—without referring to their mission. What tends to happen is that the image becomes impractical when it is not grounded in the specific mission of the organization. Because the mission statement is directly linked to a broad analysis of the customers and environment, it makes sense to base the vision on the mission. It is extremely important that the organization's mission and vision be consistent and mutually supportive.

A comparison of the mission and vision in terms of purpose, use, emphasis, focus, nature, and time dependence is shown in Figure 1-4.

Comparison of the Strategic and Cultural Planning Processes

As can be seen from Figure 1-2 and 1-3, the processes for strategic and cultural planning are very similar. Both start with an assessment of current strategy (or culture). Following the assessment, both perform an internal and external analysis before developing and evaluating alternative strategies (or cultures). As described above, the content of the internal and the external analyses are quite different, even though the processes by which they are conducted are similar. Normally the cultural planning process trails the strategic planning process somewhat, since one of the inputs to the external cultural analysis is made up of the organization's mission, strategic objectives, and strategic plans—the outputs of the strategic planning process.

Figure 1-4
Comparison of Mission and Vision

Characteristic	Mission	Vision
Purpose	States what the company intends to *do*, intends to *achieve*.	States what the company intends to *be* like, intends to *become*.
Use	Guide the development and implementation of **strategic** plans.	Guide the development and implementation of **cultural** plans.
Emphasis	On what the company is *to do*, *in the external environment, on a one-time basis*.	On what the company is *to be*, in the *internal environment, on a continuing basis*.
Focus	On customers, products, competitors, and other elements of the *External* Environment.	On people, principles, values, beliefs, and other elements of the *Internal* Environment.
Nature	Highly specific, detailed, and measurable, so that execution of strategic plans can be accurately assessed.	Very short, simple, and vivid, so that *everyone* can understand, remember, and visualize it for motivational purposes.
Time Sequence and Dependence	The mission should be developed first, since it relates the company to the external environment, over which the company has little control.	The vision should be based upon and should support the mission. It should be developed to help accomplish the mission.

Integrating Strategic Planning and Cultural Planning

The interplay between the organizational culture and the organizational strategy is of great importance. Indeed, culture and strategy support, complement, and reinforce each other like a husband and wife. An innovative company does not seek a mere balance between the culture and strategy; it seeks to develop both to their highest level at the same time, all the time.

The organizational culture supports organizational strategy by providing a base of continuity around which an innovative company can evolve, experiment, and change. By being clear about what is core in values and beliefs (and therefore relatively fixed), a company can more easily seek strategic change and movement in all that is not core. The strategy supports the culture, for without continual change and forward movement, the company—the carrier of the core—will fall behind in an ever-changing world and cease to be strong or perhaps even to exist.

The Innovative Culture Development Process

Integrated strategic planning and cultural planning, as discussed above, comprise the two major stages of the innovative culture development process. However, strategic and cultural planning will not be effective without organizational planning and process reengineering. An innovative culture cannot be implemented unless there are appropriate changes in organizational behavior and structure. In a similar fashion, an organization cannot optimally achieve its strategy without streamlining or reengineering its major processes.

Thus, the innovative culture development portion of the corporate innovation process contains all four of these stages, as shown in Figure 1-5. Although discussed in four separate chapters of Part I, these stages of an organization's culture development are closely related. The strategic planning, cultural planning, organizing, and reengineering efforts must be properly aligned with each other and with the effort to develop new products and new businesses, if the organization is to be successful. They must be implemented in parallel, not in series.

Figure 1-5
Innovative Culture Development Process

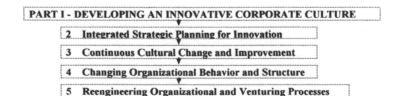

PART I - DEVELOPING AN INNOVATIVE CORPORATE CULTURE

2   Integrated Strategic Planning for Innovation

3   Continuous Cultural Change and Improvement

4   Changing Organizational Behavior and Structure

5   Reengineering Organizational and Venturing Processes

DEVELOPING THE CORPORATE VENTURING PROCESS

What *Is* a Product?

As the first step in developing the corporate venturing process, we will define what we mean by a product and a new product. Products are the building blocks of a company's offering in the marketplace. A **product** is an individual unit offered for sale as either a good or service. Examples of products are a Ford Taurus and an insurance policy. We all know what a product is, but the definition of a product is much more complex than it first appears. A product is not just its physical characteristics, attributes, or ingredients. It has a much more complex meaning, which can be understood by referring to the illustration of the product concept in Figure 1-6.

The **product concept** includes the supporting **tangible benefits (goods)** and **intangible benefits (services)** as well as the **core benefit**, which may be either a good or a service. The core benefit is delivered to customers supported by the two surrounding layers of tangible (goods) and intangible (service) benefits. All three of these benefits make up the product concept. Many refer to the core benefit as the product and refer to the total product concept as the **product bundle** or **commercial product**, since all benefits are needed to make a product commercially viable. The term *product* covers both services and goods. Whether a product is considered a service or a good depends on the tangible elements' share of its total value. If less than half the total value is made up of tangible elements, it is called a **service**. If more than half the product's value is provided

Figure 1-6
Product Concept

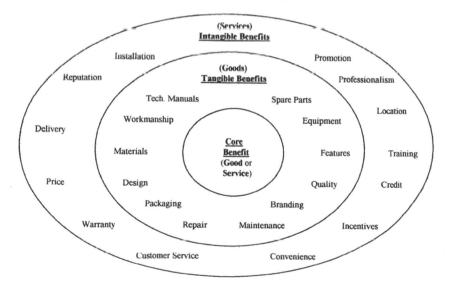

Commercial Product. The commercial product includes not only the actual core product, but also all the supporting services and goods needed to make the product concept commercially viable, as shown in Figure 1-6. In particular, it includes the necessary marketing programs (pricing, promotion, and distribution) to bring the product to the attention and use of buyers. It also includes technical services needed to assist buyers in making the buying decision and installing after buying. Very often, operating instructions and manuals must be prepared for the buyer's use. Thus, instead of simply providing a product, a firm must provide a *commercial product bundle* that includes a mixture of services and physical items in addition to the main product.

Stages of the New Product Development Process

The *stage* of the new product development *process* describes the actions by which the *product* concept is moved from one *level* to the next. When the *product* concept has advanced so that it is ready to go to the next *level*, that is the signal for the new product development *process* to proceed to the next *stage*. This relationship is summarized in Figure 1-7. For clarity, we will use "level" when referring to the refinements of the *product* concept, and we will use "stage" when referring to the steps in the new product development *process*.

Idea Generation. The purpose of this stage is to generate a large number of new product ideas that will be evaluated in the next stage of Concept Evaluation. New product ideas can be generated through both search and creative synthesis approaches. To enable an effective search for new product ideas, we will first identify the best sources and then describe the optimum procedures for searching. We also investigate generating new product ideas through creative synthesis using general, need-based, and technology-based techniques. Under general procedures, we will discuss brainstorming, checklists, and focus groups. Under need-based procedures, we will cover problem analysis, scenario analysis, and perceptual map analysis. Under technology-based procedures, we will discuss applied research and product improvement.

Figure 1-7
Relationship between Levels and Stages in Product Development

Level of Product Concept	*Stage of Product Development*
Idea	Idea Generation
Concept	Concept Evaluation
Design	Preliminary Design
Prototype	Prototype Build and Test
Product	Final Design and Pilot Production
Commercial Product	New Business Development

Concept Evaluation. The ideas generated in the previous stage must first be reduced to a number that the firm can feasibly pursue through concept evaluation. We will use rough screening techniques to reduce the quantity of ideas to a number suitable for detailed analysis. We then develop each of the retained ideas into concepts that are detailed enough they can be evaluated by prospective customers, marketing, engineering, and operations personnel. The detailed concept analysis may include such tests as need and market analysis, economic viability analysis, technical feasibility analysis, and organizational fit test. If the decision is to go ahead into technical evaluation, the team involved should write a **performance specification** for the new product, for example, what the product should do for the customer. Additionally, a **venture plan** is normally prepared to provide high-level management with the information needed to decide whether to go into technical development or not.

Preliminary Design. The first action of this stage, if not already done, is to form the venture team that will manage the venture through its entire life. The next step is to prepare the product design specification, based on the performance specification from the previous stage, that will guide and coordinate the entire design effort. The product architecture (top-level design) follows. Basic but critical tradeoffs (e.g., reliability versus cost) are considered and made at this stage. The preliminary design of the production process is also performed in this stage. The primary outputs of this stage are product and process designs in sufficient detail to build prototypes and with enough supporting analysis to convince decision makers that the optimum designs have been selected.

Prototype Build and Test. With the design completed, the next step is to build and test prototypes of the product. A prototype is model or simplified representation of the actual product. For simple products, a clay or wooden model may be adequate to test appearance, and a simple model may be sufficient to test technical performance and customers' reactions and tastes. In more sophisticated products, the prototype is the first version of the actual product that is subjected to a full range of engineering and operational tests by company personnel and prospective buyers. The prototype design, build, and test sequence may be repeated several times if the prototype is very complex or if it fails its tests.

Final Design and Pilot Production. Based on the results of the prototype tests and other valid inputs, final product and process designs are developed with full drawings, specifications, procedures, policies, and other information needed for production. If the changes to the prototype design are extensive, a new prototype may be constructed and tested. With the final design of the product and production process completed, a pilot (limited) production of the final product on the final process is conducted that may be test marketed before launching the product.

New Business Development. The new business development stage represents the high point to which every prior stage of the venturing process has been building—the full-scale market introduction of the new product. Selecting and implementing the optimum introductory marketing program is extremely important and represents the principal task of marketing during this stage. Although manufacturing has been involved in the technical development process from early on, it is during this stage that they really come under the gun to ramp-up production to meet demand. Because of limited capacity, the New Business Development stage may be divided into an initial regional introduction, followed by a nationwide rollout as capacity expands. Although this stage constitutes the culmination of the New Product/New Business Development process, it also marks the beginning or introductory phase of the product's life cycle.

Relating Stages of Product Development to Levels of Product Concept

As can be seen from Figure 1-7, there is a direct relationship between the levels of product concept and the stage of product development. The stage of product development must be appropriately completed for the product concept to proceed to the next level. For example, the idea generation stage must be completed for the product concept to advance from the idea level to the concept level.

Extensions of the Corporate Venturing Process

There are several vital concerns about the product venturing process that could not be readily included in the preceding description. These are: How can and should a company tailor the corporate venturing process to best fit its situation? How can and should a person behave in order to be successful in the corporate venturing process? Answers to these concerns are included in the last two chapters to complete the corporate innovation process.

Chapter 11, "Customizing the Corporate Venturing Process": In order to describe the new product development process in depth and still be concise, we have described the process for one situation only. Specifically, we describe the process for a medium-sized (about 1000 employees) high-tech (e.g., computers) company following a revolutionary product strategy (specifically, a diversified product). The product venturing process can and should be customized for differences in organization size, product type, and product development strategy. Additionally, developing new services is considerably different from developing new goods; this subject is discussed in detail. In Chapter 11 we discuss how the new product development process can be customized to take advantage of the firm's situation in these four areas of interest:

Chapter 12, "Guidelines for Innovators and Intrapreneurs": provides the reader with information for interfacing with the parent organization, developing an intrapreneurial management style, and managing the venture team. Also, the reader is given an understanding of the sources of power, how to use power, and specific techniques for using power in the venturing process. This chapter is designed to help intrapreneurs achieve success in a corporate venturing environment. It shows what they can do to minimize organizational and professional risks and to maximize both the performance of their ventures and their own career development. The probability of venturing success can be improved by understanding and following several principles discussed in this chapter.

THE CORPORATE INNOVATION PROCESS

By combining the four stages of the Innovative Culture Development Process with the seven stages of the corporate venturing process and the two extension areas of the venturing process, we obtain the overall guide for the Corporate Innovation Process shown in Figure 1-8. We will use this top-level guide throughout the book.

NOTE

1. Alvin Toffler and Heidi Toffler, *Powershift* (Bantam Books, 1990), p. 213.

Figure 1-8
The Corporate Innovation Process

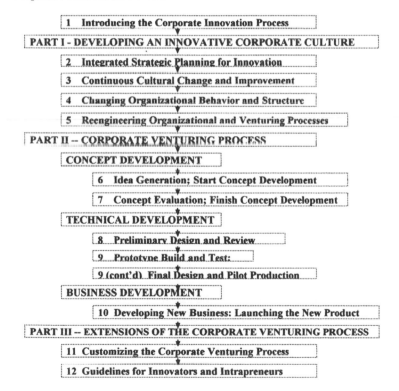

Part I

Developing an Innovative Corporate Culture

Part I covers those actions that a corporation must take in order to provide the proper environment for a successful corporate venturing process. The corporation must have a strong aggressive strategy, a culture that supports innovation and intrapreneurship, an organization and work force that will change as needed, and well structured and managed processes, especially the venturing process.

Chapter 2

Integrated Strategic Planning for Innovation

In this chapter we provide a detailed method for determining the nature and timing of new product developments. Since new product developments can not be planned without also considering new market and new process developments, strategic planning must be performed in an integrated manner.

ROLE OF HIGH-LEVEL LEADERSHIP IN STRATEGIC PLANNING

When we speak of high-level leadership or high-level management, we are referring to the executives at the top of an enterprise, including the president or general manager as well as the heads of major functions (marketing, operations, engineering, finance, human resources, etc.) and other people reporting directly to the president. In the traditional company of the past, leaders primarily exercised command authority. Managers were technical experts who defined the jobs of their employees. In many cases, they literally wrote out job descriptions for them. In doing so, these managers asked their employees to park their brains at the door. Most of the time, the employees had no idea how their efforts fit into the bigger picture.

The innovative company and the role of the leader in it are dramatically different. Innovative leaders' success will hinge largely on their ability first to plan and then to empower other people to implement the plans. An innovative organization must be led by a leader who develops and aligns the organization with the mission and vision, develops and maintains trust, ensures that coordinating and communicating occur, and encourages creativity and learning. What truly makes an organization innovative and keeps it that way, though, is *innovative intent*. Only the leader can infuse the organization with this intent and keep it burning brightly no matter what the circumstances.

While formulating and implementing strategy is very much a high-level manager's responsibility, the task of generating fresh ideas, identifying new opportunities, and being responsive to changing conditions in order to achieve that strategy is even more important in an innovative organization. It is an organization-wide task that must be aggressively led by the high-level leaders. One of the toughest parts of exerting strategic leadership is generating a dependable supply of fresh ideas and promoting an entrepreneurial, opportunistic spirit that permits continuous adaptation to changing conditions. The leader must take special pains to foster, nourish, and support people who are willing to champion new ideas, better services, and new products and product applications.

FOUNDATIONS OF VENTURE STRATEGIC PLANNING

In discussing strategic planning for innovation we will be referring many times to new *product* development projects, new *market* development projects, and new *production process* development projects. For conciseness, we will refer to all these development projects as ventures. *We define a* **venture** *as a product, market, or process development project that goes all the way from an abstract idea to a commercial product, market, or process.* When we discuss the *venturing process* we are discussing the *development process* for new products, new markets, and new production systems.

Many of today's most successful organizations continue to survive because many years ago they offered the right product at the right time. Most product, market, and process venture decisions of the past were made without the benefit of strategic thinking or planning. However, present-day managers increasingly recognize that venture decisions must be made in the context of a venture strategy. As they find themselves in ever more complex and turbulent environments, their past internally oriented, reactive approach to decision making is giving way to an externally oriented proactive approach that requires more analysis. They must analyze both the internal and external environments in a well-defined strategic framework to develop a corporate strategy and a venture strategy. This long-range, strategic, and proactive orientation to decision making is an important element of the innovative culture.

Without an effective understanding of venture opportunities at the strategic level, a company is forced to make decisions on new ventures without seeing the entire spectrum of new opportunities. The ventures they select typically have too many or the wrong features, instead of being competitively positioned. Without the context that a venture strategy provides, development takes place one venture at a time rather than as a coordinated strategy, and the result is a patchwork of individual ventures rather than an integrated array of ventures.

Need for Integrated Strategic Venture Planning

Although this book is primarily devoted to product development, we can not intelligently discuss product development ventures without also considering market and process ventures. This is particularly true at the strategic planning level. What we do in one type of venture significantly affects the other venture types. Venture strategic planning is the beginning of all development effort, and it is particularly important that our efforts be integrated at this level. Thus we are advocating the development of an integrated venture strategy where the plans and resources of marketing, engineering, and production are tied together in a single integrated plan.

Basics of Strategic Planning for Ventures

In conducting our venture strategic planning, we will endeavor to answer, and answer very specifically, three basic questions. *What* do we plan to develop? *How* do we plan to develop it? *When* do we plan to develop it? The *what* question asks, what will our area of focus be? Product? Market? Process? All three? or two of the three? In answering the *how* question we must decide what *type* of development venture we intend to conduct. We will find that one approach to development will not fit all situations. We need to tailor our development approach to the situation at hand.

Flowing generalities in response to these questions are not much help to people on the front line. They need to know exactly what products we want to develop, what markets we are going to sell these products in, and what specific production processes are going to make them. We have developed a method whereby these very important questions can be answered with very specific answers. We will first describe some possible types of development ventures, before outlining the approach that will enable us to organize the many facets of venture strategy.

Possible Types of Development Ventures

In order to better understand the venture strategic planning process, we need to understand the various *types* of ventures that could be undertaken as a result of our planning. Listed in Figure 2-1 are the various types of ventures that can be undertaken for *products*, *markets*, and *processes*. Not all of these will be useful for your firm. Later in this chapter, we discuss how a company determines which ventures are most suitable for them. The three-letter abbreviation after each type will be used later in preparing the Integrated Venture Map.

The venture strategies are arranged in increasing order of difficulty, with the more basic strategies first. They are also categorized as *evolutionary* or *revolutionary*. The revolutionary strategies require considerably more effort, more risk taking, and a greater outlay of commitment and capital than do the evolutionary strategies. For example, in the most advanced evolutionary product strategy, *imitation*, the firm waits until a competitor successfully markets a product before entering the market with an imitation. In the simplest revolutionary strategy, *differentiation*, the firm aggressively takes action to develop and market a

Figure 2-1
Types of Venture Strategies

Product	Market	Process
	Evolutionary	
Cost Reduction (COST)	Penetration (PEN)	Cost Reduction (COST)
Repositioning (POS)	Enlargement (ENL)	Enlargement (ENL)
Modification (MOD)	Modification (MOD)	Modification (MOD)
Consolidation (CON)	Consolidation (CON)	Consolidation (CON)
Imitation (IMI)		
	Revolutionary	
Differentiation (DIFF)	Segmentation (SEG)	Focused (FOC)
Diversification (DIV)	Completely New (NEW)	Completely New (NEW)
Breakthrough (BRK)	Platform (PLAT)	Platform (PLAT)
Platform (PLAT)		

differentiated product to capture a specific market niche ahead of the competition.

Description of Venture Strategies

We will describe each of the venture strategies of Figure 2-1 in each area (products, markets, and processes), starting with the easiest in the *evolutionary* category and ending with the most difficult in the *revolutionary* category. We will provide the following basic information in each short description:

- Purpose of the venture strategy
- Nature of the venture strategy
- Situation for which this type of venture strategy is appropriate
- How does this development venture strategy affect other areas
- Does this venture strategy increase or decrease the number of products, product families, markets, or processes
- What developments should be conducted in parallel with this venture strategy
- Nature of the venture team conducting the venture strategy
- An example of the venture strategy

Evolutionary Product Venture Strategies

Product Cost Reduction (COST). This venture is undertaken on an existing product. There is no intent to change the performance of the product—only its cost. Very often a technique known as *value engineering* is used. Value engineering endeavors to reduce the cost of a product without changing its performance, by using less expensive materials, using fewer parts, making it easier to fabricate and assemble, and employing other cost reduction techniques. A product cost reduction venture is often scheduled for a product during the mature phase of its life cycle, when it is facing fierce cost competition from its competitors. Very often, a *process* cost reduction venture is initiated in parallel with a product cost reduction.

Product Repositioning (POS). These are existing products that are retargeted for a different market. These products are not new to the developer, but they are new to the customer. There is essentially no technical change to the product and only minor changes in branding, packaging, and the like. Most of the development effort involves developing new marketing programs for the new market. A marketing development effort should be scheduled concurrently with the product repositioning. The classic example of this type of new product is Arm & Hammer baking soda, which was repositioned several times as drain deodorant, refrigerator deodorant, and the like.

Product Modification (MOD). A product modification involves altering one or more features of an existing product. The existing product is then discontinued, and the altered product is marketed in its place. In a product modification, both the number of products and the number of product families remain unchanged. Examples are annual changes in existing automobile models and changes in a cereal to reduce fat. A product modification does not represent a high degree of newness for either the developer or the customer. The development is relatively simple and straightforward. The developer is simply making a modification to an existing product. The customers will use the altered product in essentially the same manner as they used the old product.

Product Consolidation (CON). In product consolidation, we endeavor to develop one product that will replace two or more existing products. The primary purpose in consolidation is to develop a product that can be produced more efficiently and effectively. Very often, a firm that is starting to compete on a cost basis in a broad market will turn to consolidation to achieve a competitive advantage. Product consolidation is often used in conjunction with market consolidation during corporate retrenchment or the latter phases of a product's life cycle, when competition on price becomes paramount.

Product Imitation (IMI). A product imitation is based on quickly copying another firm's product before the originator can achieve success and dominate the market. This imitator or "me too" effort is common practice in the fashion and design industries for clothes, furniture, and small appliances. Product imitation requires primarily a good capability in *reverse engineering*, where the imitating firm dismantles and analyzes the originator's product and designs one slightly different, and hopefully better, that does not violate patent law. For example, once Cuisinart demonstrated that a market existed for expensive food processors, many of the major appliance companies followed with product that imitated Cuisinart.

Revolutionary Product Venture Strategies

Product Differentiation (DIFF). Product Differentiation involves developing a new product that is sufficiently different from its parent that both models are retained in the product family. Differentiation extends existing product families by offering additional versions of the basic product concept. In product differentiation, the number of products increases, but the number of product families remain unchanged. The differentiated product would represent a fair degree of newness for both the developer and the customer. In product differentiation the development would be somewhat complex since the developer is creating a whole new product, but the development would still be in the area of the firm's technical and marketing expertise. In most cases, it is performed by a venture team. Product differentiation is often undertaken in parallel with market segmentation to provide new products especially tailored to each new market segment. Examples include new automobile models, such as the Ford Mustang, the Ford Taurus, and the Chrysler minivans.

Product Diversification (DIV). Product Diversification involves developing a product so different from existing products that a new product *family* is created. Very often this new product family is sold in a completely different market and produced by a completely new production process. The diversified product is not necessarily new to the customers or the world, but it is completely new to the developing firm and involves both a product development and a market development. Diversification increases both the number of products and the number of product families. Examples are an auto manufacturer developing a farm tractor and a cereal manufacturer developing a new soft drink. Not only are these products considerably different, but their markets are different also. A product diversification would require a very complex development effort since the development is outside the company's area of engineering and marketing expertise. It would most definitely be handled by a venture team. In most cases the venture team would be composed of highly qualified people, and the venture would have a lot of visibility.

Product Breakthrough (BRK). Product breakthroughs are inventions that are completely new to the whole world. Examples are the steam engine, first automobile, radio, television, personal computers, and the like. A product breakthrough increases both the number of products and the number of product families. Developing a breakthrough product has all the complexities of diversified products, with a few new ones. Since the product breakthrough is new to the world, both the developer and the customers are completely unfamiliar with the product. The developer must not only perform the normal development, but must also determine how the customer can use the product and convey this information to the customer in a non-intimidating manner. The development of a breakthrough product would most definitely be handled by a highly qualified and highly visible venture team.

Platform Product (PLAT). Platform products provide the base for a new product family or even a new product line. The technology developed for a platform product can be applied to many future products over a long time period. Although a platform product may not be as radically different as a breakthrough product, it is usually more important and more profitable since it acts as the progenitor for a whole new family or families of products. A platform product is more than just a single product; the technology used to develop the platform product is usually much more important than the product itself. The supporting technology enables the initial product to be differentiated into a number of children to form a large family of products. The development effort for a platform product involves the development of extensive advanced technology that will support a whole new family of products. The first, or platform product, is not the most important output of the development effort—the comprehensive body of technology that will support the development of an entire family of products is the primary thrust.

Evolutionary Market Venture Strategies

Market Penetration (PEN). Market penetration involves increasing the sales of a firm's present products in its present markets, thus acquiring a greater percentage of a given market. This is usually accomplished by new and increased advertising and other forms of promotion. The firm may try to increase the customers' rate of use or to attract competitors' customers or current non-users. Since market penetration is strictly a marketing effort, it is usually managed by the product management group within the marketing department.

Market Enlargement (ENL). Market enlargement involves increasing sales by selling present products in new markets. This may only involve advertising in different media to reach new target customers or adding channels of distribution or new stores in new areas. It may involve a search for new uses for a product. A market enlargement project is primarily the responsibility of marketing; but if the sales increase is large enough, production may have to follow with a *process enlargement.* Engineering may become involved in determining new uses.

Market Modification (MOD). A market modification involves any *major* change to the marketing approach implemented for purposes other than market enlargement, market segmentation, or market consolidation. Such changes as changing the sales force organization, changing channels of distribution, or changing the advertising and promotion approach, all of which are implemented primarily to improve quality and efficiency rather than increase sales, would qualify as a marketing modification. Marketing modifications are normally handled completely by the marketing department.

Market Consolidation (CON). Market consolidation is the opposite of market segmentation. In market consolidation we endeavor to fold several small market segments into one or fewer composite markets. With market consolidation broader or mass market approaches will have to be developed and used to reach all the customers in the composite market. Market consolidation is often used in conjunction with product consolidation during corporate retrenchment or the latter phases of a product's life cycle, when competition on price becomes paramount. Market consolidation is primarily a marketing responsibility.

Revolutionary Market Venture Strategies

Market Segmentation (SEG). Market segmentation is a process that clusters people with similar needs into a market segment or niche. A market should be segmented so that (1) customers in the same segment would have similar buying needs, (2) customers in different segments would be as different as possible in terms of buying needs, and (3) each segment would be large enough to be profitable. Upon completion of the segmentation, a marketing approach will be developed for each segment. A market segmentation project is primarily the responsibility of marketing. If successful, it is often followed by *product differentiation* ventures to develop products that will exactly meet the needs of each market segment.

Completely New Markets (NEW). A completely new market development can result from several causes. The most common cause is the development of a diversified, breakthrough, or platform product. It can also come from a purely marketing effort to move into virgin markets, such as marketing in a new country or marketing globally.

Platform Marketing (PLAT). Platform marketing developments provide the base for a series of new marketing efforts over time. The technology developed for platform marketing can be applied to many future marketing efforts over a long time period. The first, or platform marketing effort is not the major thrust of the development effort. The comprehensive body of technology that will support the development of an entire family of marketing efforts and markets is the primary thrust. An example would be a firm's initial marketing effort on the Internet.

Evolutionary Process Venture Strategies

Process Cost Reduction (COST). In process cost reduction, an effort is made to improve the efficiency and productivity of the production system, without modifying its basic design or changing the quality of manufacturing. In performing a cost reduction streamlining, the concepts of Just-in-Time and Total Quality Management are often applied. Process cost reduction can usually be performed while the production system is operating, so it is not necessary to shut down the system. A process cost reduction venture is most appropriate for firms following either the low cost strategy or a retrenchment strategy. A *process* cost reduction project is often undertaken in parallel with a *product* cost reduction venture.

Process Enlargement (ENL). Process enlargement involves modifying the production system so that it can deliver a larger output. Such a venture is normally undertaken after a market enlargement has been successful or some other action has increased the demand. High market growth of a new product may necessitate a process enlargement. Given sufficient planning time, the enlargement can be made without interrupting production.

Process Modification (MOD). A process modification involves a major change to the production system that is large enough that it involves shutting down all or part of the system in order to make the change. Such a change will involve detailed planning and meticulous coordination with other activities going on in the organization. Such a change in the production system may be required by a diversified, breakthrough, or platform product.

Consolidated Process (CON). Process consolidation is the opposite of process focusing. In process consolidation we endeavor to fold several small unique processes into one or fewer larger, more standardized processes. With process consolidation, mass processing approaches are developed to make all the products in the firm's product line. Process consolidation is often used in conjunction with market and product consolidation during retrenchment or during the latter phases of a product line's life cycle, when competition on price becomes paramount.

Revolutionary Process Strategies

Focused Process (FOC). A focused factory assigns products with similar processing needs to a subdivision of the factory that is especially designed to satisfy those needs. A focused factory is designed so that (1) products using the same process have similar processing needs, (2) products using different processes have very different processing needs, and (3) each process is large enough to be efficient. A focused process development venture involves determining how an existing factory can best be reorganized to match current or planned products with appropriate processes. The concept of the focused factory was developed more than twenty years ago by Wickham Skinner[1] to counter the existing philosophy of making everything in one factory. A focused process venture is often conducted in parallel with market segmentation and product differentiation ventures.

Completely New (NEW). A completely new process development can result from a number of causes. The most probable cause is the development of a diversified, breakthrough, or platform product that requires a completely new production process. Another possible source is the imitation of a process from another firm or country. A completely new process will be more disruptive than a process modification, since the old production system is essentially disbanded when the new one is started up.

Platform Process (PLAT). Platform process developments provide the base for a series of new production processes over time. The technology developed for platform process can be applied to many future processes over a long time period. The first, or platform process, is not the major thrust of the development effort. The comprehensive body of technology that will support the development of an entire family of processes is the primary thrust. The initial installation of computer controlled equipment would be an example of a platform process venture.

INTEGRATED VENTURE STRATEGIC PLANNING PROCESS

After the corporate mission, vision, strategic plans, and cultural plans have been developed, the next step is to develop the venture strategy concurrently with the development of other supporting strategies. The venture strategy is but one of several supporting strategies that every company should develop. For an innovative company, it is probably the most important supporting strategy, since it outlines how the company intends to move forward through development efforts. The venture strategy is the beginning of all development effort; and if the development effort is to be integrated, the venture strategy must be integrated.

We propose developing an integrated venture strategy by following the process shown in Figure 2-2. First, we assess the current and past ventures to ascertain the pattern and success rate of ventures and decide whether to continue or change the pattern. Second, we analyze the corporate mission and strategies to determine the implications for venture strategy. Third, we conduct an analysis of the external environment to determine the opportunities and threats pertinent to us. Fourth, we analyze our internal environment to identify strengths and weaknesses in various parts of the organization. And fifth, we combine all the inputs for the previous four steps to develop an initial venture strategy. We then employ various techniques to improve this initial strategy before it is approved and implemented. In the remainder of this chapter, we will provide the details for each of the above steps.

ASSESS CURRENT AND PAST VENTURES

Assessment Using the Integrated Venture Map (IVM)

We start the strategic planning process for ventures by identifying and assessing the strategies employed in our current and past ventures. To assist in making this assessment, we suggest using the Integrated Venture Map (IVM)[2] described in the Appendix. The IVM enables us to put all our information concerning current and past ventures into a common format to facilitate assessment.

Analysis of Current and Past Ventures

As a part of the assessment, the current and past ventures for each of the firm's businesses, as displayed on the Integrated Venture Map, should be analyzed. The importance of each venture to specific products, processes, and/or businesses should be analyzed. Also, the policies dictating past and current venture strategies should be reviewed. This will normally involve some rethinking about the rationale for setting priorities and the basis for determining level of effort.

Figure 2-2
Integrated Venture Strategic Planning Process

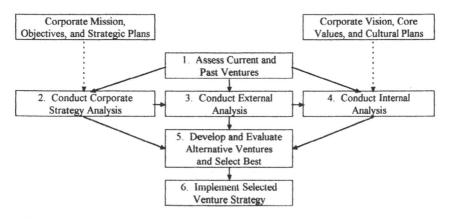

To perform a detailed analysis of product ventures, the following steps are suggested:

- Identify types and timing of ventures the firm has undertaken in the past.
- Identify which ventures succeeded. Failed. Why?
- Determine the new product survival rate, revenue, and profit performance.
- Assess new product performance against objectives and determine success rate.
- Determine the underlying causes behind new product success or failure.

What we have done or not done in the past in terms of ventures is a good gauge of what we can do in the future. This is not to say that we cannot or should not improve, but only that it is a starting point for determining our future strategy.

CONDUCT ANALYSIS OF CORPORATE STRATEGY

After the assessment of current and past ventures, the next step is to analyze the corporate strategy. Our venture strategy must be consistent with and support the corporate mission, objectives, and strategies. To accomplish this, we must analyze our corporate strategy and determine the implications for our venture strategy. To make this analysis more definitive, we have described four often-used corporate strategies and have indicated their implications for venture strategy. These corporate strategies are (1) growth versus retrenchment, (2) aggressive versus conservative, (3) time of market entrance-exit, and (4) low cost versus differentiation. By identifying where your company stands with regard to these corporate strategies, you can determine the implications for venture strategy. You should be forewarned that all of these corporate strategies may not be explicitly covered in your written mission and strategies, in which case you will have to infer from past actions what the strategy is. Also, your company may have a special corporate strategy that is not covered by the four well-known strategies described here.

Growth versus Retrenchment Strategy

A **growth strategy** seeks to increase an organization's overall size by increasing its volume, market share, or number of markets served. *Internal* growth can include development of new or changed products or expansion of current products into new markets. *External* growth typically involves the acquisition of businesses that are related to current product lines or take the corporation into new areas. We are primarily interested in *internal* growth, which requires the initiation of ventures to achieve it.

A **retrenchment** strategy normally consists of two phases: *contraction* and *consolidation*. In the *contraction* phase an effort is made to reduce size and costs in order to improve efficiency. It typically involves a general cutback in personnel and all noncritical expenditures. Hiring stops, and across-the-board cuts in R&D, advertising, training, and services are usual. The second phase, *consolidation*, involves the development of a program to stabilize the now-leaner corporation.

Implications. From the standpoint of the venture strategist, a corporate strategy of rapid *internal growth* would be the most desirable. Such a strategy would tend to support revolutionary product ventures such as *differentiation, diversification, breakthrough,* and *platform* ventures, and *completely new* market and process ventures. If the corporate strategy speaks of *retrenchment*, this does not bode well for an aggressive venture strategy. However, firms following a retrenchment strategy could undertake product *modification* and process *streamlining* ventures for cost reduction. If the retrenchment was deep, the company might elect to perform a combined product, market, and process *consolidation*.

Aggressive versus Conservative Strategy

This strategy has more to do with the value system of high-level management than it does with the external environment. This aspect of corporate strategy has been given a number of names by various authors. In addition to *aggressive versus conservative*, it has also been called *proactive versus reactive, risk taking versus risk avoiding, offensive versus defensive,* and *revolutionary versus evolutionary*. Regardless of the terms used, the concept is essentially the same.

Aggressive Strategy. If the environment in which a firm operates is dynamic and has great potential for growth, the aggressive strategy makes sense. Aggressors are leaders, not followers. They take risks and pursue innovation to develop new products and new markets. For example, Federal Express has always been aggressive, blazing new trails in the package delivery market.

Conservative Strategy. In a slow growth or stable environment, the conservative strategy makes sense. A conservative company avoids changing its current products and markets. It seeks to hold on to existing market share through improvement in efficiency or incremental quality improvement. The conservative company is concerned with internal efficiency and control to produce reliable products for steady customers

Implications. A *conservative* company, which avoids changing its products and markets, is anathema to a revolutionary venture strategy. The conservative company, if it supported ventures at all, would tend to support the less risky evolutionary ventures, such as product *modification* and *imitation*, market *penetration* and *modification*, and process *modification* and *enlargement.* An aggressive corporate strategy would be most conducive to a revolutionary venture strategy. An aggressive company would support the riskier types of ventures such as the product *differentiation, diversification, breakthrough,* and *platform* ventures, *segmented* and *completely new* market ventures, and *focused, platform,* and *completely new* process ventures.

Probably the most revolutionary venture strategy would be to develop *platform* products with their supporting core technologies. The supporting core technology enables the platform product to be *differentiated* into a number of children to form a large family of products. By achieving and retaining leadership in a core technology, a company can develop successive generations of products, continually adapting to changing customer needs and taking advantage of new markets.

Time of Market Entrance-Exit Strategy

A company's market entrance-exit strategy indicates when it intends to enter a market and when it intends to leave it. Choosing one of the three basic strategies described below has important implications for product and process development.

The **early, first-to-market** or leader strategy aims to get the product to the market before the competition. It provides the advantages of a *temporary monopoly* in exploiting a new technology during the period preceding the adoption of the new technology by competitors. When the product reaches the maturity stage and profit margins begin to shrink, the firm either sells or abandons the product and focuses on new products. An excellent example of a firm following this strategy is the Intel Corporation.

Implications. An early-to-market strategy normally requires a strong commitment to applied product research and development, in order to achieve a position of technological leadership. Throughout the product life cycle, manufacturing maintains a small, flexible production system that can readily be adapted to changing products, and thus little process development is required. The early, first-to-market corporate strategy would support the more advanced ventures such as the product *differentiation, diversification, breakthrough,* and *platform* ventures, *segmented* and *completely new* market ventures, and *focused, platform,* and *completely new* process ventures.

The **second-to-market** or fast follower strategy involves entry early in the growth stage of the life cycle and quick imitation of innovations pioneered by a competitor. Marketing emphasis will generally be more on winning customers away from the technological innovator. All of the "follow-the-leader" strategies try to learn from the innovator's mistakes, so as to develop an improved, more reliable product that may include "advanced features" while avoiding entirely the mistakes made by the innovator.

Implications. This strategy generally requires a strong and nimble development and reverse engineering capability, with little attention to applied or basic research. Normally followers stay longer in the product cycle than leaders, which means manufacturing must evolve from a low-volume, flexible production system into a high-volume, low-cost system. Such a shift is a challenge because it means changing over to a whole new way of doing things, sometimes in a short time period if the product life cycle is short. The second-to-market strategy would strongly support the product *imitation* venture and would provide some support for product *modification*, market *penetration* and *enlargement*, and process *enlargement* and *modification* ventures.

In the **late-to-market** strategy, entry into the market is generally late in the growth stage, to allow market volume to grow to the point where significant economies of scale can be achieved and to avoid investment in capital-intensive plant before product designs have become reasonably standardized. Firms following a late-to-market strategy are extremely efficient and offer a standard, no-frills product. Large companies, in particular, may accompany their entry with preemptive pricing. An example of a firm using this strategy is Toyota.

Implications. In firms following a late-to-market strategy, all product developments must use cost as one of the major screening criteria in selecting new product and process ventures. For products they would tend to use a combination of *imitation* and *cost reduction* ventures. To achieve the low-cost product, a *process modification* or *cost reduction* venture might be employed. Excellent product and process engineering skills are required to achieve a low-cost position. Also, production must be more involved in the product development to ensure they can produce the resulting product at low cost.

Low Cost, Differentiation, and Focus Strategies

Michael E. Porter studied a number of business organizations and proposed three business-level strategies: cost leadership, differentiation, and focus.[3] **Cost leadership** is a strategy in which the organization aggressively seeks efficient facilities, cuts cost, and employs tight cost controls to be more efficient than competitors. A low-cost position means that the company can undercut competitor's prices and still offer comparable quality and earn a reasonable profit. To be successful a low-cost company should have good process engineering skills, products designed for ease of manufacture, and tight cost control.

Implications. For a companies pursuing a low-cost strategy, most of their development efforts would be evolutionary, with periodic product *modifications* to update their products and product and process *cost reductions* that would reduce the cost of their products. If the company wanted to be more aggressive in the low-cost strategy, it might elect to perform a combined product, market, and process *consolidation*. It is not expected that a firm pursuing a low-cost strategy would undertake any of the revolutionary ventures.

Differentiation is a strategy with which the organization seeks to distinguish its products or services from those of competitors. The firm may use advertising, distinctive product features, exceptional service, or new technology to achieve a product perceived as unique. The differentiation strategy can be successful because some customers are willing to pay extra for desired features. To be successful a company employing the differentiation strategy must have excellent marketing abilities, strong capability in basic research, and a corporate reputation for quality or technological leadership.

Implications. Firms following the *differentiation* strategy would tend to follow an overall revolutionary strategy, utilizing the product *differentiation*, market *segmentation*, and process *focus* ventures as a minimum. If the firm truly wants to differentiate itself from the competition, there is no better way than to embark upon a product *diversification*, product *breakthrough*, or product *platform* venture.

Focus is a strategy that emphasizes concentration on a specific market segment, a group of customers with specific needs. To use a focus strategy, the firm must be able accurately to identify the detailed needs of a specific group of customers and then satisfy those needs exactly. Customers will tend to buy from those firms that can satisfy their needs exactly.

Implications. If a firm pursued the focus strategy exclusively, it would be expected to undertake product *differentiation*, market *segmentation*, and process *focus* ventures singly and in combination. The recommended way to pursue the focus strategy is first to perform a market *segmentation* venture, then a product *differentiation*, and finally a process *focus* (if needed). It is possible to start with the product *differentiation* venture, but this way is somewhat more risky, since you may not find customers that want what your product provides.

CONDUCT EXTERNAL ANALYSIS FOR VENTURE STRATEGY

Competitor Analysis

The external analysis begins with the analysis of the market and industry, particularly competitors that can procure or are producing the same type of products as we do. With the key competitors identified in each market segment, managers must understand each rival's goals, strategies, and probable course of action and strategies that might provoke retaliation. To gain market share without retaliation, managers must understand the rival's weaknesses better than the rival itself. The external competitive environment must be scanned to pinpoint the development patterns of competitors in process and market development, as well as product development. The competitor analysis will identify the primary *threats* in the external environment.

Trend Analysis

In the trend analysis, we are primarily looking for two things: **future** *opportunities* or *needs* that our products or other ventures could fulfill and **future** *technological solutions* that would enable us to fulfill those needs. We do not want to answer today's needs with today's technology. Rather, we want to answer tomorrow's needs with tomorrow's technology. To find these future needs and solutions, we must conduct a systematic analysis of the external environment for relevant trends. *Social* trends include long-term changes in cultural attitudes, values, and behaviors such as permissiveness, conservatism, family structure, entertainment leisure time patterns, health and environmental consciousness, educational achievement, cultural diversity, and so on. *Technological* trends include major technological drivers such as miniaturization, digitalization, and automation that are making all activities more information intensive, speeding up innovation, and shortening product life cycles. *Economic* factors to be monitored include inflation, consumer confidence, the business cycle, interest rates, exchange rates, and globalization.

CONDUCT INTERNAL ANALYSIS FOR VENTURE STRATEGY

The primary purpose of the internal analysis is to determine the relative strengths of the marketing, engineering, production, and other departments of the firm in order to determine what type of ventures the firm is best capable of undertaking. We will accomplish this analysis in three phases: (1) look at the capability of marketing to develop need-based product concepts, (2) assess the capability of engineering to develop technology-based new products, and (3) evaluate the overall capability of the firm for product development.

The first step of the analysis assesses our capability to determine the needs of our customers and to develop need-driven new product ideas. The marketing department must have the experienced people and procedures that will enable them to identify the true needs of a selected group of customers accurately and rapidly. Knowing the customer's needs, they must have the people and procedures that will enable them to develop need-based product concepts. The ability to determine the needs of customers and to conceptualize products that will satisfy those needs is required for both evolutionary and revolutionary product ventures.

The second step in our analysis is to determine our capability to develop new products through technology. Our technical people—their knowledge, experience, and commitment—are the most important measure of our technical capability. Intimately related is a strong technological and research history, as any lack there might make new product development difficult. Technical personnel must understand all levels of technology, from the product venture strategy to the technical details of the components. They must understand the market and competition as well as the technology. *If the firm does not have the required technical capability, undertaking any of the revolutionary product ventures (differentiation, diversification, breakthrough, or platform) would be ill-advised and possibly disastrous.* Without the necessary technical capability, the firm is advised to implement one of the evolutionary ventures.

The internal analysis should also assess the firm's overall capability to meet current and future customer needs and its ability to build future capability. The ability to build distinct competencies (strengths) that generate new products and processes faster and better and the ability to train and empower the workforce to adapt quickly provide the ultimate source of competitiveness. Previously we emphasized the functions of marketing and engineering, but these are not the only functions required to develop new products. It is important that cross-functional processes, such as the new product development process, be analyzed to determine strengths and weakness of the company's processes. By reviewing and enhancing its cross-functional processes, a company can often develop a competitive advantage over other firms. *Competitive benchmarking* is a new technique for evaluating and improving internal processes. In this analysis, managers determine the firm's critical processes and outputs, determine baseline performances for those processes, then compare the performance of each process against a standard outside the firm and often outside the industry.

DEVELOP, EVALUATE, AND SELECT INTEGRATED VENTURE STRATEGY

In the next several pages we describe an iterative approach for generating a very specific and doable venture strategy using the following outline: First, we develop an initial venture strategy based on an analysis of current and past venture strategies using the Integrated Venture Map (IVM). We improve upon this initial strategy in the following steps. Second, we utilize the information from the external and internal analyses to evaluate and improve the initial strategy. A SWOT (Strengths, Weaknesses, Opportunities, Threats) analysis is conducted as part of this step. Third, we improve the initial strategy by using the relationships between types of ventures in the three areas of products, markets, and processes. In step four, we compare our venture strategy with the corporate mission and strategies to ensure the two are consistent, before documenting the venture strategy in step five. It should be emphasized that this process is an iterative one, subject to doubling back and multiple loops, that very seldom proceeds in the straightforward manner described above. However, if pursued diligently using the IVM, it will provide a very specific, realistic, and integrated venture strategy.

The development of the integrated strategy should be accomplished by an integrated team of personnel, with representatives from engineering, marketing, and production as a minimum. It should also have representatives from finance, purchasing, human resources, and others as appropriate. For best results, the planning for products, markets, and processes should be done concurrently and not sequentially.

Develop *Initial* Venture Strategy Using Integrated Venture Map

We suggest using the Integrated Venture Map (IVM), described in the appendix, in three steps to develop the initial version of your firm's development strategy. First, enter the current products, markets, and processes with their development history, if known. Second, add the product, market, and process ventures that are currently underway. Third, tentatively determine what product, market, and process ventures should be undertaken in the future and add them to the chart.

The IVM summarizes what the business is doing today and what it plans to do tomorrow in a very simple and graphic format. After the first step, the company has a snapshot of what it is doing today. After the second step, it has a picture of how the company will change in the near future. After the third step, the company has a blueprint of what product, market, and process ventures are contemplated for the future.

This third step is by far the most important and most challenging of the three. This blueprint for the future need not specify in detail the concepts, features, and content of future product, market, and process ventures—such detail should be left to the venture summaries (described later). The IVM should lay out the evolution of the company's ventures, map the relationship between current and future product, market, and process ventures, and lay out the type and timing of future ventures. It must do so in a way that fits the marketplace, the competitive environment, and the firm's resource realities.

From the past, certain development patterns can be discerned. If these patterns have been successful, they can be extended into the future. If they have not been successful, then it would be advisable to investigate alternative development paths. Future plans must be based on past accomplishments. If last year's plans have not been successful or have not met schedule, then this year's plans will have to be altered. The need for these kinds of changes is readily apparent from the IVM.

Four issues must be addressed to extend the map into the future and create the best product, market, and process map for the business:

1. *Area of Focus*. What products, markets, and processes should be developed? Where are the opportunities, and where do we have the capability to develop new products, markets, or processes? For products, what part of the product line should be developed? New markets can be defined by their customer type and location. Answering this question focuses attention on opportunities in the market; possible competitive moves; gaps in the product, market, and process lineup; and the breadth needed to accomplish the business objectives.

2. *Type*. What *type of ventures* will be most effective in meeting the need?

Should we strive for *revolutionary* ventures or should we settle for *evolutionary?* The various types of ventures were discussed previously. Although these types may not fit your situation exactly, they will provide a common language during the early phases of development planning.

3. *Timing.* When should the ventures be introduced? The pace of technological change, price/performance economics, and market rhythms, as well as the ability of customers to make the transition from the old to the new and the ability of the business to fund development at a sustainable pace, all must be factored into such time deliberations. The time between the introduction of platform products and that of their children in a product family is critical; the timing of product differentiation (in a cluster or spread out over time) has financial and market perception implications as well.

4. *Relationships.* How will the new product, market, and process developments be related? As we see in the example presented in Figure A-1, there are many important relationships between ventures in the three areas of products, markets, and processes. The Integrated Venture Map makes these relationships more evident, and they are easy to portray by the use of dotted lines between developments in two or more areas.

Use Results of External and Internal Analysis to Evaluate and Improve Venture Strategy

With an initial venture strategy developed using the Integrated Venture Map, the next step is to use the results of the external and internal analyses to improve this initial strategy. The trend analysis in the external analysis is a very important input. Customers are a very productive source of new product ideas, but they provide very few radically new ideas. If the focus of new product ideas is restricted to the analysis of customer needs, the company will more than likely end up with product modifications and imitations and not with radically new products such as differentiations, diversifications, breakthroughs, or platforms. Customers can convert performance gaps in current products into explicit needs, but these gaps are rarely the source of needs that give birth to the *revolutionary* product ventures.

Revolutionary new product concepts can come from the identification of *implicit* needs that stem from the interpretation of *future* trends. The key to the creation of revolutionary new products is the ability to look into the future and anticipate what trends or events will shape the industry in which the corporation operates. The second skill is the ability to match the strategic capabilities of the company with the revolutionary new products and exploit them before the competition does.

Formulation of a successful venture strategic plan requires planners to have an accurate and complete understanding of the external environment and the internal capabilities of the organization. This can be done by conducting a SWOT (Strengths, Weaknesses, Opportunities, Threats) analysis. *The SWOT analysis consists of compiling and sizing up a firm's internal strengths and weaknesses from the Internal Analysis and its opportunities and threats from the External Analysis.* The SWOT analysis emphasizes the basic principle that strategy must produce a good fit between a company's internal capability (its strengths and weaknesses) and its external situation (reflected in part by its opportunities and threats). An organization will achieve strategic success by integrating and increasing strengths and opportunities and by countering and reducing weaknesses and threats.

Once a company's SWOT have been identified, the four lists should be carefully evaluated. From a strategy-making perspective, a company's strengths are important, because they can serve as the cornerstone on which strategy and competitive advantage can be built; there's something to be said for grounding strategy on a company's strongest skills, competence, and resources. An organization's venture strategy must be well suited to what it is capable of doing. Market opportunity is definitely a big factor in shaping a company's strategy. Unless a company is in position to pursue a given opportunity and unless the opportunity is fruitful enough to pursue, it usually makes sense to choose some other strategic course.

The SWOT analysis is much more than just making four lists. It is essential to evaluate the strength, weakness, opportunity, and threat listings in terms of what conclusions can be drawn about the company's situation and what the implications are for venture strategy. Some of the more pertinent questions to consider, once the SWOT listings have been compiled, are:

- Does the company have any internal strengths around which an attractive venture strategy can be built? In particular, does the company have a distinctive competence (strength) that can produce a competitive edge?
- Do the company's weaknesses make it completely vulnerable, and do they disqualify the company from pursuing certain opportunities? Which weaknesses does strategy need to be aimed at correcting?
- Which opportunities does the company have the skills and resources to pursue with a real chance of success? Remember, opportunity without the means to capture it is an illusion. An organization's strengths and weaknesses make it better suited for going after some opportunities and not after others.
- What threats should management be worried most about, and what strategic moves does management need to consider in formulating a good defense?

Improve Strategy by Analyzing Relationships between Venture Types

The relationship that exists between various types of ventures in different areas can be used to assist in formulating the company's venture strategy. As we have seen from the example, certain types of developments often occur concurrently in three areas. The types of ventures that have the strongest relationship among the three areas are market *segmentation*, product *differentiation*, and process *focusing*. If a market is *segmented* (divided into smaller markets, each with unique needs), then it is often necessary to *differentiate* the firm's products (develop several versions to satisfy the unique needs of each market segment), and it is often advisable to develop a *focused* factory to optimally manufacture the differentiated products. This relationship can also be initiated by product *differentiation*, which then requires market segmentation, but this sequence is less prevalent.

Another set of strongly related ventures is product, market, and process *consolidation*. These three types of development projects are often conducted in parallel when a firm's market share is shrinking and the firm is retrenching. In retrenchment, firms often endeavor to reduce the variety of products produced, the variety of markets served, and the variety of factories operated by initiating market, product, and process *consolidation* ventures.

The production processes used by a firm should be closely matched to the product being produced. Every time there is a major product venture (such as a *Product Modification*, *Differentiation*, *Consolidation*, *Imitation*, *Diversification*, *Breakthrough*, or *Platform*), the situation should be examined closely to determine if there should be a parallel process venture.

Any marketing venture that increases the size of the market (*Penetration* or *Enlargement*) should normally be paralleled or followed by an *Enlargement* venture in production. There is no point in developing a larger market if you can not produce the products to satisfy it.

Certain product developments carry a requirement for a concurrent market development. For example, *Product Imitation*, *Diversification*, *Breakthrough*, and *Platform* developments generate new products that are capable of satisfying the needs of new customers. However, they will not be available to new customers unless a market development venture is undertaken.

Test Venture Strategy against Corporate Mission and Strategies

We will use the corporate mission, objectives, and strategies as our first and last criteria for determining our venture strategy since it is such an important factor. Before we promulgate our venture strategy we must ensure that it is consistent with and supports our corporate mission and strategies. To do so, we will analyze and evaluate our development strategy using the four dimensions of corporate strategy defined previously: (1) growth versus retrenchment, (2) aggressive versus conservative, (3) market entrance-exit, and (4) low cost versus differentiation. The venture team must determine where its company stands on these four dimensions and ensure that the proposed venture strategy is consistent. Implications of these various dimensions are discussed in the section on Corporate Strategy Analysis.

Document the Integrated Development Strategy

In addition to the Integrated Venture Map, the documentation of the Venture Strategy should include (1) an overall Executive Summary of the strategy and (2) Venture Summaries (brief synopses of each current and planned venture).

The **Executive Summary** should be prepared after the Integrated Venture Map and the Venture Summaries have been completed, so that the salient features of each can be included.

Venture Summaries should include the following information:

- *Background.* Provide pertinent information and ideas from the External and Internal Analyses and other sources.

- *Area of Focus.* For each proposed venture, state at least one clear technology dimension (such as a science, a material, or process skill) and one clear market dimension (such as a user, a use, or an activity). Without both a product and a market focus, the concept will be weak.

- *Product (Market or Process) Concept.* Concepts are essentially descriptions of the envisioned product, market, or process in a form that can be readily understood and investigated by the people primarily responsible for development: high-level management, marketing, engineering, and production. For example, a *product* concept should outline the **need**, **solution**, and **features** of a proposed product.

- *Goals—Objectives.* Be as specific as possible. Think about what a project team should really be held accountable for.

- *Type of Venture.* Identify the type of venture envisaged using the categories described previously. If there is something different about this particular venture, point out this uniqueness.

- *Estimated Time and Cost of Development.* Provide an estimate of when the project might start, how long it will take, and how much it will cost. At this point in time, these are "ball park" estimates that will be refined during the budgeting process and the preparation of the venture plan.

IMPLEMENTING INTEGRATED VENTURE STRATEGY

Develop the Aggregate Venture Plan

To implement our integrated venture strategy, we must develop and manage the *Aggregate Venture Plan (AVP)*, which contains two portfolios: the *portfolio of* **ventures** and the *portfolio of venture* **resources**. The portfolio of ventures contains all the individual ventures that are planned for accomplishment. The portfolio of venture resources describes all the firm's resources that are available for development. In managing the AVP, we must match venture requirements with venture resources, in terms of both the aggregate capability to perform all ventures and the needed mix to perform each venture. In developing and managing the Aggregate Venture Plan, we must perform two tasks: defining the venture portfolio and matching ventures with capabilities and capacity.

Defining the Venture Portfolio

The Integrated Venture Map outlines the planned evolution of market, product, and process ventures. But the IVM is not the only source of ventures. Venture proposals will also come in from many additional sources. The challenge is to select the most productive ideas from those proposed and those planned and to shape and influence the development and collection of ideas into productive ventures. Putting the right development ventures in the right places requires a combined bottom-up and top-down approach. The result will be a portfolio of ventures, some of which will be done now (or are already under way), some of which will be done soon, and some of which will be done down the road. A clear and integrated market, product, and process venture strategy is required to provide the guidance needed to select the best proposed and planned ventures.

Matching Development Ventures to Capability and Capacity

To accomplish all development ventures we must ensure we have all the resources necessary to meet all venture requirements. In addition to making sure we have the right number of people and other resources, we must make sure that they have the right set of skills, tools, and methods to carry out the development venture plan. The matching process requires that we build a base of information so we can estimate what is necessary to conduct a venture of a certain type and thus determine the impact of individual ventures on available capacity. Maintaining discipline by focusing resources and limiting the number of ventures under development to the capacity available to execute them to avoid overloading, confusion, and congestion are extremely critical tasks for high-level management.

NOTES

1. Wickham Skinner, "The Focused Factory," *Harvard Business Review* (May-June 1974), p. 113.
2. Adapted from Steven C. Wheelwright and Kim B. Clark, *Revolutionizing Product Development* (Free Press, 1992), pp. 57–85.
3. Michael E. Porter, *Competitive Strategy* (Free Press, 1980), pp. 36–46.

Chapter 3

Continuous Cultural Change and Improvement

Cultural change is very difficult to effect in organizations, particularly in mature organizations. An existing strong culture can often resist a weak change effort. However, if innovation and intrapreneurship are to be successful, they must be supported by an appropriate corporate culture. To be successful, our plans for change must be firmly focused on developing a culture that is aligned with the firm's intended strategy. Trying to implement a cultural change that is counter to the strategy is almost certain to fail. It is the high-level leader's responsibility, once strategy is chosen, to bring the corporate culture into close alignment with strategy and keep it there.

The many reasons cited for the failure of organizational behavior change efforts can be reduced to one sentence: *The culture of the organization remained unchanged.* Any attempt to introduce management practices or organizational behavior changes that are radically different from the existing culture will almost certainly fail if these changes are incompatible with the existing culture. The culture—that sum of values, beliefs, and assumptions that is the core of any organization—must support the new initiatives if these behavioral changes are to take hold. Without a change in the culture of the company, no new set of skills or work processes will bring about the kind of reform that is needed.

Developing an innovative company will require many changes in organizational behavior and business processes. However, before we even think about making these changes, we must change the organizational culture so it will support these changes. That is the subject of this chapter. We will first explore how a company should be organized for cultural improvement. Then we look at the planning process for determining the company's vision, values, and principles. And finally we look at the most difficult task of all, implementing a cultural change.

THE ROLE OF HIGH-LEVEL LEADERSHIP IN CULTURAL PLANNING

High-level managers have an important role in formulating and implementing an innovative culture for their company. First, they set direction and get people in the organization aligned. Drawing on their own insights and the ideas from others, they develop a sense of what is possible, articulate their *vision*, and work with people to align them with it. Furthermore, they select, train, and develop people capable of realizing thát vision. Through these people, they create, shape, and influence how work is done in order to ensure that it gets done in the best way possible. In essence, they are endeavoring to create their version of the company's culture.

At the heart of the innovative culture lies the vision of the leader. This vision includes the broader sense of who we are, why we are doing this work, why it's important, the promises we have made to customers, and the code of conduct governing how we operate with each other. Developing the vision, though, is not enough. The leader must be able to inspire others with the vision so that others want to say yes to it. In articulating the broader sense of vision, the new leader must be able to touch the hearts of the employees. The first person the new leader must convert to his or her vision is himself. If he is not sold on the company's vision, it will be next to impossible for him to effectively convert his employees.

As innovative companies move into the twenty-first century they will be operating with a culture of greater employee autonomy and self-direction. Teams will be less controlled by management and will exercise more autonomy in completing tasks from start to finish. It will be the leader's job to ensure that the team's efforts are bound together by a shared commitment to the mission and vision. Paradoxically *more* leadership will be required—not less. A unique reciprocal relationship should evolve between leadership and the front line. As the front line takes on greater tactical and operational authority, leaders should become ever more responsible for being the source and interpreter of the vision.

The single most visible factor that distinguishes major cultural changes that succeed from those that fail is competent leadership at the top. In all ten of the cases Kotter and Heskett studied, major change began after an individual who already had a track record for leadership was appointed to head the organization.[1] Each of these individuals had previously shown the capacity to do more than manage well. In their new jobs, they did this again, albeit on a grander scale. Each new leader created a team that established a new vision and set courses of action for achieving that vision. Each new leader succeeded in persuading important groups and individuals in the firm to commit themselves to that new direction and then energized the personnel sufficiently to make it happen, despite all obstacles. Ultimately hundreds (or even thousands) of people helped make all the changes in strategies, products, structures, policies, personnel, and eventually culture. But often, just one or two people seem to have been essential in getting the process started.

The necessity for three characteristics in the high-level leader—effective leadership, outsider's perspective, and insider's resources—helps explain why major cultural change does not happen more often in large organizations. It requires an effective leader on top. He or she must have both an outsider's openness to new ideas and an insider's power base. This leader must create a perceived need for change even if most people believe all is well. He must create and communicate effectively a new vision and set of strategies and then behave accordingly on a daily basis. He must motivate and increasingly large group of people to help with this leadership effort. These people must find hundreds or thousands of opportunities to influence behavior. The resulting action on the part of a growing group of people must produce positive results; if they do not, the whole effort loses critical credibility.

ORGANIZING FOR CULTURAL IMPROVEMENT

Establish a Cultural Improvement Council (CIC)

Although implementing a major cultural change requires a dynamic and committed CEO, he cannot do it alone. He must enlist the support of other members of the high-level management team. The best way to do this is to create a Cultural Improvement Council, composed of appropriate members of high-level management, that is responsible for planning and leading the cultural improvement program. Some substantial meetings will be called for—for education and to work through major decisions together—as well as regular meetings to review progress and make routine decisions. Rather than schedule this work in an ad hoc fashion or attempt to combine it with other scheduled meetings that have different purposes, it is better to give this team a separate identity and title. Doing so gives the team more visibility and power and implies that this team will continue to operate for some time.

The purpose of the Cultural Improvement Council (CIC) is to oversee the planning, implementation, and continuing support for a Cultural Improvement Program. The CIC acts as a steering committee for the cultural improvement program, providing overall direction for the program and specific direction for the Cultural Improvement Manager. It establishes policy, sets goals, reviews progress, and provides authority to modify existing programs and organizations to comply with the Cultural Improvement program.

The CIC should include the key decision makers in the organization. It may also include others who represent important stakeholder groups. For example, the council may decide that it needs to involve representatives of staff associations or unions. The council should have the same level of decision-making authority as any other group of high-level managers. It should not have to seek high-level management approval for its decisions; it is high-level management.

Appoint a Cultural Improvement Manager (CIM)

As soon as possible after the start of the Cultural Improvement Program, the council should select a Cultural Improvement Manager (CIM). The CIM occupies a full-time position in the company and is a full-fledged member of the Cultural Improvement Council, usually acting as chair of the council. The principal duties of the CIM are as follows:

- Coordinates the development of the vision, core values, and guiding principles by the council
- Develops and implements a plan for achieving the vision, core values, and guiding principles
- Coordinates the meeting schedule of the council to ensure that important decisions are made in a timely manner
- Provides guidance to the council on technical issues concerning cultural improvement
- Proposes and organizes educational activities for the council and the organization
- Plays an active part, as any other member of the council, in issues before the council
- Serves as a gathering point for information about cultural improvement techniques
- Organizes an assessment of the status of the organization
- Transfers success from one part of the organization to another
- Monitors progress and brings problems areas to the attention of the council

CULTURAL IMPROVEMENT PLANNING

Brief Description of Cultural Improvement Planning

Brief Description of Planning Results

The four outputs of cultural planning are *vision, core values, guiding principles*, and *cultural improvement plans*.

A **Vision** states what a company intends that its *internal* (cultural) environment should *be* or should *become* on a *continuing* basis. A vision is a picture of a preferred future state, a description of what the organization would be like some years from now. The vision provides an image of what the organization intends to be in the future, to provide the guidance for designing and managing the cultural changes that will be necessary to achieve those intentions. By providing a few broad concepts rather than a multitude of precise details, the vision becomes a simple guide, allowing many levels of the organization to make decisions without the necessity of consulting with their superiors.

Core Values are the organization's essential and enduring tenets—a small set of general values, not to be compromised for financial gain or short-term expediency and not to be confused with specific practices, which are included in the guiding principles. Innovative companies tend to have only a few core values, usually between three and six. Indeed, we should expect this, for only a few values can be truly *core*—values so fundamental and deeply held that they will never change and will never be compromised.

Guiding Principles describe *how* the vision and core values will be achieved. They establish the professional standards for the work done inside the organization. They specify the relationship between people in the organization—on all levels. In short, they outline how all members of the organization will behave to achieve the core values, the vision—and the mission.

Cultural Improvement Plans are specific time-phased plans for improving the company's culture in a logical and systematic manner in order to achieve the culture specified by the vision, core values, and guiding principles. These plans are discussed in detail in the implementation section of this chapter.

Responsibility and Process for Cultural Planning

The Cultural Improvement Manager, with the advice and support of the Cultural Improvement Council, is responsible for carrying out the cultural planning process. The procedure for cultural planning, shown in Figure 3-1, was described in Chapter 1. In this chapter, we will discuss each of the steps in the process in more detail. Cross-functional task groups may be assembled to perform various phases of the planning process.

Identify and Assess the Current Culture

Once high-level management commitment has been obtained and the organization has been established, it is tempting to immediately begin developing the planned culture and the plans for implementation. However, such planning is premature. We first need to determine what that current culture is so that we ascertain the direction and magnitude of the required change. We first need to do an organizational assessment (or diagnosis, as it is sometimes called) that has several objectives:

Figure 3-1
Cultural Planning Process

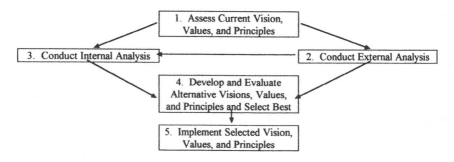

- To explore all aspects of organizational functioning in order to identify the values, beliefs, and assumptions currently held by the organization's employees
- To identify major opportunities for cultural improvement
- To identify possible barriers to a cultural change program
- To promote cultural change

A broad-based assessment project usually employs one or more of the following data-gathering techniques:

Personal and confidential interviews with a cross section of employees. The interviewer can probe personal experiences, explore critical issues in depth, and obtain useful anecdotes. In addition, the confidential, one-on-one nature of the process ensures a greater degree of openness than can be obtained in a group setting. The drawback of the personal interview approach is that it is costly and time-consuming to interview a large number of employees.

Group interviews. The major benefit of the group interview is that a larger number of employees can be involved in a cost- and time-effective manner. The trade-offs are that confidentiality concerns may inhibit some participants and that issues cannot generally be explored in as much detail as in the individual interview.

Written surveys. The written survey is clearly the most cost-effective way to involve very large numbers of people in the assessment process. If input from an organization of several hundred or more people is desired, a written survey is perhaps the only practical technique. A survey provides quantifiable data to support (or contradict) the conclusions that have been reached through some other format. On the down side, a survey requires some interpretation and does not permit an in-depth evaluation of the issues. The written survey contains questions such as the following:

- Is there cooperation among employees?
- Do employees feel recognized and rewarded?
- Do employees feel they have a say in how the work is done?
- Do employees feel free of unnecessary policies and procedures?
- Do employees feel challenged by the work they do?

It is generally advisable to employ a combination (if not all) of these techniques in the assessment process. Group interviews might be used, for example, to allow for the active participation of a sizable number of employees and to identify the major cultural values, beliefs, and issues. More detailed information on the issues could be obtained through individual interviews, and a written survey would provide quantitative support for the conclusions reached.

Conduct External Analysis

Analyze Corporate Strategy

Our culture must be consistent with and support the corporate mission, objectives, and strategies. To accomplish this, we must analyze our corporate strategy and determine the implications for our corporate culture. To make this analysis more definitive, in Chapter 2 we defined four often-used aspects of corporate strategy with their implications. These aspects are: (1) growth versus retrenchment, (2) aggressive versus conservative, (3) time of market entrance-exit, and (4) low cost versus differentiation. Identifying where your company stands on these four aspects will help in determining the general nature of the corporate culture. A detailed analysis of the company's actual mission, objectives, and strategies will enable us to deduce the general nature of the culture that would best support the corporate strategy.

External Culture Analysis

Business organizations are immersed in cultures much larger than their own—those of the region and nation of which they are a part. In improving their corporate culture, they must keep these larger cultures in mind, since these larger cultures have considerable influence over the people they employ. What is our national and regional culture, and how is it changing? How might these changes affect what our corporate culture is or should be?

We should also look for trends that might affect these cultures—primarily social and political trends. *Social* trends include long-term changes in cultural attitudes, values, and behaviors such as permissiveness, conservatism, family structure, entertainment, leisure-time patterns, health and environmental consciousness, educational achievement, cultural diversity, and so on. *Political* trends concern political party changes (especially at the national level), shifts from liberal to conservative views (or vice versa), and any other major change in political views.

Conduct Internal Analysis

This analysis follows the initial assessment of culture and uses much of the data gathered during the assessment, but it looks at the data from a different perspective. In the initial assessment we were trying to find out what the corporate culture is. In this analysis we are primarily trying to determine the *readiness* or *willingness* of the organization and its various parts to *change* its culture. We need to know this in order to intelligently develop plans for cultural change. The following questions are useful in conducting the analysis:

- Are the present cultural change efforts succeeding?
- Why are the cultural change efforts succeeding or failing?

- Has the organization taken advantage of all opportunities?
- Can the organization overcome obstacles?

Develop New Vision, Core Values, and Guiding Principles

The Desired Results of Cultural Planning

We provided a brief description of cultural planning outputs above. We will now expand upon these brief definitions.

The Vision. A vision is usually not as concrete and measurable as a mission. It is not a specific objective or strategy. Rather, it tends to be a broad statement that inspires, integrates, and controls an organization. One of the roles of the vision is to promote and protect organizational values. A vision enables people in the organization to know the general purpose or role of their organization and the reasons why they should be proud of their organization. We will discuss the four most persuasive reasons for having a vision: inspiration, unobtrusive control, focus, and integration.[2]

- *Inspiration.* A vision can energize people by legitimizing the organization's existence and satisfying a basic human need: the need to be important, to make a difference, to feel useful, and to be part of a worthwhile enterprise.
- *Unobtrusive Control.* A vision may provide an effective, yet unobtrusive, form of control. A vision may help to ensure that people will make decisions that are consistent with the organization's overall needs. Since managers cannot be everywhere at once, many decisions are made without their knowledge. A vision provides employees with a compass that points their feet in the right direction.
- *Focus.* A vision can channel the energy of the organization, preventing employees from dissipating their energy in a variety of unrelated directions. By focusing individuals' attention on what is most important to the organization, a vision helps people uncover and eliminate a myriad unproductive activities.
- *Integration.* A vision is also an integrating force in organizations, a mechanism for coordinating the efforts of groups with divergent interests. A vision can lift people out of their petty private preoccupations and unify them in pursuit of objectives worthy of their best efforts.

Core Values are the organization's essential and enduring tenets—a small set of general values that should not to be confused with specific cultural or operating practices, which are included in the guiding principles. Core Values are perhaps the most difficult element to define, but they are also one of the most important. We found that even beyond a shared sense of purpose or vision, the people share values, which guide not only the way individuals treat their work but also how they treat one another. Most excellent companies have established an internal culture based on trust and participation. This culture fosters creativity and productivity and enhances both the employees' work and their lives.

Guiding Principles. The most successful companies worldwide are values-driven. That means a bedrock of common, positive values underlies the thinking and the creativity of everyone in these organizations. The Vision defines the desired culture in general terms. The Principles provide the guidelines that will enable us to *achieve* our desired culture.

First, the Principles establish the professional standards for the work done inside the organization. Without clear standards, the organization may suffer inconsistent efforts because people do not know to what level they should strive. The Principles establish a clear level of quality and excellence that every employee can understand and aspire to maintain.

Second, the desired relationships among all people at all levels in the organization need to be defined. If ignored, these relationships will emerge by themselves and will often be counterproductive. If consciously defined and nurtured, they will add vital strength and creativity to the organization.

The Principles are especially important as top-down hierarchies give way to self-managed teams. As you unleash authority to the front line, the Principles are often all people have left (and all they need, if done correctly) to show them *how* to achieve the organization's vision. Many innovative companies have adopted the following principles, which were discussed in Chapter 1.

- Far-sighted High-Level Strategic and Cultural Leadership
- Emphasis on Innovation, Intrapreneurship, and Achievement
- Strong customer focus
- Emphasis on Total Quality Management
- Flexible and Adaptable Organizations
- High Levels of Collaboration, Teamwork, and Trust
- Participative Management Style and Employee Empowerment
- Emphasis on Human Resources
- Continuous Learning, Change, and Improvement
- Effective Information, Communication, and Decision-Making Systems
- Emphasis on Process Management
- Emphasis on Corporate Venturing Process

Developing the Initial Vision, Core Values, and Guiding Principles

After completing the assessment of the current culture and conducting the internal and external analyses, it is time to develop the vision, values, and principles. The Cultural Improvement Council, under the leadership of the Cultural Improvement Manager, is responsible for developing the initial drafts of the vision, core values, and guiding principles. The CEO should be considered an ex-officio member of the Council for these deliberations. The more the CEO participates, the better. A corporate vision does not come down from the mountaintop engraved in stone. Rather it is shaped, crafted, and developed in cooperation with those who will live it. Shared visions are developed in much the same way that a painter paints a picture or a potter crafts pottery—through an interactive process.

A necessary input to developing the vision, core values, and guiding principles of the organization is the mission statement from the strategic planning effort. If a corporate mission statement is not available, the CIC should take steps to have one developed before proceeding. The mission and vision should definitely be consistent and supportive, but they will not be exactly alike since they serve two different purposes. A mission states what a company intends to *do*, to *achieve*, in the *external* environment on a *one-time* basis. A vision states what a company intends that its *internal* (cultural) environment should *be* or should *become* on a *continuing* basis. The mission statement names the game we are going to play. A vision is more a philosophy about how we are going to play the game.

Normally the mission should be developed first, with the vision of what the organization should be like to achieve the mission being developed second. Because the mission is directly linked to the customers and external environment, it makes sense for the vision to be based on the mission. It is extremely important that the organization's mission and vision be consistent and mutually supportive.

Testing and Improving the Vision, Values, and Principles before Implementing

One of the better methods of testing the vision, core values, and guiding principles is through employee *focus groups*. The focus group approach involves leading a group of employees, from various divisions and levels in the company, through an open, in-depth discussion of the proposed vision, core values, and guiding principles. Members of each group session would be chosen from a list of volunteers, so that each group represents a valid cross section of the company's employees. A session is usually conducted as a casual roundtable discussion with eight to twelve participants. The setting should be relaxed and casual to encourage a free and uninhibited flow of ideas. The CIM or some members from the CIC would normally act as facilitators for the group discussion.

The focus group meetings should have a threefold purpose: first, to determine if all employees *understand* the vision, values, and principles; second, to determine if all employees *accept* and are willing to carry out the vision, values, and principles, and third, to determine if there are any recommendations for *improvement*.

IMPLEMENTING AN INNOVATIVE CULTURE

Introduction

In the following pages we will discuss three powerful approaches for implementing an innovative culture: (1) initial kick-off conferences, (2) periodic deployment efforts, and (3) as-needed task group efforts. Each of these methods has an important role to play in implementing a company's vision, values, and principles; all can be used in the same company at different times. The Initial Kickoff Conferences are used to initiate a new or major change in the vision, values, and principles; they enable a company to get a fast start on cultural improvement. The Periodic Deployment Efforts are less dramatic, but they are highly efficient and effective for implementing cultural change over the long haul. The As-Needed Task Group approach can be used to implement cultural change wherever and whenever change is needed. It is a very effective and flexible tool for implementing specific changes.

The Role of High-Level Leaders in Implementing Culture

Getting Ready for Kickoff

Do not let the existing culture dictate your implementation approach for the new culture. You will have trouble creating a new culture if you insist on implementing it in ways that are consistent with the old one. Culture change moves at a slow crawl if the existing culture gets to call the shots on methodology. Remember, the old culture is designed to protect and perpetuate itself, not to bring about its own demise. From the very outset you must free yourself from the existing culture and conceive a plan of action that starts to liberate the organization from its past.

The kickoff should be dramatic enough to jar your organization from its past. High-level management must hit the organization with a change big enough to shatter the status quo and dislodge the old culture. Heavy-duty intervention is required because the existing corporate culture has a very strong defense system. Unless you can overwhelm its defenses—weaken the culture somehow—it launches a fierce counteroffensive and usually wins. Attempts at incrementally changing the culture are doomed to failure. Significant culture change should start to occur in months, not years. Start out fast and keep trying to pick up speed. There are many good reasons for a high-velocity approach to culture change. There are no valid arguments for going slowly.

Actions Speak Louder than Words

High-level management must realize that actions are much more convincing than words. Management should be clear on the actions that reflect the company's vision, values, and principles and demonstrate them personally.[3] For example, if you want to encourage decentralized decision making, you should find a way to delegate high-visibility decisions currently being made. Above all, live the vision, values, and principles consistently. Your people study your every move. If they catch you following the vision today and then not following it tomorrow, they will resist following it. Not only must the messages be consistent, they must be omnipresent. Act out your vision, values, and principles continuously. Take every opportunity to drive home the message. Leaders live the vision by making all their actions and behaviors consistent with it and by creating a sense of urgency and passion for its attainment.

High-Level Leaders Involve Everyone in Implementation

High-level leaders must learn to let others take responsibility (and credit) for implementing the company's vision, values, and principles; they should check their egos at the door and be less of a guru/hero and more of a facilitator/coach. Following are some concrete suggestions for implementing the company's Mission, Vision, Values, and Principles (MVVP):

- Encourage others to take responsibility for executing the MVVP in their area. Get each person to set goals and action plans and then follow up with them.
- Set up regular multiple communications channels where supervisors discuss the new MVVP with their people.
- Refer questions and comments about the new MVVP to supervisors, rather than answering them directly.
- Lionize others; constantly communicate about the heroic actions of others in multiple mediums.
- Talk about "the team" and "our vision" and "our results." The leader's language has a dramatic empowering impact.
- Avoid answering all questions/problems/difficulties. "I don't know" is a legitimate answer. Employees will respect you for not giving glib, and often incorrect, answers just for the sake of giving an answer.

Initial Kickoff Conferences

The implementation kickoff for cultural change involves a series of three high-powered conferences for high-level management, middle management, and all employees. These three conferences, which can be scheduled within a three- to six-month time frame, constitute an intensive organization-wide intervention that constitutes a form of shock therapy. They are intended for kicking off either a new program or a major change in cultural improvement. They enable the organization to come out of the gate running, rather than having to wait several years for anything to happen. The kickoff approach should *not* be used for a continuing effort or for long-range change efforts. Other methods described later in the chapter are more appropriate for these situations. The Cultural Improvement Manager, with the advice and support of the Cultural Improvement Council, should plan and conduct these conferences.

High-Level Managers Conference

Members of the Cultural Improvement Council and selected other high-level leaders of the organization come together at an off-site location for a one- or two-day workshop to discuss and approve the company's Mission, Vision, Values, and Principles (MVVP). High-level leaders should return from the session with a clear sense of direction and a commitment to achieving their MVVP.

Once the high-level management team is ready, it's time to begin to lay a foundation of trust among the front-line employees. The most important element in this foundation is credibility. The management team's actions must be consistent with their words. When the MVVP are released, they proclaim that certain values are paramount in your organization. These values *must* be reflected in the actions of high-level management. Chief among these is creating a fear-free environment in which every employee is encouraged to participate in a spirit of equality and teamwork.

Nothing will sabotage the entire effort faster than for a manager to say one thing and do another. An obvious example of this is the manager who encourages participation and open communications, then does not listen to anything his/her subordinates have to say, or worse yet, punishes an employee for proposing an idea different from his/hers.

Middle Managers Conference

The most likely source of resistance to the "new thinking" will be middle managers and supervisors. A retreat where fears and concerns can be expressed and answered will pay a rich dividends. Our approach for implementing an innovative culture must take into account the feelings of vulnerability on the part of middle managers. These middle managers can and will sabotage implementation if not given a chance to buy in. An implementation strategy that bypasses the middle managers is doomed to failure.

The change to an innovative culture requires a new mind-set, new behaviors, and a new skill-set for middle managers. We must convince middle managers to accept and embrace these new behaviors if we are to implement an innovative culture. A brief description of the shift that must take place at each of the three levels is provided in Figure 3-2.[4]

Change does not come easily to managers who have climbed the corporate ladder through sheer personal drive and a hands-on style that borders on benevolent dictatorship. It is difficult psychologically and philosophically for those managers to recognize that their role has shifted from being a director and order giver to becoming more an educator and motivator. One of the toughest things for them to learn is that empowerment of subordinates does not mean loss of responsibility. It's just that execution is different.

This new way of operating is not something that can be forced on middle

Figure 3-2
Mind-Set, Behavior Style, and Skills of Middle Managers: Old and New

The Old Mind-Set	The New Mind-Set
I am the boss.	I am a coach.
People are a liability.	People are an asset.
I must have the answers.	We need to find answers.
You do as I say.	How can I help you?

Old Behavior Style	New Behavior Style
Acts as "lone ranger."	Acts as team player.
Tightly controls information.	Shares information.
Demands conformity.	Encourages diversity.
Maintains the status quo.	Encourages innovation.

Old Skills	New Skills
Ability to set goals.	Ability to follow shared vision.
Ability to speak well.	Ability to listen.
Ability to develop self.	Ability to develop group.
Ability to solve problems.	Ability to facilitate team problem solving.

managers. All managers must be given support as they move through the change process. The primary purpose of the Middle Managers Conference is to indicate to the middle managers that the company understands their difficult problem of change and will provide all the support needed to make the change easier. We should also stress the very important part they are expected to play in achieving the new mission, vision, values, and principles.

All-Employee Conferences

After the high-level management and the middle management conferences have been completed and other preliminary work has been completed, the organization is ready for the all-employee conferences. Included in the all-employee conferences are members from all levels and departments. Participants explore common ground, develop a shared understanding of the direction for the future, and identify ways of increasing the responsiveness of the organization to its mission and vision.

Ordinarily a conference lasts two days. Each conference should contain 75 to 150 participants; large organizations will require several conferences. Participation should be voluntary, except for management. The goal is to get a critical mass committed to the new direction. Those who do not participate are given a complete briefing on what transpired at the conference. The data supplied to the conference participants provide a basis for the exploration of ways to improve the way the company operates. The data provided come primarily from the cultural planning effort that generated the vision, core values, and guiding principles. By the end of the conference, each participant:

- Has a clear understanding of the direction for the future
- Has a strong commitment to helping the company achieve its mission, vision, core values, and guiding principles

Planning and executing an all-employee conference is not something that can be reduced to a list of dos and don'ts. It is a highly dynamic event that needs to be skillfully managed. With effective management, it has the potential for generating extraordinary enthusiasm and commitment. The conference can become the defining moment as the organization moves from the old way of doing things to the innovative culture.

Every detail of the two-day conference should be planned. To the casual observer, the conference many seem like a spontaneous unstructured experience. However, the most creative and energizing learning experiences are usually the direct result of a scenario that has been carefully planned. Preplanning includes everything—the number and mix of people in break-out groups, guidelines for discussions, and the amount of time for reporting back to the conference.

While it does not have to resemble a religious revival meeting, a well-planned conference should generate excitement and enthusiasm. It should be fast paced to maintain the momentum. No activity should be scheduled to last more than one hour, presentations to the group should generally not exceed fifteen minutes, and reports from break-out groups should be limited to less than five minutes.

The all-employee conferences generates openness and enthusiasm throughout the organization. It is important that arrangements be made to provide a detailed briefing for employees who did not attend one of the conferences. The major challenge at this stage is to get all employees to accept and embrace the company vision, core values, and guiding principles and to maintain the momentum generated.

Deployment: A Periodic Approach to Implementation

The Kickoff approach to implementation, discussed above, is intended as a one-time effort to initiate a cultural improvement effort. The approach described below is an annual or periodic effort that extends over a number of years. Just as a military commander must deploy his men and armaments to win the military battle, we must deploy our people armed with ideas to win the cultural battle. Our message will be deployed level by level throughout all departments until every man and woman in the organization understands and is committed to the Mission, Vision, core Values and guiding Principles (MVVP).

Overview of Deployment

The purpose of deployment is to discuss the company's mission, vision, values, and principles with every employee in the company in an efficient and effective manner. Deployment involves each manager sitting down with his or her immediate team and having a series of meetings. These meetings should accomplish the following purposes:

• Leader explains and discusses the company's MVVP. Team members ask questions and discuss for understanding

- Team members discuss further for understanding and *commitment*, with the leader acting only as a facilitator and explainer
- Teams develop their own team-specific Mission and Vision
- Teams plan action to achieve company's and own MVVP

Who Should Lead the Deployment Meetings?

Managers should lead these meetings themselves. Do not use an outside facilitator. It is important for team members to hear about the company's MVVP directly from their leaders. Managers must understand and be committed to the Mission, Vision, Values, and Principles in order to properly explain and support them.

The leader's purpose in these meetings is to promote discussion among team members. You should stay out of the discussions as much as possible after the initial explanation. Talk only as necessary to keep the team members talking. You do not want to give the impression that the Mission, Vision, Values, and particularly the Principles are being rammed down their throats by management. Commitment will come only after they have voluntarily accepted them following open and frank discussions. That means you should explain, give examples, and discuss what they mean to you, but you should not engage in a long tirade about why they should be adopted.

The Deployment Process

Deployment is a top-down, bottom-up discussion process that proceeds through the organization one level at a time. The first series of discussions is between top managers and their next level of managers. At the end of each series of discussions, the company's MVVP (plus the missions and visions of higher levels) are passed down to the next level for discussion. Proposed changes and unanswered questions will go up until they are resolved or answered. Attendees at one series of discussions will become the leaders of the next series. In the following guide, we have divided the discussions into four *types* of meetings. The actual number and length of the meetings should be determined by the local situation.

1. Leader explains and discusses the company's MVVP and missions and visions of higher levels.

- Establish the purpose of this portion of the meetings: to learn and understand the purpose and content of the company's MVVP and the missions and visions of higher levels. This first group of meetings is primarily educational.
- Explain the need for and the relationship between the Mission, Vision, Values, and Principles.
- Distribute copies of the draft of the company's Mission, Vision, Values, and Principles

and missions and visions of higher levels. Read them with the team, explaining concepts and terms, providing examples, and answering questions, as appropriate.

• Discuss how the MVVP and missions and visions of higher levels apply to the work of the team and how they will enable us to do a better job.

2. Team members discuss further for understanding and commitment.

• Establish the purpose of this portion of the meetings: to have a full, honest, no-holds-barred discussion (and possible modification) of the corporate MVVP and missions and visions of higher levels to ensure that every team member will fully support them without reservation.

• In particular, have them examine each of the Principles in detail, since they will be most pertinent to the team members. Can they be followed? Do they make sense? Will they require changes on the part of team members.

• Explain that the current MVVP and missions and visions of higher levels are only drafts. They are subject to continuous improvement like everything else. Ask if anything should be added or subtracted. Ask if they could be written more clearly.

• At the conclusion we would like to obtain a voluntary commitment from each team member that they will do everything in their power to follow the company's MVVP and missions and visions of higher levels. This commitment must be voluntary and honest to be worthwhile.

3. Teams develop their own team-specific Mission and Vision.

• Establish the purpose of this portion of the meetings: to develop a Mission and Vision that are unique to this team and a draft mission and vision for each member's team.

• The leader distributes draft copies of the team's mission and vision. Read them with the team, explaining concepts and terms, providing examples, and answering questions, as appropriate. Emphasize that they are first drafts that should be modified and improved.

• The team discusses the mission and vision, starting with the mission statement, which should answer the questions: *What* are we now doing? *What* do we intend to **do**? for whom? when? and why?

• The team discusses the vision statement that should answer the following questions: *Who* are we? *Who* do we intend to **be**? why? and how? What kind of place will this be to work?

• Members prepare draft mission and vision in preparation for meeting with their team.

4. Plan the action to achieve the company's MVVP and your mission and vision.

• Determine your current position in regard to the company's MVVP and your mission and vision. Be as specific as possible.

• Discuss where the team is accomplishing its Mission and Vision and where it is not.

Encourage the team to identify and develop plans to close the gap between the current situation and the intended situation.

- Compare your current position with the final intended position and define the gap between them.

- Develop time-phased plans to close and ultimately to eliminate the gap.

Making the Deployment Process Successful

In the above guide, we divided the discussions into four types of meetings. We did not intend to imply that only four meetings would be required. It may take a greater number of meetings, particularly if the Mission, Vision, Values, and Principles are brand new. Do not try to rush the process. This is a major change for everybody in the company. It takes time for people to examine and absorb the MVVP and decide how they feel about them.

The deployment process should be repeated whenever there is a change in the company's MVVP, or annually if there are no changes. If there is a *major* change, the Kickoff approach may be advisable. The annual deployment is primarily a review and can be accomplished much more rapidly than the initial deployment.

As-Needed Task Group Implementation Efforts

Introduction

An *organization-wide* task group is one of the most effective tools for sustaining involvement and commitment after completing the Kickoff Conferences and the Deployment Meetings. Following are a few simple guidelines to keep in mind in establishing a task group:

- Include representation from all major constituencies, including high-level management.
- The mandate for the task group should be stated in a clear written statement. The statement should originate with the CEO.
- The time frame for accomplishing the task must be clearly specified.
- Resources needed to accomplish the task must be provided. This will include time to hold meetings. Some groups will need the services of a trained facilitator.

The task groups take up where the Kickoff Conferences and the Deployment Meetings stop. An effective follow-up to the Kickoff Conferences would include task groups in the following areas.

Cultural Assessment

The purpose and procedures for conducting a Cultural Assessment are given as the first step in the cultural planning process described at the beginning of this chapter. The Cultural Assessment should be conducted before any of the Kickoff Conferences are scheduled.

Customer/Supplier Conference

This one- or two-day conference brings together a team made up of representatives of key departments and a representative group of customers and suppliers. Quality Function Deployment (described in Chapter 8) provides a useful methodology for clearly identifying the wants and needs of customers and suppliers. Despite long involvement with particular customers, managers, and employees, companies will always learn something new from this conference. This task group should definitely be convened before the *all-employees conference*, and perhaps even before the high-level management conference.

Business Process Reengineering Study

This study group, representing all employees, has the responsibility for identifying key business processes that need improving. They establish and provide support for teams involved in the redesign of key processes. This task group can evolve into a steering group for the process reengineering effort that is discussed in detail in Chapter 5.

Competitive Benchmarking Study

This study compares the company's operations with those of other firms. Typically, the comparison is made with those firms believed to exhibit the most efficient operations. Speed to market is a particularly useful benchmark.

Company Information Study

This study group, composed of representatives of all major employee groups, has the responsibility for developing systems and procedures for ensuring that all employees have access to all information on the business. They analyze current communications channels and develop recommendations.

Additional Task Group Studies As Needed

We have described the most-used task group efforts. However, the list of topics that would be worthy of a task group effort is almost endless. Additional task group efforts based on the local situation should be authorized if they will be productive. All task group efforts should be coordinated by the CIM and CIC to ensure there is no duplication or conflict of effort.

Summary of Implementation Efforts

Shown in Figure 3-3 is a summary of the implementation methods we have discussed. Each of the three different methods has a specific role to play in implementing a company's vision, values, and principles. The Initial Kickoff Conferences are used to initiate a new or major change in the vision, values,

Figure 3-3
Summary of Culture Implementation Methods

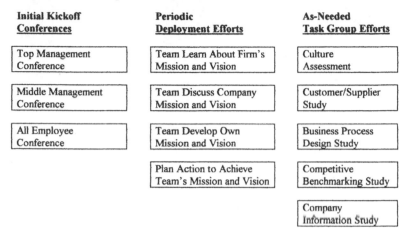

Initial Kickoff Conferences	Periodic Deployment Efforts	As-Needed Task Group Efforts
Top Management Conference	Team Learn About Firm's Mission and Vision	Culture Assessment
Middle Management Conference	Team Discuss Company Mission and Vision	Customer/Supplier Study
All Employee Conference	Team Develop Own Mission and Vision	Business Process Design Study
	Plan Action to Achieve Team's Mission and Vision	Competitive Benchmarking Study
		Company Information Study

and principles; they enable a company to get a fast start on cultural improvement. The Periodic Deployment Efforts are less dramatic, but are highly efficient and effective for implementing cultural change over the long haul. The As-Needed Task Group approach can be used to implement specific change wherever and whenever change is needed. It is a very effective and flexible tool for implementing specific changes.

CONCLUSIONS

Just because a company has well-defined, well-known, and well-accepted Mission, Vision, Values, and Principles doesn't mean that it will necessarily be an innovative company. Developing the MVVP is a necessary first step, but it is not the end. The essence of an innovative company comes in the translation of its culture—the MVVP—into everything that it is and does. A company's culture must permeate everything in the company: organizational structure, leadership style, management practices, employee behavior, human resources, management, policies, processes, procedures, information systems, reward systems, pay systems, job design, product design, and even building design. An innovative company creates a total environment that envelops employees, bombarding them with a set of signals so consistent and mutually reinforcing that it's virtually impossible to misunderstand the company's Mission, Vision, Core Values, and Guiding Principles.

NOTES

1. John P. Kotter and James L. Heskett, *Corporate Culture and Performance* (Free Press, 1992), pp. 84–92.

2. Alan L. Wilkins, *Developing Corporate Character: How to Successfully Change an Organization without Destroying It* (Jossey-Bass, 1989).

3. Burt Nanus, *Visionary Leadership* (Jossey-Bass, 1992).

4. Edward Deevy, *Creating the Resilient Organization* (Prentice-Hall, 1995).

Chapter 4

Changing Organizational Behavior and Structure

In an innovative organization human resources—and not financial and physical capital—are an organization's competitive edge, and management must maximize the output of highly educated workers. As the "organization man" becomes a dying species and workers owe their livelihoods primarily to professional training and brain power rather than membership in industrial labor unions, *participatory management* styles are becoming increasingly important. The rise of the knowledge worker is requiring a shift from an authoritarian management style to a networking, participative style of management. Participatory management evolves into *self-management*—employees taking responsibility and initiative, monitoring their work, and using managers and supervisors as teachers and facilitators. Self-management presumes that workers are competent, self-confident, and independent and that people perform better when they manage themselves.

This chapter presents methods for changing the behavior of both managers and employees to support the innovative culture. The change in organization from the traditional organization to the organization needed to support an innovative culture is also described.

PARTICIPATIVE MANAGEMENT AND EMPLOYEE INVOLVEMENT

In the next several pages we will discuss employee involvement. However, we must realize that employee involvement can not happen unless management adopts a more participative management style. Employee involvement can not survive and thrive in an atmosphere of autocratic management and hierarchical organizations.

The majority of today's managers have been trained and have managed in the traditional hierarchical/autocratic style of management. They have learned to get things done using their authority through the well-defined lines of the traditional hierarchy. If employee involvement is to succeed in the long run, that management style must change. Ingrained attitudes and entrenched systems must change. Otherwise employee involvement will ultimately be rejected by an organization whose systems and practices are unsupportive.

Changes in Management Style

Managers as Teachers and Facilitators

The critical skill that is desired in workers in the innovative organization is the ability to think—to synthesize, make generalizations, divide into categories, draw references, distinguish between fact and opinion, and organize facts to analyze a problem. Education must continue beyond early formal schooling because knowledge of any subject that is not continually updated will become obsolete.

Managers in the innovative organization must be teachers and facilitators who do not control the workers but liberate them. This is a fundamental reshaping of the traditional managerial prerogative of giving orders. To be a coach, teacher, and mentor means creating a nourishing environment for personal growth. Because this is so contrary to the traditional military-style management thinking, the big challenge is not to retrain workers but to retrain managers.

Whatever else the leader does, his/her ultimate goal is to focus the organization's energies on *learning* and *innovating*. We say "ultimate goal" because trust, coordinating, and communicating must come first; they make or break the organization. In the long run, the organization prospers only when it innovates continually—and to accomplish this it must learn continuously.

Managers as Intrapreneurs

Managers will increasingly be required to be innovators and intrapreneurs in addition to being teachers and facilitators. We look at intrapreneurship as a form of management that transfers resources from an area of low productivity to an area of high productivity. Control-oriented administrators will be less and less in demand.

The more the leader can turn the organization's members into intrapreneurs, the more learning and creativity will increase—ownership and intrapreneurship support learning and innovation. An individual or team with ownership of its results and anticipating rewards for achieving them cannot afford to reject good ideas from any source. They will be motivated to learn from any and all sources as quickly as possible.

Employment Empowerment

Involving people in decisions relative to their work is a fundamental principle of good management. In the innovative organization, this principle is taken even further. First, employees are involved not only in decision making but also in the creative thought processes that precede decision making. Second, not only are employees involved, they are also empowered. Employee involvement and empowerment are closely related concepts, but they are not the same.

Employee involvement is a way of engaging employees at all levels in the thinking processes of an organization. It's the recognition that many decisions made in an organization can be made better by soliciting the input of those who may be affected by the decision. It's an understanding that people at all levels of an organization possess unique talents, skills, and creativity than can be of significant value if allowed to be expressed.

Employee empowerment is employee involvement that matters. It's the difference between just having an input and having an input that is heard, seriously considered, and followed up on, whether it is accepted or not. The objective of empowerment is to tap the creative and intellectual energy of everybody in the company, not just those in the executive suite, and to provide everyone with the responsibility and the resources to display real leadership within their own individual spheres of competence.

Most employee involvement systems fail within the first year. The reason is simple; they involve but do not empower employees. Without empowerment, involvement is just another management tool that does not work. For empowerment to occur, companies must undertake two initiatives: (1) identify and change organizational conditions that make people powerless, and (2) increase people's confidence that their efforts to accomplish something important will be successful.

The need to do both of these implies that organizational systems often create powerless employees and that these systems must be changed first. Systems especially needing change are those that specify who can (and cannot) make certain types of decisions. Even when systems are changed to permit empowerment, some individuals who have lived under the old system for a long time are not readily able to operate in an empowered manner. Everyone needs to be convinced that they can really make a difference and should therefore fully utilize their empowerment.

Empowerment is important primarily because it improves organizational performance. Everyone in an organization is an asset, albeit an asset whose value is not automatically realized. If money is put into a closet instead of a bank, it will not produce results (interest). Similarly, if employees are locked into an organizational closet by restrictive rules that make them powerless, they cannot produce creative and productive results.

Empowerment may sound easy, but there is a lot more to it than telling employees they are empowered. A number of principles are involved in successfully giving power to employees[1]:

* *Empower sincerely and completely.* It should go without saying that empowerment must be done sincerely. It cannot be done superficially. To gain its benefits, managers must empower for its improvement value, not for its public relations value. This does

not mean there should be no limits. On the contrary, managers must be clear on exactly what responsibility and authority rest with employees.

* *Provide employees with business information.* For empowerment to succeed, it must focus on making the organization more competitive. Empowerment can contribute to organizational performance only if employees have access to the necessary information about the business and its performance. In the absence of appropriate information, empowered employees may waste their power on problems that are not very important.

* *Ensure that employees are capable.* You cannot empower incompetence. If employees are going to take on important organizational responsibilities, they must be prepared to do so. To operate in an empowered innovative environment, employees must possess not only technical skills but also interpersonal and problem-solving skills.

* *Do not ignore middle management.* Managers must consider how empowering lower-level employees will affect middle managers. If the needs and expectations of middle managers are ignored, empowerment will be confusing at best and disastrous at worst. In an empowered organization, middle managers should be encouraged and assisted in taking on the following new roles: (1) acting as project team managers and network managers, (2) managing solutions to system-level problems—those that involve many functions—and (3) acting as teachers and coaches.

* *Change the reward system.* Rarely can substantial organizational change be created without changing the reward system. The reward system includes all of the rewards that employees receive, as well as the criteria for distributing these rewards.

* *Establish Mutual Trust.* The managers must trust the work force enough to be willing to make the delegation, and the work force must have enough confidence in the managers to be willing to accept the responsibility. Trust is not created just by saying you trust someone; it must be backed up by action. Trust is indicated to employees by opening up heretofore closed company records such as personnel, budget, and the like. The element of trust is so important in employee empowerment that we devote the following section to it.

Methods of Employee Involvement

The real power of employee involvement lies in its ability to bring about cultural change by fostering a more participative management style in an organization. Participative management does not equate to quality circles or any specific involvement method. Rather, participative management is an organized set of ideas about *how* to manage an innovative business enterprise. While participatively managed organization certainly utilizes methods like quality circles to involve employees in problem solving, involvement goes much deeper.

Employee involvement should be viewed as an organizational culture change effort, which must be supported by a strong management commitment, a long-term perspective, and reinforcing organizational systems. Although we should never assume that merely using involvement methods will result in employee involvement, involvement techniques do play an important part. We cannot hope to achieve a change in management style without them. Methods provide us with mechanisms that enable employees to become involved in a structured way. Ultimately, we would like to reach a state where employees are involved in problem solving and decision making informally on a day-to-day basis. Until we get there, we must facilitate involvement through organized, structured mechanisms so the organization can gain some experience and skills in employee involvement.

Because involvement methods are vital elements in our cultural change strategy, it is important that we utilize them intelligently. There are a wide variety of involvement methods, and they vary greatly in terms of their sophistication, organizational support requirements, and effectiveness in supporting change. Given the wide variety of employee involvement methods, it is useful to organize them along a continuum from *information sharing* to *work and organization design* as indicated in Figure 4-1.

At the upper left of the continuum are those methods that are relatively simple, can be implemented without a major commitment of management time and resources, and can reasonably be effective in a traditional hierarchical organization. The work redesign methods at the lower right of the continuum represent the state of the art in employee involvement—they truly represent *employee empowerment*. They are highly sophisticated; and because they represent a radical departure from traditional management practices, they require extremely high levels of management commitment. They should not even be considered by an organization that is a novice in employee involvement.

Information and Idea Sharing Methods

Information Sharing. This most basic of all employee involvement methods should be a fundamental feature of all involvement efforts. Lacking information about organizational performance, the nature and challenges of the business, and

Figure 4-1
Employee Involvement Methods

Information Sharing Methods
- Information Sharing
- Education and Training
- Survey Feedback

    Idea Generation Methods
-     Suggestion Systems
-     Idea-Generation Groups

        Group Problem Solving Methods
-         Ad Hoc Task Teams
-         Project (Matrix) Management
-         Quality Circles

            Work/Organization Redesign Methods
-             Process Management
-             Autonomous Networked Teams

the rationale behind decisions that affect their jobs, employees become alienated and resentful. They feel no loyalty toward the organization and are not committed to its objectives and endeavors. Improved communications is a low-risk tactic and can serve to unfreeze the organization.

Survey Feedback. The survey is a useful method because it is a cost-effective way to involve a large number of employees and gain useful information about the enterprise. Surveys can take a variety of forms. The written instrument is best known, but surveys can also be conducted through personal interviews. Surveys can also serve a variety of purposes. They can be used to gather opinion, probe attitudes, gauge organization climate, or identify improvement opportunities. Surveys are especially useful as a means of monitoring progress in efforts to change organizational climate; survey results from several successive periods can be compared as a measure of process.

Once a survey has been administered, it is imperative that the organization do two things: feed back the results and take action on the issues identified. By administering a survey, management raises employee expectations. The work force expects to learn of the survey's conclusions and anticipates that management will take appropriate action. If management is not prepared to provided full and honest feedback and to address the key issues raised by the survey, it would be wise to forego this method, as the involvement benefits will largely be lost and employee resentment may well result.

Idea Generation Methods

Suggestion Systems. Suggestion systems are organized approaches to obtaining and evaluating employee ideas for improvement. One of the most widespread employee involvement methods, suggestion systems unfortunately are often ineffective in practice. Ineffectiveness is not an inherent trait of suggestion systems, but instead stems from poor design. Certain features are invariably found in *successful* suggestions systems:

- *Supervisory support.* Supervisory assistance in defining and developing the ideas can significantly increase the quality and quantity of ideas submitted.
- *Prompt feedback.* Lack of feedback to suggestors will ensure the failure of the system.
- *Recognition and reward.* Employees whose ideas provide benefit to the company are certainly not unreasonable in expecting recognition for their contributions.

Group Idea Generation Methods. A number of group idea generation methods are available. They are all very similar in that they attempt to unleash the creativeness of group members by employing specific group procedures. These group idea generation methods are described in detail in Chapter 6, where they are used extensively in generating new ideas for products. They will only be listed here: brainstorming, nominal group method, checklists, focus groups, problem analysis, scenario analysis, and perceptual map analysis.

Group Problem-Solving Methods

Moving from idea-generation methods to group problem-solving methods is not a trivial undertaking. Both supervisors and employees must be trained in problem-solving methods. Facilitators are required to organize problem-solving groups, provide the training, and support the group's efforts. As a result, problem-solving methods require a greater commitment of the organization's time and resources. However, they can result in significant improvements and, more important, can begin to foster meaningful organization culture change.

Ad Hoc Task Groups. The least demanding of the problem-solving techniques is the ad hoc task group. An ad hoc task group is simply a group of managers and employees that have been brought together to solve a particular problem. The problem is defined by management, and the groups are typically disbanded after a solution has been developed and presented. Some group leadership and problem-solving training is often provided, but not always. Since a task force has only a limited life and little or no discretion in choosing its problems, it is a relatively low-risk means of engaging employees in problem solving. As such, it can serve as a useful bridge between information sharing methods and the more sophisticated problem-solving methods.

Project (Matrix) Management. Project or matrix management leaves the hierarchy in place, but superimposes a horizontal structure in order to achieve some coordination and integration. The horizontal structure may be defined in terms of products or projects. A product or project manager assumes responsibility for the horizontal flow. He or she coordinates, integrates, and expedites work among the functions. Matrix structures vary in terms of how power and authority are divided between functional managers and product/project managers. Companies using matrix management tend to have a large number of projects underway at all times, with the composition of the projects changing continuously

Quality Circles. Quality circles are permanent problem-solving teams consisting of employees from a common work area. Participation in quality circles is voluntary, and circles meet on a regular basis on company time to identify and solve problems. Circles choose their own problems to solve and thus enjoy a greater degree of autonomy than the project group. Despite the name, problems addressed are not limited to quality, but typically include product ideas, productivity, quality of work life, and other work issues.

Work and Organization Redesign Methods

The problem-solving techniques discussed above are not actually integrated into the structure and practices of the organization. Involvement occurs "off line," rather than within the context of employees' day-to-day jobs. The problem-solving groups are not found on organization charts; they are *parallel* to the formal organization. If we wish to achieve the ultimate in employee involvement, commitment, and effectiveness, that is, achieve *employee empowerment,* we must *redesign* jobs, and the organization itself, so that maximum involvement is built into day-to-day work practices. As an interim step we can improve employee involvement within the traditional hierarchical organization by designing permanent "process teams" that cut across functional boundaries. However, if we truly wish to maximize involvement, we must redesign both the jobs and the organization structure.

Process Team Management. Implementation of *process team management* starts with the identification of horizontal work processes within the organization. Horizontal processes are those that are made up of a continuous chain of supplier, producer, and customer relationships. The process team consists of a number of employees organized around a single work process, who are interdependent in their functioning and have a common leader. Everyone in the organization is a member of a team, and the teams extend all the way up the hierarchy, that is, every team leader is a member of a higher-level team. Process teams differ from ad hoc task teams and matrix management in that they are a permanent part of the organization.

Process team management is a horizontal approach that focuses on the achievement of corporate-wide goals and objectives. It works on the process to change the procedures and culture to achieve smoother flows and better achieve operational goals. An innovative organization knows that people feel ownership for processes for which they have shared in the creation. Consequently experienced process managers tend to be alliance builders who influence others in the organization to work together as a team to accomplish organizational goals and objectives. Process team management is described in greater detail in Chapter 5.

Autonomous Networked Teams. Autonomous *networked team management* is based on autonomous teams and businesses networked together across the enterprise. Rather than a rigid structure, it is a modular organizational architecture in which business teams operate in a network of what we call *customer and producer* functions. Teams form, expand, contract, and disband in response to operational needs. Teams are both customers and producers for other teams, who are both internal and external to the organization. As producers, they receive requests or directions from customers, make requests of other producer functions, and add value for the purpose of serving these customers.

The autonomous work team is essentially a self-managed work unit. Members of the team select their own leader and are involved, on a routine basis, in decision making, goal setting, hiring, planning, peer reviews, and problem solving. They determine how they will work together, for instance, and how they will rotate through the various jobs. In a traditional work group, a process is divided into various tasks and a task is assigned to each employee. By contrast, employees in the autonomous team are cross-trained to execute all the jobs in the process.

Beyond Empowerment: Every Employee an Intrapreneur

Empowering all employees is an important step in improving the effectiveness of an organization. But we should not stop there. We should go beyond empowerment and make every employee an intrapreneur[2]. As an intrapreneur, the employee will act as the owner of his or her own business. An intraprise is a business still legally owned by the larger organization but operated and controlled internally by one or more employees of the organization. An intraprise may serve internal or external customers or both.

The right to form an intraprise liberates the energy and intelligence of the ordinary employee. A team of people who believe they can do something better than it is currently being done are free to try to sell their idea as a product or service. The right to form an intraprise is the right of intrapreneurial individuals and teams to exchange their jobs in the bureaucratic chain for autonomous jobs in a small company, without leaving their parent company.

In a free intraprise system, would-be intrapreneurs do not have to sell their ideas to their chain of command. Bureaucrats can be champions of the competing old way and are liable to resist the new ideas that may make their skills, systems, and capital equipment obsolete. Instead, in a free intraprise system, the intrapreneurs must sell their ideas to the customers who will benefit from them. This shift from the power of the chain of command to the power of the network of customers is the power shift that ends the dominance of bureaucracy.

With imagination, every job can become an intraprise. The intrapreneural job must be such that the employee essentially runs his or her own business. Intrapreneurial jobs have the following characteristics:

- composed of mainly self-initiated projects
- perform ad hoc problem-solving directly for individual internal or external customers
- work in multifunctional configuration, with self-initiated access to experts inside and outside the company
- performance is measured on bottom line result, based mainly on customer and teammate evaluations rather than a boss's subjective judgment

EMPHASIS ON HUMAN RESOURCES MANAGEMENT

If the innovative organization is to be effective, the systems and processes put in place must be staffed by highly qualified people. People must be regarded as critical system elements that must be managed with quality and consistency. In traditional organizations, human resources managers identify, prepare, direct, and reward employees for following rather narrow objectives. In innovative organizations, human resources managers develop policies and procedures to assure that employees can perform multiple roles, improvise when necessary, and direct themselves toward continuous improvement of both products and processes. Human resources has evolved from a support function to a leadership function. This requires a significant adjustment not only on the part of human resources professionals, but on that of line managers as well.

Human Resources Practices in an Innovative Organization

For an innovative organization to operate effectively, human resources professionals must recruit, develop, motivate, and retain its most valuable resource—creative people. In order to carry out their important responsibilities, human resources managers have developed a number of new policies and practices. We will explore some of the policies and practices of innovative organizations.

They integrate all their human resources plans and policies into a coherent design that supports the corporate mission, vision, values, and principles. Human resources plans must follow and support the highest-level direction of the company, the mission and the vision. Long-term plans concentrate on developing the continuous-learning environment and developing new systems for empowering and developing employees. Periodic deployment meetings, discussed in Chapter 3, provide a means for ensuring that human resources plans are aligned with the company's mission and vision.

They develop a comprehensive and concerted effort for hiring creative people. They develop such a reputation for having a creative, exciting place to work that the line forms outside their door. To keep up the talent flow, they encourage and reward employees for recommending new hires. They continue to recruit from colleges and universities, but they also consider work-study programs and making contact with potential hires in high school, then following the outstanding ones through college before hiring them permanently.

They continually improve key personnel management processes such as recruitment, hiring, training, performance evaluation, and recognition. A key approach to improving human resources practices is the use of employee surveys and measurement of key indicators. Employees also participate in focus groups to identify causes and work toward solutions.

They empower individuals and teams to make decisions that effect innovation, quality, and customer satisfaction. Many companies talk about empowerment, but few truly practice it. Empowerment requires substantial training. All employees should be provided general training in such areas as communication techniques, problems solving, statistical quality control, leadership, and team building, in addition to being provided specific training to do their jobs.

They hire individuals to make a lifetime contribution, not to fill a specific position. Many of the better companies, such as Hewlett-Packard, look for a specific set of skills, for instance, electrical engineering, math ability, or experience in dealing with the public. But the criteria that really matter to them are personal attributes and abilities that will contribute to the company for years, not just for weeks or months.

They train constantly and integrate the training into ongoing operations. Training can solve a multitude of ills, but only if it is related to the present and future activities of the person being trained. Even when the training is designed to develop employees (management, leadership, etc.), it's built around how work is actually performed.

They teach creativity to all employees. Most companies consider that creativity can be improved by training. Such training programs run the gamut from introductory classes in traditional brainstorming to elaborate sessions that include games and horseplay. Obvious, but often overlooked, is training in the company's products, markets, competition, and technologies.

They measure creativity and innovation. Although creativity and innovation are not easy to measure, an attempt is well worth the effort. People tend to strive to excel in those areas in which they are measured. So even if the measurement results are not definitive, the fact that you attempted to measure will improve creativity and innovation.

They make the challenge and worth of the work itself the most important motivator for high performance—for everyone. Effective performers should earn well, but should never think of pay as the primary motivator. Everyone, from the most junior clerk to the CEO, should view his or her job as an intriguing challenge. Everyone should want to and be expected to contribute to the fullest from his or her very first day.

They are expert at balancing people and work, creative and routine work, and individual and team work. If companies have followed the previous guidelines, they will be flexible enough that individuals will find their places. If teams are working effectively, they will accomplish much of the balancing. The more self-managing the teams become, the more skilled they will become at balancing tasks and people.

They maintain a work environment conducive to the well-being and growth of all employees. Happy employees are innovative and productive employees. By maintaining an enjoyable, bureaucracy-free environment, one that encourages innovative thinking and honest communication, people are free to concentrate solely on the needs of the customers.

They foster new interaction patterns. They create a physical environment that (a) lets people express their personalities, (b) allows project teams to form at a moment's notice, (c) encourages getting together and hanging out, and (d) intentionally snubs traditional functional groupings. Space is a powerful force for reflecting (and shaping) organizational culture. This fact is recognized by too few managers.

They ensure that work is fun. We do not mean that work is a barrel of laughs, but rather that the company is a fun place to go to work, even on Monday morning. Work is exciting, and there is always something to look forward to—in short, it is enjoyable. People who enjoy their work and their fellow employees will stay with the company even under adverse circumstances.

They do not motivate by money, but they ensure their compensation system is congruent with the emphasis on creativity. Creativity cannot be motivated by money alone. However, money rewards must be consistent with individual and team contributions, or they will act as powerful demotivators. Actually, in an innovative organization, money can cause more problems than it solves. A company should start with the challenge. If the employees rise to the challenge, pay them for it.

They ensure that all incentives fit together to support creative performance. In the previous item, we noted that financial incentives should follow, not lead, creative performance. There are many other elements of the compensation plan that should follow creativity as well, such as promotions, bonuses, key jobs, and choice assignments. In an innovative organization, employees who do not strive to be proactive and creative will find themselves at the end of the line for everything, including parking spaces.

They ensure that demotivating situations, such as the following, do not occur.

- The organization stresses teamwork and gives special plaques honoring it, but appraises and promotes on the basis of individual performance.
- The organization stresses the importance of front-line performers, but does nothing to help them in dealing with customers.
- The organization stresses quality and innovation, but gives bonuses based on profitability alone.
- The organization stresses autonomy and initiative, but key spots go to those who never make waves.

Human Resources Management Must Support Employee Involvement

Employee involvement requires changes in human resources practices. Monetary rewards over and above basic wages should be tied to organizational accomplishment. Additionally, skill-based compensation systems become a basis for determining compensation based on *potential* contribution to the organization. A person is paid on the basis of certified skills. Usually tiers of skill clusters are established. A new employee is paid at an entry-level pay rate when he or she first enters a work unit. Once capable of performing a basic set of functions, the employee receives the next higher rate. A third tier is reached when the employee can perform all the tasks or functions within the work unit or team. A fourth tier might reflect special skills that are periodically needed at the the work site. This is in contrast to the traditional job-based compensation systems that pay the individual employee based on the specific job he or she is actually doing at a particular point in time. Skill-based pay encourages the development of a range of skills and rewards employees for the flexibility they provide the work unit.

Cross-training becomes a significant element of employee involvement and an important responsibility of human resources. It must be effective and available to all employees. In organizations making extensive use of teams, the development of technical and team competencies is a team responsibility. Usually a team member ensures that all members have the requisite training, but the training must be planned and provided by human resources.

DEVELOPING INNOVATIVE ORGANIZATIONS

The Changing Nature of Organizations

Under industrialization, bureaucracy was the dominant form of organization. The factory was designed to produce standardized products; the bureaucracy, to produce standardized decisions. Most major corporations developed in an industrial society, based on a bureaucratic model of machine-like division of function, routine activity, permanence, and a very long vertical hierarchy. It was a world of mass markets, uniform goods and services, and long production runs.

There is growing recognition that yesterday's hierarchical bureaucracies do not work in the new knowledge society. The hierarchical structure where everyone has a superior and everyone has an inferior is demeaning to the human spirit—no matter how well it served us during the industrial period. The authoritarian organization has a stultifying effect on initiative and innovation. People feel they cannot change their environment and thus never seek the information that might change it. The top-down authoritarian management style is yielding to a networking style of management, where people learn from one another horizontally, where everyone is a resource for everyone else, and where each person gets support and assistance from many different directions.

Problems with the Traditional Functional Organization

Functional Structure Overemphasizes Vertical Relationships. The functional structure promotes the idea that one's boss is the prime customer that *must* be satisfied. Each manager is more interested in satisfying the next-level manager than the real customer. Managers in functional organizations are usually rewarded for satisfying functional goals, such as meeting design deadlines and limiting manufacturing costs, rather than for providing value to customers. This emphasis on vertical reporting relationships to the exclusion of horizontal coordination has led many authors to refer to departments in functional organizations as ''chimneys'' or ''silos.''

Functional Structure Separates Employees from Customers. Few employees in the functional organization have direct contact with the customers or even a clear idea of how their work combines with the work of others to satisfy customers. The functional structure tends to insulate employees from learning about customer expectations and their degree of satisfaction with the service or product the firm is providing. Being insulated from customers encourages workers to hold a narrow conception of their responsibilities.

Functional Structure Inhibits Process Improvement. No organizational unit has control over a whole process, although many processes involve a large number of functions. This is because the breakup of the organization into functions is usually unrelated to the processes used to deliver a product to the customer. This structure is likely to create complex wasteful processes as people do things in one area that must be redone or undone in another. This deficiency is especially important, since the product development process is one of the major processes of an innovative organization.

Functional Structure Hinders Creativity and Innovation. The functional structure not only hinders an organization's innovativeness but also has a strong negative effect on the creativity and innovativeness of the individual. People feel they cannot change their environment and thus never seek the information and ideas that might change it. The top-down authoritarian management style is yielding to a networking style of management, where people learn from one another horizontally, where everyone is a resource for everyone else, and where each person gets support and assistance from many different directions.

The Structure of Future Innovative Organizations

The Rise of Participation. If hierarchy was central to traditional organizations, the lack of hierarchy is central to the future innovative organization. This shift away from hierarchy does not spell the death of order, despite the fears of many corporate managers. The opposite of hierarchy is not anarchy. What is emerging in place of the rigid structure of the traditional organization is a variety of flexible new forms with a single feature in common: all value and practice more participatory decision making.

Participation is inevitable in environments that must accommodate rapid and endless change. Participation in industry is not an idealist conception but a hard necessity in those areas where changes are ever present and creative scientific enterprise must be nourished. Participation is the only system of organization that is compatible with perpetual change.

Participation is essential in organizations that rely on the creativity of all workers to produce continuous innovation. Innovation requires participative processes: the sharing of information across departments, functions, and organizational levels; team decision making; conflict resolution; and deference to the person with the best idea rather than the most senior title.

The Networked Organization. Many people are struggling to determine the shape of the innovative organization. A variety of new forms are emerging. Whatever their shape, all are loose, *organic* arrangements of people and technology—flexible, adaptive, capable of reconfiguration to meet the requirement of the moment. Within these fluid structures, employees work in self-managing teams, functioning with great autonomy as long as their work is compatible with the mission, values, and objectives of the organization. Some teams are more or less fixed, working together over long spans of time. Others form spontaneously—across functions and levels, even across organizational boundaries—to solve problems and produce innovations, then disband once they have achieved their goals. The product development team is one of the more important of these temporary teams that form and function long enough to achieve their purpose and then disband.

Many see the organizational structure of the future as some form of network in which employees are free to move in any direction, even across boundaries of function and level, to link up with anyone to accomplish a task. *However, we should not fall into the trap of thinking that an innovative organization will assume only one form.* The same organization may adopt many different forms over time, and many different structures may emerge within a single organization as it attempts to accommodate continuous change. It is probably more true to say that *networking* will be the glue that holds the organization together than to suggest that a *network structure* will be the primary form of organization.

The Networked Organization

Networks offer what bureaucracies can never deliver—the horizontal link. Networks cut across the organization to provide genuine cross-functional approaches to people and issues. Within the networking structure, information itself is the great equalizer. Networks are egalitarian, not just because every member is a peer. On the contrary, because the networks are diagonal and three-dimensional, they involve people from every possible level. What occurs in a network is that members treat one another as peers—because what is important is the information, the great equalizer. Structurally, the most important thing about a network is that each individual is at its center.

The Free Intraprise Network

The alternative to corporate bureaucracy is not merely training managers to behave in an empowering way within a bureaucratic structure; it is developing a system of freedoms and institutions analogous to free enterprise, a system of organization that we will call the *free intraprise network*. Free intraprise empowers ordinary employees to start a "business" (or intraprise) within the organization if they can find the customers and the capital to do so.

When employees create an intraprise, the form of control changes from dependence on the hierarchy to interdependence with customers and suppliers. Customers, not bureaucrats, are the basic controllers of the free enterprise and free intraprise systems alike. Rather than having a bureaucrat decide, free choices by buyers and sellers throughout the network determine what is needed, what is cost-effective, and what creates the most value. Because there are many different potential customers, an intraprise no longer rises or falls on the opinion of one bureaucrat.

The overall pattern of an innovative organization is a network of interdependent intraprises and their associated internal and external customers and suppliers. Some intraprises focus on serving external customers directly, such as the product order and delivery system. Others focus on serving internal customers. Internal intraprises created to serve internal customers can do so more efficiently than bureaucratic departments ever could. Large businesses can consist of a relatively small number of externally focused intraprises served by a network of internal intraprises.

Including external contractors in the network can lead to some interesting relationships. There may be times when a company is simultaneously providing a service to a customer, subcontracting a service from that customer, and competing with the same firm. Company personnel have to remember which relationship they're working on when they're talking. If they can manage these three relationships in an effective manner, they will come out winners.

The network organization has the advantage that it can achieve business focus, responsiveness, and, at the same time, reasonable economies of scale. Externally oriented intraprises have a choice among external and internal suppliers, which goes a long way toward ensuring responsiveness. Because of the flexibility of the network, technology and market information moves easily among the intraprises and among various parts of the organization.

Although there is considerable room for personal preference and even idiosyncrasy in the free intraprise network, all of these choices are ultimately aligned with the external customers' needs and wants. Intraprises serving external customers subcontract to other intraprises that give them a good deal on what they need to serve those external customers better. Only those intraprises whose work adds value for the external customer, well in excess of its cost, will long survive. For all its freedom, free intraprise produces a powerful customer focus no other organization can begin to match.

The Network Style of Management

What is evolving now is a *network style of management* to manage in our free intraprise form of organization. The new management style is inspired by and based on networking. Its values are rooted in informality and equality; its communication style will be lateral, diagonal, and bottom up; and its structure will be cross-disciplinary. The vertical to horizontal power shift that networks bring about will be enormously liberating for individuals. Hierarchies promote moving up and getting ahead, producing stress, tension, and anxiety. Networking empowers the individual, and people in networks tend to nurture one another. In the network environment, rewards come by empowering others—not by climbing over them.

Networking allows us to pull people together to work cross-functionally on market opportunities, instead of dividing the various aspects of those opportunities into stiff and rigid hierarchies. This allows us to size up a problem's patterns and make this learning available to others in our company. Networking does not homogenize people into bland commonality. Rather, it sharpens our perceptions of one another's talents and abilities. We learn of value differences and to play off each other's strengths. We become more important as individuals as we participate on multiple teams, because our knowledge and talent are sought after by the other members.

Networking requires a different coordination strategy from that of the traditional hierarchical organization; otherwise, indecision will rule the day. As people make decisions in a networked environment, there has to be some commonality of context. We need to understand how our own activities are going to fit into a larger whole and how to draw upon common information resources (knowledge) so that we can see significant patterns, adding value through our own insights and wisdom.

Networking does not eliminate the hierarchy; it just recasts its role and function. Companies still need some levels of authority. There are times when decisive leadership from the top is necessary. Executives of the flatter hierarchy move away from our preoccupation with the prerogatives of decision making. Instead, we find we get better results when we actively listen to our teams, ask challenging questions, define the context for the teams, and build our resources.

Transitioning to the Networked Organization

Following are a number of changes that must be made for an organization to transition from a traditional hierarchical organization to an innovative networked organization.

Chain of Command to Networking. Networking is an ongoing process of reaching out and getting in touch with others to get tasks done. As we become nodes in a network—knowledge resources—we tap into this available knowledge, and our effectiveness increases. Instead of being confined by the chain of command, we can go directly to the sources of knowledge, whether they are inside or outside the enterprise. When a worker joins a certain large innovative organization, he is told a good news, bad news story. The good news was that he had 120,000 people working for him. The bad news was that they do not know it. It was up to him to determine how he could best network himself and build working alliances.

Power of Position to Power of Knowledge. In traditional hierarchical organizations, position and power are defined by boxes and lines: the higher up the position, the more powerful it is. The prerogatives of position legitimize an arbitrary attitude toward subordinates. Superiors need not listen; they merely monitor and control subordinates.

The power of knowledge is fast becoming more important for success. This is not knowledge doled out in tiny bits like pennies, but knowledge that is available to all. As traditional hierarchies are replaced by multiple teams, the individuals' knowledge becomes both more important and more accessible, and a lack of knowledge can no longer be hidden behind the walls of organizational boxes. People quickly learn who has knowledge and who will share it. They are the ones who become key players on teams.

Vertical Communications to Horizontal Communications. The shift to horizontal communications should be an obvious one, especially as we see people not as turf owners but as knowledge resources within the network. There will still be vertical communications, of course, but the predominant communication will be horizontal in nature as the core teams leverage knowledge wherever it may be in the enterprise.

Horizontal communication in a networked environment is freer and more fluid, with few bureaucratic barriers. It also facilitates serendipity, where key patterns may be unexpectedly discovered. Perhaps a request from one team to another will provide a clue to the pattern the other team is trying to discern. If we see our work as information processing, we will stay open to discovery, observe the interplay of multiple patterns, and achieve our visions.

The emphasis on horizontal work processes in the innovative organization results in an emphasis on horizontal communications also. Work cannot become more horizontal unless communication also becomes more horizontal.

Distrust and Compliance to Trust and Integrity. The fragmented structure of traditional hierarchies breeds distrust among functions. It is common to hear people complain of how another department throws information over the wall. In the knowledge era, trust and integrity are critical. When people work closely together as resources in a network and as members of teams, it quickly becomes obvious who can be trusted and who cannot.

CONTINUOUS LEARNING, CHANGE, AND IMPROVEMENT

To keep pace with changes in the external environment, managers have to improve their organization. Managers have always made improvements. However, with rates of change increasing in the external environment, managers must improve more frequently than in the past. They must pursue *continuous improvement*, which is a constant striving to change and make things better. *Any* activity directed toward improvement falls under the continuous improvement umbrella. Activities to install robotics and advanced technology, implement employee suggestion systems, implement statistical process control, and even maintain equipment are included under continuous improvement.

Approaches to Continuous Learning, Change, and Improvement

Constant reaching for continuous improvement may be achieved in two ways, through big steps (breakthroughs) or little steps (increments). The breakthrough approach, which represented the American thinking until recently, focuses on large, short-term, and radical changes in products or processes. Often the breakthrough approach requires substantial investment in equipment or technology, with major rebuilding of entire plants. Breakthroughs are dramatic and are often championed by a few proponents.

The incremental approach, championed by the Japanese, concentrates on small and gradual, though frequent, improvements over the long term. Financial investment is normally minimal. Everyone, not just high-level management, participates in the process; many improvements result from the knowledge and experience of workers. People, not technology, are the principal source of incremental improvements.

The most powerful approach to continuous improvement is to combine the breakthrough and the incremental approach, since they complement each other, as shown in Figure 4-2c. Between the big steps, repeated small steps ensure perpetual progress with no backsliding. With no breakthroughs, the incremental approach would reach a point of diminishing returns, as shown in Figure 4-2a. Without incremental improvements, the breakthrough approach tends to backslide between breakthroughs as shown in Figure 4-2b. Combining the incremental and breakthrough approaches prevents backsliding between breakthroughs, and prevents the incremental approach from reaching a point of diminishing returns.

Every day, in every organization, people have *ideas* about how to make things work better, and every day we take a lot of actions based on these ideas. Still, the same problems keep rearing their ugly heads, over and over again. We keep ''solving'' these problems and reinventing the same wheels because we lack effective procedures for *learning*. Without effective learning, we lack sufficient knowledge to *improve rapidly*.

Rapid learning is critical capability for an innovative organization, because it creates the foundation for translating theory into effective action. Smart companies will invest a lot of time, money, and effort in learning how to learn faster: how to gather data and use it effectively to shape decisions, how to root out the deep causes of problems, how to run experiments to determine the optimal operating condition of complex machinery, and how to improve design

Figure 4-2
Improvement Rate for Incremental, Breakthrough, and Combined Approaches

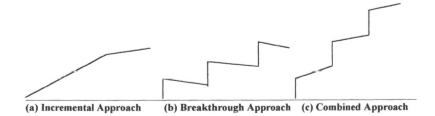

(a) Incremental Approach   (b) Breakthrough Approach   (c) Combined Approach

processes rapidly. These companies will be better able to adapt their operations, to learn new technologies quickly, and to *improve* on the new technologies than those organizations that have not learned how to learn rapidly.

We need to make sure that all employees learn as much as possible about the systems with which they work. They need to know about the needs of the organization's customers and suppliers as well as about the needs of their immediate customers and suppliers. They need to understand the basic "theory" behind the work they do. This knowledge, plus an environment receptive to rapid improvement where managers are eager to learn and to try new ideas on a small scale, helps develop a "fire in the belly" for creativity, learning, and improvement.

No worker can improve a procedure he or she was involved in without also comprehending the whole process. It makes no sense for a worker to detect a problem at his or her moment of performing a task without being able to correct the source of the problem, which might originate several stages earlier in the customer chain. Continuous improvement has to be holistic in order to detect and correct problems.

The Learning Organization

The most successful companies of the future will be *learning organizations.* These are adaptive enterprises where workers are free to think for themselves, to identify problems and opportunities, and to go after them. In the learning organization people share a passion for personal and corporate improvement. People feel a sense of responsibility to learn how to do things better and are proactive in seeking ways to improve what they do. The person who is willing to question the old assumptions is admired. There is a curiosity about what other companies are doing. The idea that "if it ain't broke, don't fix it" is rejected.

The need to constantly improve work processes and systems is accepted as standard operating procedure. The organization is constantly studying itself and its marketplace. Everyone, from the CEO to the lowest worker, is constantly striving to improve his or her skills. Learning becomes an integral part of the work environment. The mission and vision are used as guides to determine what learning needs to take place. Learning should focus on developing the knowledge and skill needed to make the mission and vision a reality.

A learning company learns as it works. The work environment should be a lab where learning becomes an integral part of the work experience—not something added on. The most important information that is communicated in the learning organization is derived directly from the experience of work. Too many business leaders mistakenly think that by offering an occasional seminar or workshop they are creating a learning organization—not so. In a true learning organization, people at every level are hungry for new ideas every minute of the day.

Companies should foster a perpetual learning culture. Learning should become a continuous process that is institutionalized into the everyday life of the company. The impetus for institutionalizing learning must come from the leaders at the top and must include a willingness to share information with people who were formerly excluded from the organization's database. The belief that continuous learning leads to new knowledge, skills, and understanding that is necessary for maintaining the competitive edge must become an integral part of the learning organization's culture. People who are learning are more open to improvement, change, and risk-taking—this is the kind of people that are needed.

Since early in life, we have all been taught to break problems down into parts to better understand and solve them. The resulting thought fragmentation has left us unable to see the consequences of our own actions, creating an illusion that we are victims of forces outside our control—and that the only type of learning that is possible is learning to react more quickly. However, if we learned systems thinking, which is about understanding wholes and not parts, we could grasp the whole situation and be able to formulate a systems, or total, solution to our problems. One of the most important types of learning in innovative organizations is systems learning. With it we can gain insight into our complex environment and complex problems and formulate a long-range change program to shape our destiny.

To employ systems learning, an innovative organization must have an effective feedback system to know how well it is doing. Actually two types of feedback are required: *operational* and *strategic. Operational* feedback comes directly from results-producing operations and indicates whether these operations are being performed correctly or not. *Strategic* feedback comes from many sources, but usually from internal or external customers, and indicates whether we are pursuing the right goals or not.

Traditional organizations typically have deficient feedback systems. For all but the more routine operations, feedback on an operation goes, not to the performers, but to the managers one, two, or even three levels above them. Such operational feedback as exists is usually highly summarized and seldom available in time to correct current operations. Such strategic feedback as exists is channeled through a few specialized departments, primarily marketing. If it points to significant differences between the organization's products and market needs, it may take months or even years to influence organizational goals.

Innovative organizations use feedback effectively and extensively. They understand the difference between the two forms of feedback and the need for both. They provide operational feedback to performers that is accurate, specific, prompt, direct, reliable, and appropriate. They provide feedback from the market at all levels, but particularly at the strategic level. They truly emphasize "listening to the voice of the customer."

Success in the marketplace today is directly proportional to the knowledge that an organization can bring to bear, how fast it can bring that knowledge to bear, and the rate at which it accumulates knowledge. Learning is the new form of labor. It's no longer a separate activity that occurs either before one enters the workplace or in remote classroom settings. Learning is the heart of productive activity. Market power derives primarily from one's skill at bringing together the best network of insiders and outsiders—to take advantage of the fleeting opportunity.

NOTES

1. David L. Goetsch and Stanley Davis, *Introduction to Total Quality* (Macmillan, 1994).

2. Tom Peters, *Liberation Management: Necessary Disorganization for the Nanosecond Nineties* (Knopf, 1992), pp. 226–228.

Chapter 5

Reengineering Organizational and Venturing Processes

In this chapter we will apply the concepts of reengineering at two levels in an innovative organization: (1) at the level of the overall organization and its major processes and (2) at the level of the venturing process and its associated organizations. Reengineering can be defined as: "*the radical redesign of broad, cross-functional business processes with the objective of order-of-magnitude performance gains, often with the aid of information technology.*"[1] At the level of the overall organization we will primarily be discussing why and how to shift from a functional organization to a process organization.

The venturing process definitely meets the criteria in the reengineering definition for a "broad, cross-functional business process." There is probably no other process, except perhaps the strategic planning process, that is broader or more important. As noted in Chapter 2, a venture is any development project, whether it be for a new product, a new market, or a new production system. In this chapter, when we discuss the *venturing process* we are primarily discussing the *development process* for new products. We will be using the concept of integration to improve the venturing process.

REENGINEERING THE OVERALL ORGANIZATION AND ITS PROCESSES

Definitions

Before beginning our discussion of reengineering the work of the overall organization, we must be sure we understand the terms used. The lowest level of work that we will discuss is the **task**. A task is specified work that achieves a specific goal. The next level is the **operation**. An operation is a group or sequence of similar tasks that are performed in close time and space proximity with identifiable inputs and outputs. A **function** is a grouping of similar operations with similar inputs and outputs that can be performed by people with similar skills using similar equipment. In a business organization, three of the primary functions are marketing, engineering, and production. **Processes** are sets of work operations that are logically related and executed to create a business outcome such as producing a product, delivering a service, negotiating a contract, or processing an order. They occur when an individual or group takes input from support and supply groups and adds value—creating outputs to be consumed by customers.

The difference between a **process** and a **function** should be clearly understood. A **process** is a sequence of operations that produces a useful product for a customer. Not only does it produce an identifiable product, but it produces a product that has value to a customer. A **function** is a grouping of similar operations with an output, but the output normally is not an identifiable product and normally has little immediate value to a customer. Functions must usually be sequenced in a process to produce a product of value to a customer.

In this section we will describe, discuss, and compare **process management** and **functional management**. The terms lateral, cross-functional, and horizontal have all been used for **process**. We elected to use the term **process management**, since it provides a better indication of what we really mean. Similarly, the terms vertical, hierarchical, and traditional have been used for **functional**. Again we elected to use the term **functional management**, since it is the more meaningful term. With these terms it is easy to remember that *process management is designed to manage processes, while functional management is designed to manage functions.*

Overview

Many organizations are currently organized as functional organizations. Functional organizations tend to establish barriers that thwart the creativeness and problem-solving abilities of employees. A functional organization has departments such as marketing, engineering, production, and human resources, with strong boundaries between departments. Employees look to their bosses for direction and authorization for actions; they are loyal to their own disciplines, and little communication occurs across functional boundaries. For example, in many traditional companies, marketing managers do not understand the problems of the production manager, production managers do not talk to engineers, and there is little coordination between the human resources department and all the other functional areas.

In the process organization, hierarchy is reduced, departmental boundaries are eliminated, and the organization is run by multidisciplinary process teams. The idea is to manage *across* functional areas rather than managing *down* the functional structure. The organization might have only three or four layers of management between the CEO and the members of a team. The focus in these organizations is the customer, not the interests of the functional areas.

The move from functional to process management is an essential part of becoming an innovative organization. It is difficult to serve external customers well when the company is organized to serve internal functional managers. The *customer-focused company* has no choice; it must look at itself from the customer's perspective and then reorganize to improve the processes that satisfy the customer's requirements.

Process management has a common overriding purpose: to produce a product for the customer. This purpose is the key to weaving a *process* horizontally across the firm so that all parts work in unison and not at cross-purposes. Although the term **process management** has been used to describe multidisciplinary teaming, the real practice and methods of process management are new to most American firms. *Process management and organization* is a *horizontal technique and structure that operates across vertical functional boundaries to achieve corporate-wide goals and objectives. It provides an approach to implementing important boundary-spanning solutions to meet organization-wide needs.

The Need for Process Organization and Management

In process management, the stress on process, or how to align all the operations of the company in order to best produce a product for the customer, is far different from the emphasis in functional management. In a functional organization, each function is primarily interested in maximizing the output of its function rather than maximizing the total output of the entire process. For example, marketing tries to maximize revenues, engineering tries to produce the best designs, and manufacturing tries build products most efficiently with little regard to the other functions or the total process. Process management, on the other hand, is horizontal. It focuses on how marketing, engineering, and manufacturing and other vertical functions can work together to satisfy a customer requirement.

Without process management, performance, in the eyes of the customer or shareholder, is suboptimized, because under functional management specialized departments plan and execute policy insulated from one another. One department's activities may work at cross-purposes with those of another department. Without process management, such major processes as new product development, quality, cost, and delivery are rarely optimized.

In a functional organization, there are many company problems that cannot be effectively solved by any one vertical division or department or simply by issuing top-down executive orders. One example is the meeting of customer expectations in regard to quality or warranty management. In a functional organization there is no single department solely responsible, and certainly no single department is a "quality or warranty assurance department." Only by coordinating all pertinent departments through process management can the customer's need be adequately satisfied.

Even though project teams have existed on an ad hoc basis and *project* management has been broadly discussed by academics and practitioners for many years, managing the total company-wide product development process has received little attention until lately. We need to learn how to manage the whole new product development process, and not just a specific new product development project. This helps explain why many product-development projects are too slow, too costly, and not always able to meet customer and quality requirements. One project may get it right; another may not. There is no consistent method of conceiving and improving a whole new product development process.

Description of Process Organization and Management

Process management focuses on managing the critical processes that cut across the whole enterprise. These include such major processes as *new product development, quality, cost control*, and *delivery*. A variety of other processes such as *purchasing, personnel, training, research*, and *information management* are also amenable to process management. Each is treated as a horizontal process.

Process management activities are woven through the vertical structure of a firm by teams with company-wide representation. The most effective process teams consist of line people, with day-to-day responsibilities, taken from across a company's divisions, departments, suppliers, or customers. Through such teams, one part of the company must take the needs of another into account and must treat this other part as its own customer. A "cost control" process team, for example, will not consist of specialists in cost accounting or finance. It will consist of representatives, with direct line responsibility for results, from each of the company's functions involved in cost control. Line people take on two responsibilities: to manage departmental operations and to coordinate company-wide processes (cost control) across departments.

A process management team's responsibility is to optimize information flows across departmental barriers. This runs against decades of corporate (and broad cultural) development that actively encouraged specialization and compartmentalization as a desirable end. Greater and greater specialization of activities breeds withdrawal into smaller and smaller social units more and more insulated from one another. The counterpoint to this trend is the belief that, rather than limit contact, *the purpose of the process organization is to maximize the opportunity for human interaction*. Since one purpose of human interaction is to exchange information, a corollary could be that *the purpose of the process organization is, also, to maximize the opportunity for information exchange*.

It must be emphasized that process management is not the conventional two-boss matrix management, with the vertical functions on one axis and project teams on another. Neither is it a patchwork of disciplines brought together as an ad hoc team. It is a deliberate effort to build a structure and a process that enable communication and action to occur horizontally across the organization. The ability to undertake coordinated horizontal action and communication is crucial.

For process management ideas to flourish, several rules need to be widely understood by managers and workers. The first rule is that product and service requirements are *customer focused*. Doing only what the producer thinks best is no longer viable in markets crowded with competitors. The second rule is *continuous process improvement*, or the steady monitoring and correction of problems as they occur. Standing still is not a competitive strategy. The third rule is *collaboration, concurrency*, and *integration* in the management of work activities across the entire process. This leads not only to improved horizontal communications, but to shorter development cycle time and to greater quality of work.

These new rules of the game—customer focus, continuous improvement, collaboration, concurrency, and integration—are forcing a new management style upon us. Central to it is the joining of managers and workers horizontally in process teams across their companies. To do this, more and more firms are turning to process management as the principal method for making improvements and stimulating innovative solutions.

Focusing on the Customer

To be competitive, a company must be attuned not only to the customer demands for today's products and services but also to what the customer will want and need in the marketplace of tomorrow. Simple as this may sound, it is difficult to do on a consistent basis. The larger the company becomes and the further management is removed from direct customer contact, the harder it is. Becoming—and remaining—customer focused requires effort and discipline. Shifting to process management enables a company to regain their focus on the customer.

Customer focus is first and foremost a business philosophy—a way of looking at the world. It requires focusing outward, not inward. It requires always keeping customer wants and needs at the center of decision making. It demands a genuine commitment to satisfying the customer, no matter how much effort is required. Without this kind of outlook—and perhaps even obsession—a firm cannot be customer focused, no matter what techniques it employs.

We use the term *customer* in its broadest sense to include both internal and external, consumer and industrial, product and service, purchaser and user, and intermediary and final customers. Everyone who produces any kind of economic good has a customer, who either adds value and passes the good on to the next customer or who are final consumers or users of the good. By the same reasoning, virtually all workers are suppliers to one or more customers, either internal or external.

For customer focus to be implemented, most firms must make two major changes in the way they operate. First, the monitoring of the customer and market environment must be *continuous*. It must be a continuous process of listening, documenting, analyzing, sharing, and acting. It must be an integral part of the way in which the firm operates. It must be considered a necessity, not a postponable discretionary item.

Second, the customer-focused firm must manage cross-functionally, or process manage, in an integrated, cooperative manner and not in a confrontational, competitive manner. Cross-functional, or process, decision making is necessary to speed products and services to market. It helps to avoid redesign, rework, and more generally the NIH (Not Invented Here) syndrome that can make the introduction of new products and processes agonizingly slow. In an age of ever-shorter product life cycles, the organizational disunity that stems from narrow functional perspective cannot be tolerated.

Implementing Process Organization and Management

Process management should be an integral part of any innovative organization. Process management reorients the communication and information flows horizontally across the company into more effective value-adding activities. This overcomes a fundamental flaw of the functionally organized firm in that what you do is presumed to be of no interest and to have no impact on any other activity.

To implement process management, the firm faces a difficult challenge: to horizontally integrate all the vertical activities so that non-value-adding vertical barriers, such as dysfunctional reward systems, are eliminated. Process management methods of teaming are used to induce horizontal communication and to establish uniform performance standards company wide. Through horizontal interdepartmental collaboration, the fulfillment of corporate objectives can be made far more effective. The members of a company-wide process team work best if constituted from all line operations, divisions, or departments. A line person does not have to be an expert in the horizontal function to be chosen.

The implementation of process management involves not only the redesign of business processes but also changes in other management domains to create a process orientation. They include process-based measurement and information systems, process-based organizational structures, and process-based management approaches (e.g., budgeting and resource allocation). Most firms undertake these only after reengineering their business processes, but changing them may offer more benefit than reengineering some of the less important business processes.

A process management team is empowered to treat a process in its totality, and not with narrow departmental jurisdictions. The process may be quality assurance, managing cost reduction, or managing delivery of products in quantities and time desired by a customer. Or the team may focus on an internally important process such as safety and training, research and development, management information systems, or purchasing. A team may also work to improve a product development process. In each case, the group is the responsible activity, not some specialized unit within a functional department.

A mature innovative company might have several process teams, each one responsible for managing a specific process. In time, each acquires operational knowledge that is strategically valuable to the firm: where the strengths and weaknesses are, how things are done, and how procedures can be improved. Together these company-wide teams constitute the eyes and ears of the whole system's capability. They embody a new form of corporate intelligence that cuts across departmental boundaries. Since total quality activities are aimed at merging company-wide intellectual power, all information contained in the teams must become the possession of the entire organization. This, in turn, leads to the generation of new ideas.

Successful process management requires behavioral changes as well as structural changes. Structural changes can be made very quickly, but behavioral changes take time and nurturing. Process management helps to break down the traditional functional barriers that impede smooth-flowing and collaborative work in the organization. Process management is designed to reduce the vertical dictator syndrome. If the company does not change the mentality and associated behaviors of those involved, it will end up with horizontal dictators instead of vertical dictators. Organizations that have implemented process management without paying attention to behavioral change have been amazed at how fast vertical dictators become horizontal dictators.

The process of changing from authority and control to consensus and collaboration as a regular way of running a business requires more than just tipping the organization on its side and calling it process (or horizontal) management. Following are some specific guidelines for implementing process management and organization:

Implement the most critical processes first. Often, three to five processes are crucial to the success of the organization. For example, a manufacturer's core processes may be product development, customer support, and sales and delivery.

Form teams to manage the process. Teams are the major building blocks of the process organization. The top-level team would consist of the CEO and the high-level managers from all disciplines, who would be responsible for the operation of the entire company. Below that level are teams made up of managers and employees from various disciplines, each organized around a core process.

Flatten the organizational hierarchy. Have teams analyze processes so as to reduce the number of levels in each to a minimum and to eliminate vertical work that does not add value to the product or service.

Let customers evaluate performance. Customer satisfaction is the key performance measure in a process organization. Since the process teams deliver the product directly to the customer and deal directly with the customer on a daily basis, customer satisfaction is the most valid measure of their performance.

Reward team performance. The appraisal and pay systems should be designed to reward team efforts rather than individual efforts. Employees acquiring multiple skills needed by their team should be rewarded for their efforts.

Have teams maintain supplier and customer contact. Team members should be in nearly constant contact with customers and suppliers. When appropriate, customer or supplier representatives may take active roles on the teams.

Provide training programs for all employees. Employees should be offered training programs to improve their general skills in problem solving, leadership, communications, and administrative skills. Such training will make them more productive team members.

Cautions in Implementing

Focusing on the work processes, or horizontal work flows, is the key to achieving the cross-functional teamwork needed to provide superior customer value. However, the vertical flow of information and work between layers of management should not be ignored. In attending to the vertical flow of work, managers must realize that the work that flows up and down the chains of the hierarchy does not create value for the customer. When managers focus on the vertical flows, they are distracted by issues of power and politics, instead of on producing superior value for the customer. Vertical flows of work, such as paperwork and reporting, should be minimized or eliminated unless they are key to providing customer value or sustaining the organization over the long term.

However, we must be careful not to go too far in eliminating vertical work flows and relationships. If we define the system entirely in terms of processes, or horizontal work flows, we are guilty of going to the opposite extreme—of partitioning the system along horizontal lines but not paying any attention to how these processes should be integrated vertically to form subsystems and then how subsystems should be integrated to form systems.

Viewing an organization as one large open system means that managers must address how to integrate the horizontal and vertical flows of work and information. The vertical flow should be bidirectional, because strategic plans and investment decisions must be based on knowledge of operational capabilities. In the horizontal work processes, the work normally proceeds in one direction, but the information pertaining to the work process is usually bidirectional.

REENGINEERING THE VENTURING PROCESS

Earlier in this chapter, we described process management and the techniques for adopting it within a company. Since the venturing process is one of an innovative company's major processes, all these concepts are applicable to the venturing process. Of special interest to us, process management permits venture teams to treat the totality of a product's full life cycle from inception to disposal. This is particularly important in drawing customer needs into the complete evolution of a product. In addition, it responds to growing pressures to address such environmental issues as toxic disposal early in the design phases. All of this can be done by bringing all the key functional players together on a single *integrated* team that will pursue the venture throughout its life process. In this section, we will discuss two very specific approaches that can be used in reengineering the venturing process: (1) integration and (2) the creation of an "Office of Venturing."

Improving the Venturing Process through Integration

What Is Integration?

Integration means to form, coordinate, or blend into a smoothly functioning or unified whole, thus causing all the parts to work together in a manner that will make the whole process most productive. In the new product development process we are concerned with two types of integration: *cross-function* integration and *cross-stage* integration.

Cross-function integration is concerned with improving how the major functions in new product development (high-level management, marketing, engineering, and production) work together to achieve optimum results in the new product development process. A functionally integrated process is characterized by joint, proactive decision making among all functional units. Joint decision making means that experts from each function work as contributors of disciplinary expertise and not as defenders of their own function's agenda or their boss's orders. An integrated process also causes team members to anticipate and manage problems and actively exploit opportunities for progress that exist at the interfaces between different technologies.

Cross-stage integration is concerned with improving the coordination of effort *across the stages of the new product development process*. Because new product development is a long and complex process, we wisely divide it into stages so that we can better understand and manage it. However, we must ensure that information is passed horizontally throughout the process, and particularly from the earlier stages to later stages, so that work will proceed efficiently from one stage to the next. We can consider cross-function integration to be integration across *technologies* in the *vertical* direction, while cross-stage integration is integration across *time* in the *horizontal* direction.

Why Do We Need Integration?

From marketing one needs thoughtful product positioning, solid customer analysis, and well-thought-out product plans; from engineering, good designs, well-executed technical tests, and high quality prototypes; and from production, capable processes, precise cost estimates and skillful pilot production and ramp-up. But there is more than this. Great products and processes are achieved when all of these functional activities mesh together well. They must not only mesh together well from a technical viewpoint, but they must be well matched in time also. In short, outstanding development requires **integration** across functions and across stages in a timely and effective way.

A Framework for Integration

Achieving integration changes what the functions do, when they do it, and how they get the work done.[2] To illustrate the impact that integration has on the role of the functions in product development, we have laid out a framework in Figure 5-1. The table examines four of the major functions involved in prod-

Figure 5-1
Integrated Framework for New Product Development

Development Stage	High Level Management	Marketing	R &D and Engineering	Production	Criteria for Stage Approval
CONCEPTUAL DEVELOPMENT					
Idea Generation	Provide Guidance for Idea Generation	Generate Need-Pull Ideas	Generate Technology-Push Ideas	Generate Process and Producibility Ideas	Sufficient Valid Ideas Generated
Concept Evaluation	Approve Criteria for Evaluating Concepts	Perform Need Evaluation of Product Concepts	Perform Technical Evaluation of Product Concepts	Evaluate Cost & Feasibility of Product and Process Concepts	Product and Process Concepts Selected. Perf. Spec. and Business Plan Prepared
TECHNICAL DEVELOPMENT					
Venture Startup and Prototype Design	Approve Business Plan Form Venture Team	Validate Performance Specifications of Product	Conduct Engineering Design of Product	Conduct Preliminary Design of Process	Venture Team Formed. Product & Proc. Designs Satisfactory
Prototype Build and Test	Authorize Prototype Build and Test	Conduct Market Testing of Product Prototype	Build and Technically Test Product Prototype	Build and Test Prototype of Process	Product and Process Prototypes Test Satisfactorily
Final Design and Pilot Prod.	Authorize Final Design and Pilot Production	Finalize Market Plans Conduct Test Marketing	Perform Final Design of the Product	Perform Final Process Design and Conduct Pilot Prod.	Product and Process Ready for Launch
NEW BUSINESS DEVELOPMENT					
New Business Development	Authorize Product Launch and Monitoring	Execute Marketing Plans and Monitoring	Implement Engineering Services	Ramp-Up to Full Production	Meet Initial Commercial Objectives

uct development: high-level management, marketing (including marketing research and sales), engineering (with a focus on product design), and production (including process development, manufacturing engineering, and plant operations). Within each function, we have identified the major activities in each stage of product development. Additionally we have identified key criteria that must be satisfied for each stage to obtain approval for the next stage.

Clearly indicating, as we do in Figure 5-1, what action each function is expected to perform in each stage will aid in cross-function integration. But this is not all. It is evident that the greater cross-functional integration requires the addition of specific activities that support cross-functional work. For example, engineering builds very early system prototypes to support marketing's desire to develop richer customer insight early in the process. To complete the circle, engineers participate with marketing in interacting with customers to strengthen and deepen their understanding of the experience the product will create for future customers. Production establishes process concepts in the concept development phase and does process development and planning in collaboration with design engineers. Moreover, prototype testing and evaluation is a business process conducted jointly by all functions involved in development.

The cross-stage integration efforts are not so obvious from Figure 5-1, but we will point out some of them. Please note that production not only plays its traditional roles in building the production system and manufacturing the product at the end of development but is also actively engaged in proposing concepts and investigating them at the very earliest stage of development. Similarly, marketing does not wait until full-scale engineering prototypes are complete to interact with customers and bring customers' insight and information into the process. The net effect of these changes in timing of activities is to pull forward in time the activity and involvement of the later functions.

Not all development projects need extensive integration. Where product designs are stable (or change only in a minor way), customer requirements are well defined and stable, the interfaces between functions are clear and well established, and life cycles and lead times are long, functional groups can develop new products effectively with only a modest amount of coordination through procedures and occasional meetings. However, where markets and technologies are more dynamic and time is a critical element of competition, an intensive cross-functional and cross-stage integration effort is crucial to effective development.

Developing and implementing a framework similar to that shown in Figure 5-1 is a start, but this does not ensure that all market plans, designs, and tools will be integrated. To be truly effective, cross-functional and cross-stage integration must be much more than a scheme for linking the activities of the functions in time, and even more than adding new kinds of activities that support integration. True integration occurs at the working level and rests on a foundation of tight linkages in time and in communications between individuals and groups working on closely related problems.

Achieving Cross-Stage Integration

Of the two types of integration in the new product development process, cross-stage integration is probably the more difficult to achieve. In discussing cross-stage integration,[3] we will refer to the group providing the output as the *earlier* group and to the group receiving it as the *later* group. For example, marketing (earlier group) provides its output to engineering (later group), which in turn provides its output to production.

A critical element of the interaction between the earlier and later groups is the pattern of communications. The quality and effectiveness of the communications pattern is primarily determined by four characteristics: richness, frequency, direction, and timing. It is desirable to have communications that are (1) direct face-to-face and rich in content, (2) high frequency, intense, and on-line, (3) two-way, and (4) early in the process. Poor communications are (1) sparse, (2) infrequent, (3) one-way, and (4) late.

A more important characteristic pertains to how the earlier and later groups link up. As shown in Figure 5-2, they can link up in **series**, in **parallel**, or **in between**. The top sketch depicts what we call the *serial*, or no cross-stage integration, method of linking up. This is the classic relationship in which the later group waits to begin its work until the earlier group has completely finished its work. Engineering does not start its design until a final, full-blown performance specification is received from marketing, and production does not start

Figure 5-2
Possible Modes of Cross-Stage Integration

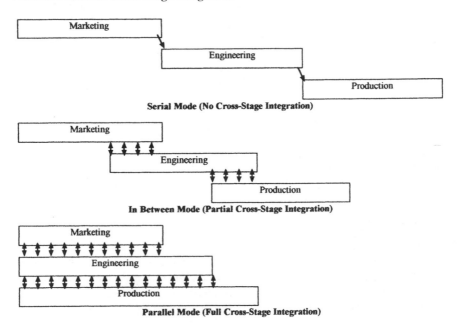

Serial Mode (No Cross-Stage Integration)

In Between Mode (Partial Cross-Stage Integration)

Parallel Mode (Full Cross-Stage Integration)

the design of the production system until the final product design is received from engineering. Not only is this serial method of operating very slow, but the later group does not get any of the background on how the earlier group arrived at their decisions.

The bottom sketch depicts the *parallel*, or full cross-stage integration, method of linking up. In this method, members of the later group not only participate in a preliminary and ongoing dialog with their earlier counterparts but also use that information and insight to get a flying start on their own work. This changes the content of the later work in the early phases of earlier effort and is also likely to change fundamentally the content and manner of communication between the two groups. Feedback will reflect actual practice in attempting to use the output of the earlier group. The parallel mode of linking up will foster face-to-face discussions, direct observations, and interactions that are needed for joint problem solving. The rich intimate pattern of communications will occur in a timely fashion so that action may be taken to avoid costly mistakes later. This does not mean the absence of conflict but rather the honest, open consideration of alternatives and resolution based on data, analyses, and joint creative problem solving.

The center sketch of Figure 5-2 depicts the *in between*, or partial cross-stage integration, mode of linking up. As the reader can surmise, there are several possible in between modes. The one shown in Figure 5-2 has the earlier and later groups engaging in an interactive pattern of communication. Although the later group develops insight about the output of the earlier group and provides feedback to the earlier group, it waits until the work of the earlier group is essentially complete before undertaking problem solving in its own domain.

Overlap is not only desirable but is inherent in the product development process, and there is no such thing as a clean hand-off. Instead, staggered concurrency of development efforts, along with interactive yet defined responsibilities, compels different groups to interface constantly. Overlap, contact, and negotiation are the norms, with no illusions about chains of command or clearly distinguished responsibilities. Even the image of stages themselves is changing. Earlier thinking suggested a sequence of relatively independent stages that follow one another much like beads on a string. The current thinking is different. The steps and processes of continuous innovation are far more interwoven, interdependent, and mutually involved. Rather than beads on a string, the stages are more like stages in a person's life, from childhood to maturity.

Further Actions to Improve Integration

Although establishing a framework, improving the mode of linking up earlier and later groups, and improving intergroup communications are powerful means for enhancing the integration of cross-functional teams, there are additional actions for improving integration.[4] We group these actions under the following five headings: co-location of team members, cross-training of team members, development of interpersonal communication skills, prototyping and simulation, and formal management protocols.

Co-location

One of the first actions after creating a cross-functional team is to locate the members in one place. Co-location has many benefits: it enables frequent interactions, quick feedback, bonding between members, mutual education, the replacement of an auditing mentality with cooperation, and an enhanced ability to conduct concurrent engineering. "Virtual co-location" in the form of computer networks, information systems, and computer conferencing provide team members with real-time interaction and parallel problem solving.

Cross-Functional Training

Even if a team can eliminate physical barriers, co-location will lead to improved communication and integration only if team members can understand and appreciate the needs and challenges of each others' work. This requires cross-training. Serving on cross-functional teams is itself one way to achieve some degree of cross-training; rotating assignments between functional areas is another. In addition to having cross-training, it is helpful to have experienced cross-functional team members and even better if team members have worked together previously. Prior team interaction can help facilitate cross-training.

Team-Building and Interpersonal Skills

Another action that leads to strong integration is deliberate development of team-building skills. All team members on a development team perform important roles as information providers, knowledge consultants, problem solvers, energizers, and ambassadors who articulate the constraints and capabilities of their respective functions. But to bring about integration, the contribution of team members must go beyond simply providing inputs; each person must constructively convert these inputs into operating parameters for the project as a whole. To do so, they must learn the languages of different functions, build relationships with other team members, receive feedback openly, and engage in give-and-take negotiations.

Prototyping and Simulation

One of the most important communication tools is using prototypes to facilitate discussions across functional differences. By focusing the team's communications on the physical reality of what they are doing, cross-functional integration is enhanced. Communications and problem solving can also be enhanced by visiting other facilities to benchmark ideas and by using graphs and models to demonstrate the concepts being discussed.

Management Procedures

Formal project management procedures can be developed and adopted that will improve integration. These procedures can be used to track progress through a series of development stages that include concept evaluation, preliminary design, prototype build and test, final product design and production, and product introduction. The procedures should do more than provide a highly organized procedure for coordinating activities; they should reflect a new philosophy premised on the importance of integration and system integrity. They should shift the center of gravity *from* the traditional focus on technology development *to* the entire development process, from idea generation through commercialization.

Perspectives on Integration

Cross-functional teams are established for most development efforts, but most of these efforts *are not integrated across stages*. The non-integrated projects proceed in a *serial* manner from task to task, achieving coordination but not integration. Information tends to flow from earlier to later functions, but there is little feedback. The burden for integration often rests with the later units or is passed on to specially created "SWAT" teams in more serious cases. Later activities often live with constraints imposed by decisions made earlier. Conflict resolutions tend to reflect the pecking order in the formal hierarchy or the preference of the dominant function.

In contrast, *fully integrated (in both function and stage)* processes are characterized by joint decision making by all team members from the start of the project. Early and late groups operate in parallel and jointly choose the constraints under which they will operate. The team's focus is anchored by the desired technical and economic performance of the end product. Integrated and parallel processes also enable teams to be more aggressive in exploiting opportunities at the interfaces between technical groups—for example, in trade-offs between software and hardware solutions, product design and field service, or electrical and mechanical subsystems. While integrated processes do utilize formal coordination mechanisms, they also benefit extensively from the real-time, spontaneous, informal interactions made possible by co-location of team members and other strategies. More important, these interactions help build a shared language, common experiences, and trust, which enable system integration issues to be addressed simultaneously with the development of functional policies.

While products can emerge from non-integrated as well as integrated development processes, the quality and efficiency of these outcomes differ markedly. Integrated projects generate solutions that are higher in quality and achieved with less cost and in less time. For integration to be truly effective, it must be pursued on multiple levels. Integration is required not only between functions and project stages but also between different scientific disciplines, business units, and external parties.

Creating an "Office of Venturing" to Improve the Venturing Process

To continuously improve a process, there must be one person and/or office that "owns" the process. It is intended that the Vice President for Venturing and the Office of Venturing be that person and office for the process of venturing. The VP for Venturing would report directly to the CEO as a staff adviser and would have a relatively small staff. The VP for Venturing would have the following major duties and responsibilities:

• continuously monitor and evaluate the venturing process
• continuously plan and implement improvements to the venturing process
• supervise and assist venture managers and venture teams
• provide a voice for venturing and venture managers in high-level management circles
• coordinate the activities of functional departments in areas related to venturing
• develop an annual plan and budget for venturing and for venturing improvement
• document and promulgate the procedures for venturing to all concerned

The most important responsibility of the VP for Venturing would be to continuously improve the venturing process and the ventures that are products of the process. The VP for Venturing would have the overall responsibility for monitoring and evaluating the venturing process and for planning and implementing continuous improvements to the process. It is anticipated that most of the improvement work on the venturing process and ventures would be accomplished by task groups composed of personnel from the functional departments, assisted and supervised by the Office of Venturing. To coordinate implementation of improvements, the VP for Venturing would prepare and promulgate a Venturing Improvement Plan.

It is anticipated that the majority of venture team leaders would report to the VP for Venturing. This would provide several benefits. First, the VP for Venturing could coordinate the activities of the various venture teams, arranging for mutual assistance where appropriate and preventing or resolving conflicts. It would provide venture leaders with a voice in high-level management, which they sorely need to resolve resource problems and political conflicts. The only ventures that would not report to the VP for Venturing would be those that were very small, which would probably report to an appropriate line manager, and those that were very large and/or critical, which might report directly to the CEO for added visibility and authority.

IMPROVING THE VENTURING ORGANIZATION

Alternative Forms of New Product Development Organization

Responsibility for new product development can be assigned to a number of organizational forms. We will look at these forms and then describe in some detail the form that has become the most popular and effective, the venture team. The alternative organizational forms for product development can be divided into the following categories:

A. New Product Committee

B. New Product Department

C. Single Function Project

D. Multiple Function Teams

E. Lightweight Project Team

F. Heavyweight Project Team

G. Autonomous Project Team

H. Venture Team

A. New Product Committee

In this organization structure, new product development decisions are made by a committee composed of members from various departments or divisions within the organization. Committees are often used to perform one-time or non-continuous functions, such as screening new product ideas, evaluating new product proposals, or coordinating the test marketing process. One particularly important committee, the *executive committee*, composed of the company's high-level executives, makes the crucial decisions that allocate resources and determine the future path of the company.

Because committees exist somewhat informally in the organization and because their membership may be temporary, the responsibility and roles of committee members are often not clearly defined. Even though the committee has its weaknesses, it is still widely used for making spot decisions since it can be easily formed and/or convened when needed. However, committees are not very useful in carrying out the detailed and continuing action needed to develop new products.

B. New Product Department

This organizational structure separates the new product planning, development, and management tasks from the existing divisions into a separate organization to centralize the new product decision-making process and eliminate redundancy across divisions. A company with autonomous divisions has difficulty managing new product development, including inefficient decision making, duplication of effort, and inefficient use of funds. The new product department ameliorates these problems by providing a central decision-making authority.

The new product department usually employs just a few people. Normally, it is not their job to actually perform all new product activities. Rather, they are to ensure that designated functional groups do the work assigned to them on schedule and within budget. Department members also interface with the R&D and marketing departments regularly on ongoing projects. Every new product department must initiate, coordinate, and control a continuous series of new product activities. It must oversee the execution of development tasks to ensure that new products come about and are launched at a steady pace.

C. Single Function Project

In this form, the venture is assigned to a manager in one of the major functions: marketing, engineering, or manufacturing. This form of organization is often used in multiproduct firms to give new evolutionary products the care and attention they need to prosper in highly competitive environments. The most used single function project manager is the *product manager* in the marketing department, who oversees the introduction of *product modifications*. Without product managers, these product modifications might well wither and die because no one would accept responsibility for them. Product and process *cost-reductions* projects are also often assigned to a project manager in engineering or a project manager in manufacturing, as appropriate.

D. Multiple Function Teams

It should be made clear at the start that we are speaking of *multiple function teams*, and not *one multifunction team*. There are independent teams in each of the functions (marketing, engineering, production, etc.) working under the direction of a specialized department manager. The work of these departmental functions is planned in advance through detailed specifications combined with occasional meetings to iron out issues that cut across disciplines. Additional coordination occurs through rules and procedures and shared traditions among professionals. Each function, however, controls the work processes it uses and seeks to apply them in a fairly uniform fashion, independent of the specific project and its nature. Responsibility for project work shifts over time from one function to the next according to prior agreement as to who controls what—a procedure that does not always run smoothly or quickly. No individual has overall responsibility for the total product or process. Functional teams are found most often in large, mature businesses that are organized by function.

E. Lightweight Project Team

Lightweight project teams are similar to the functional teams, except they are *coordinated* by the lightweight project manager, normally called the **project coordinator**. The project coordinator attempts to schedule, encourage, and track the project's various activities through representatives from each function. The basic work and the bulk of decision making takes place in the functions, and the functional representatives remain part of their disciplines, with the liaison role added to their regular responsibilities. The project coordinator is often a part-time design engineer or marketing product manager who has expertise in his or her function but has little status or influence. The project coordinator has no control over resources, including people, which remain under control of the functional manager. Thus, while project coordinators can coordinate project activities and keep the relevant functions apprised of progress, they can neither allocate financial resources nor reassign people. Project coordinators typically spend about 25 percent of their time in this role and describe their key activities as persuading, encouraging, and reminding.

F. Heavyweight Project Team

The heavyweight project leader, normally called the **project manager**, has responsibility for the total project effort and its overall success. The project manager is often quite senior in the organization and brings both expertise and organizational clout to the project. The project team consists of a core group of functional leaders responsible for work on the project and the majority of project decision in their functions. Often, the core group of people is dedicated and physically co-located with the project manager. While much of the work goes on in the functional groups, it goes on under the influence of the project manager. Project managers are responsible not only for internal coordination but also for product and process planning, concept development, and integration of the customer into the process.

G. Autonomous Project Team

Autonomous teams, often called tiger teams or SWAT teams, are dedicated teams whose members have been pulled out of the functional organizations and transferred to the project on a full-time basis. The **tiger team leader** is a heavyweight in the organization and is given full control over the resources contributed by the different functional groups. The team and its leader have great latitude as to the choices they make, the processes they use, and the sources from which they seek support and assistance (including outside the organization). As a team they will be held fully accountable for the final results of the project. Typically, such tiger teams are not required to follow existing organizational practices and procedures, but are allowed to create their own. This includes establishing incentives and rewards as well as norms for behavior. Tiger teams are often formed when the venture gets into trouble under some other form of organization.

H. Venture Team

A venture team is a group of professionals assembled on a full-time, though temporary, basis by bringing together key representatives from various line departments, with the specific task of developing and introducing a new venture. The *full* venture team is composed of two components: the *core* venture team and the *virtual* venture team. The *core* venture team consists of three to ten members who are assigned *full-time* to the venture team. The *virtual* venture team consists of an unlimited number of people who contribute to the venture on a *part-time* or *as-needed* basis. The core team is the permanent nucleus of the team, while the virtual team is the ever-changing outer layer.

At the center of the venture team is the *venture leader*. This individual has the responsibility and accountability for ensuring that the venture meets its goals for quality, schedule, and cost. The role of the venture leader varies in a subtle but significant way from that of either the lightweight or the heavyweight project manager in a matrix organization. The venture leader is more of a team captain than a part-time boss. The emphasis is on leading, not on managing. The venture leader provides the spark that ignites the team.

The core venture team is made up of members from the appropriate functional organizations, which almost always includes marketing, engineering, and production. Team members coordinate project activities for their particular functions. They act as conduits for communicating both functional needs into the development effort and project requirements back to the functional organization.

The full venture team includes additional virtual members from the various functions that are involved in a portion of the venture managed by a specific team member. These individuals may be temporarily assigned to the venture or may remain under their functional manager. The full venture team also includes members of the Office of Venturing, which provides advice and assistance, primarily in procedural matters.

There are several advantages to the venture team form of organization. First, the venture team approach allows the firm to take on promising revolutionary ventures, such as breakthrough products, that would be difficult under the existing organization. Second, the focused full-time involvement of all core team members, without the distractions of day-to-day business, improves the quality and timeliness of the development effort. Third, it is possible to synergistically combine the outstanding talents of an innovative group of people to develop a truly creative interdisciplinary group. Last, the venture team offers a fresh organizational approach that can engender enthusiasm and commitment and increase the odds for success. The venture team will be discussed in more detail in Chapter 8.

Which Organizational Form?

Determining the correct organizational form depends upon a number of factors including the firm's objectives, strategy, structure, size, type of market, types of new products envisaged, and others. The venture team approach develops new products and businesses with the highest quality within the shortest time. If new product development is an important part of a firm's objectives and strategy, the venture team should definitely be used. For a large firm with a steady stream of highly technical new products, the new product department would probably be more efficient but slower than the venture team approach. In a firm with a number of strong product lines (most likely consumer products) and strong product managers, the product manager could manage the simpler developments (repositioning and modification) within his product line. Small firms, or firms that do very little development, may use the product committee approach, simply because they do not have the qualified personnel to do otherwise.

The various types of new product organization are not mutually exclusive, but can be combined in manner most suitable for the situation in a particular firm. In particular, the new product committee approach in the form of an *executive committee*, composed of high-level managers, is often used in parallel with the venture team, product manager, and even the new product department to make the resource allocation decisions at each stage of the new product development process and especially to make the decision to launch the product. The new product department can be assigned the responsibility of coordinating various venture teams and product managers.

Positioning the Venture Organization in the Parent Organization

With the form of the venture organization determined, we still have the question of where it should be located in the organization.[5] More specifically, to whom or to what part of the organization should the venture organization report? The key issue concerns the extent to which the venture should be separated from the organization's ongoing operations. The degree to which a venture is embedded in or separated from the parent organization significantly influences a number of issues that are important for the venture's success, as indicated below:

* *Focus.* The more embedded a venture, the less its chances of being the focus of attention.
* *Priority.* The more embedded a venture, the less likely it is to receive top priority insofar as the allocation of resources is concerned.
* *Reliability of Funding.* The more embedded a venture, the less predictable the availability of funding, since the parent organization many preempt funds for emergencies.
* *Coping with Growth.* When a deeply embedded venture needs to grow, the required systems, facilities, and staff are already in place. A highly separated venture needs to find or create them.

Possible Venture Positions in the Organization

Eight positions in the organizational structure of the parent company to which a venture may report are listed below and discussed in the following section.

1. Reports to a Line Manager
2. Reports to a Division Manager
3. Reports to VP of Marketing

4. Reports to VP of R&D/Engineering
5. Reports to VP of Production
6. Reports to VP of Venturing
7. Reports to New Venture Division
8. Reports Directly to the CEO

The advantages, disadvantages, and possible applications of these eight reporting positions are discussed below.

1. Reports to a Line Manager

The venture is assigned to a line manager to execute as all or part of his or her ongoing managerial responsibilities. No venture team is assembled. In this position, the venture enjoys maximum exposure to expertise in the line organization. *However*, this position minimizes the attention received from upper management. It also leaves the venture highly vulnerable to turf brawling. This position should be used only for small or very low priority projects. This position is often used for both product and process cost reduction ventures.

2. Reports to a Division Manager

The venture is assigned full-time to a line manager, who reports to the division manager and who assembles a full- or part-time venture team to pursue the venture. The venture gains political support, enjoys maximum exposure to division know-how, and has greater access to the organization's expertise. Subsequent integration into the division is facilitated. *However*, the venture's losses detract from divisional performance, and it may be the first to suffer during periods of cost reduction. Furthermore, it faces the dangers of turf brawling and intrusion from the parent division, and it is susceptible to red tape.

3. Reports to VP of Marketing

The venture is assigned full-time to a venture manager who reports to the VP of Marketing and assembles a team of full- or part-time people to pursue the venture. This position emphasizes and assists in the marketing aspects of a venture. *However*, it tends to ignore the engineering and production aspects. They tend to become single function projects, although this is not the intent. This position would be most useful for evolutionary *marketing* ventures such as market penetration, enlargement, and modification.

4. Reports to VP of R&D/Engineering

The venture is assigned full-time to a venture manager who reports to the VP of R&D/Engineering and assembles a team of full- or part-time people to pursue the venture. This position allows the venture to be close to the evolving technology and technical information. *However*, it tends to cause the venture to ignore marketing and production aspects, which could be dangerous. They tend to become single function projects, although this is not the intent. This position would be most useful for evolutionary *product* ventures such as product cost reduction and modification.

5. Reports to VP of Production

The venture is assigned full-time to a venture manager who reports to the VP of Production and assembles a team of full- or part-time people to pursue the venture. This position allows the venture to concentrate on the production aspects. They tend to become single function projects, although this is not the intent. This position is useful for evolutionary process ventures, such as process cost reduction, enlargement, and modification.

6. Reports to VP of Venturing

The manager of the venture team reports to the VP of Venturing. This position ensures the venture leader will have a sympathetic and knowledgeable ear for any subject pertaining to the venture. It also serves to reduce turf brawling. This reporting position is recommended for most of the ventures, whether they are market, product, or production ventures. Only those ventures that are very small, single function, or extremely critical should use a different reporting relationship.

7. Reports to New Venture Division

The venture manager reports directly to a new venture division manager, who interacts directly with high-level management. This position ensures the venture of a high level of attention, protection from red tape, and minimization of turf brawling. *However*, the venture is a highly visible target that competes for resources with mainstream businesses and is vulnerable to elimination during difficult times. Exposure to organizational expertise is minimized. This reporting position should normally be used only for very large and extremely critical ventures.

8. Reports Directly to the CEO

This arrangement guarantees maximum political protection, mainstream cooperation, and the availability of resources. *However*, this position can hamper objective evaluation of the venture's progress, and failures can be costly. This position should be used only for small companies that can not afford either a staff position for venturing or a new venture division. The CEO can always become involved in any venture at any time he or she wants to, and it is probably best that the CEO not be tied down to one specific venture.

Physical Location of the Venture Team in the Parent Organization

We have discussed the form of the venture team and to whom it should report. We will now discuss a related subject: where the team should be located physically. Although influenced by the reporting position in the organizational structure, the physical location of the team is not completely determined by it.

In physically locating a venture, it makes a huge difference whether the venture's product, market, and production systems are very similar to or very different from the parent company's existing products, markets and production systems. If they are very similar, the venture should be located near the appropriate part of the parent organization in order to take advantage of the parent corporation's know-how and experience. If they are very different, a remote location is probably better to avoid organizational intrusion and interference.

All other things being equal, ventures that are primarily product or technology oriented should be physically located in or near engineering. The ventures that are primarily marketing or customer-related should be physically located in or near the marketing organization, while ventures that are production oriented should be located in or near the production organization.

Summary of New Product Organization Alternatives

Shown in Figure 5-3 is the recommended form of organization and reporting relationship for the various types of product, market, and process ventures that can be undertaken. As the reader must realize, the type of venture in itself does not completely determine the organization form or the reporting relationship. For a number of situations, more than one form of organization and reporting relationship will be possible, which must be resolved by other criteria.

NOTES

1. Richard L. Nolan et al., *Reengineering the Organization* (Harvard Business School Press, 1995).

2. Adapted from Steven C. Wheelwright and Kim B. Clark, *Revolutionizing Product Development* (Free Press, 1992), pp. 172–175.

3. Adapted from Steven C. Wheelwright and Kim B. Clark, *Revolutionizing Product Development* (Free Press 1992), pp. 175–184.

4. Adapted from H. Kent Bowen, Kim Clark, Charles A. Holloway, and Steven Wheelwright, eds., *The Perpetual Enterprise Machine* (Oxford University Press, 1994).

5. Adapted from Zenas Block and Ian C. MacMillan, *Corporate Venturing* (Harvard Business School Press, 1995).

Figure 5-3
Relationship of Venture Types to Venture Forms and Positions

	Form of Organization								Reports To							
	New Product Committee	New Product Department	Single Function Project	Multiple Function Teams	Lightweight Project Team	Heavyweight Project Team	Autonomus Project Team	Venture Team	Line Manager in Division	Division Manager	VP of Marketing	VP of R&D/Engineering	VP of Production	VP of Venturing	New Venture Division	Directly to the CEO
Product	A	B	C	D	E	F	G	H	1	2	3	4	5	6	7	8
Cost Reduction (COST)			P						A	A		P				
Repositioning (POS)			P								P			A		
Modification (MOD)						A		P	A	A				P		
Consolidation (CON)						A		P		A				P		
Imitation (IMI)						A		P		A				P		
Differentiation (DIFF)						A		P		A				P		
Diversification (DIV)	U		U	U			A	P	U		U	U	U	P	A	
Breakthrough (BRK)	U		U	U	U		A	P	U		U	U	U	P	A	A
Platform (PLAT)	U		U	U	U		A	P	U		U	U	U	P	A	A
Market	A	B	C	D	E	F	G	H	1	2	3	4	5	6	7	8
Penetration (PEN)			P								P					
Enlargement (ENL)			P								P					
Modification (MOD)			P								P					
Consolidation (CON)	U		U	U			A	P	U		U	U	U	P	A	
Segmentation (SEG)	U		U	U			A	P	U		U	U	U	P	A	
Completely New (NEW)	U		U	U	U	A		P	U		U	U	U	P	A	A
Platform (PLAT)	U		U	U	U	A		P	U		U	U	U	P	A	A
Process	A	B	C	D	E	F	G	H	1	2	3	4	5	6	7	8
Cost Reduction (COST)			P										P			
Enlargement (ENL)			P										P			
Modification (MOD)			P										P			
Consolidation (CON)	U		U	U			A	P	U		U	U	U	P	A	
Focused (FOC)	U		U	U			A	P	U		U	U	U	P	A	
CompletelyNew (NEW)	U		U	U	U	A	A	P	U		U	U	U	P	A	A
Platform (PLAT)	U		U	U	U	A	A	P	U		U	U	U	P	A	A

A = Acceptable   P = Preferred   U = Unacceptable   A blank indicates feasible but not recommended

Part II

The Corporate Venturing Process

The corporate venturing process is divided into three phases: *concept* development, *technical* development, and *business* development. In turn, the concept development phase is divided into two stages: idea generation and concept evaluation. The technical development phase is divided into three stages: preliminary design, prototype build and test, and final design and pilot production. The business development phase has only one stage: launching the new product.

The concept development phase is primarily concerned with the development and testing of product *ideas*—not hardware or even software. In the technical development phase, the hardware and software are developed, first as prototypes and then as final products. Business development is primarily concerned with ensuring that the product is a success in the commercial world.

Chapter 6

Idea Generation; Start Concept Development

INTRODUCTION

In this chapter we describe the Idea Generation stage of the Corporate Venturing Process. The Idea Generation stage is the first stage of the Concept Development phase. The purpose of this stage is to generate a large number of new product ideas that will be evaluated in the next stage of Concept Evaluation.

We discuss the generation of new product ideas through both search and creative synthesis procedures. To enable an effective search for new product ideas, we will first identify the best sources and then describe the optimum procedures for searching. We will also investigate generating new product ideas through creative synthesis, using general, need based, and technology-based techniques.

Difference between an Idea and a Concept

A product **concept** defines the core benefit and the major supporting benefits of a new product and describes how these benefits are provided. It can be a verbal or written description, an artist's rendering, or a model or appear in another suitable presentation format that depicts the idea. The concept must be defined specifically enough that it can be evaluated by interested parties: high-level management, marketing, engineering, manufacturing, and particularly prospective customers.

An **idea** does not have to be nearly as complete or as specific as a concept. An idea is usually represented as a descriptive statement, written or spoken. In the Idea Generation stage we are more interested in generating the maximum number of ideas than concerned with the form in which the idea is stated. The process of refining ideas to convert them to concepts should be delayed until the Concept Evaluation stage, so as not to crimp the creative aspects of the idea generation effort.

In practice, ideas and concepts are often intermingled in the creative process. The value in separating them is that ideas can remain relatively free in form to stimulate maximum idea generation, while concepts must be made more complete and specific to enable (1) customers to make intelligent decisions in concept testing, (2) engineering to visualize how existing technology might be applied to implement the concept, (3) marketing to define a marketing program and predict customer reactions to the concept, and (4) high-level decision makers to evaluate one concept against another in the Concept Evaluation stage.

We intentionally organized Idea Generation and Concept Evaluation into two stages to avoid the tendency to start evaluation before generation is really completed. Separating them into two stages and requiring a stage review between stages will reduce this tendency. In this stage we are interested in generating the maximum number of ideas possible, and we will pay little attention to their form. The greater the number of ideas that we have, the higher the probability that the best idea is included.

Techniques for Improving Creativity

In Part I, we discussed the nature of the culture needed to support creativity and new product development. In this section we outline some specific actions to improve creativity that are specific to the Idea Generation stage.

Selecting the Most Creative People

With an innovative culture, we would expect all our people to be above average in creativity. However, we must select the most creative for our idea generation tasks. Research has shown that cognitive abilities are essential, with intelligence, knowledge, and thinking style as most important. Intelligence, measured by IQ, is especially needed for scientific fields, but non-IQ street smarts are felt to be equally important outside of highly technical areas. Knowledge means the breadth of background in the relevant field. Thinking style puts stress on "the individual's ability to integrate, reorganize, or restructure existing knowledge."

Being creative also means lots of ideas with a high degree of usefulness. Mental patients frequently have creative ideas, but they are not very useful in the new product sense. Conversely, the inventor of the Frisbee had a great idea, but it was apparently his only invention. Most creative people are not eccentric, but they do distinguish themselves by leaving a trail of creative accomplishments. They are creative in their early years and never become uncreative. Thus, people being considered for idea generation teams can be evaluated on their past.

Using Training to Improve Creativity

Many companies consider that creativity can be improved by training. In 1990, 32 percent of the firms surveyed said they did creativity training using (1) in-house courses, (2) the Center for Creative Leadership in Greensboro, North Carolina, and (3) the Center for Studies in Creativity at the State University of New York at Buffalo.[1] Many smaller companies have good reputations as suppliers of the training. Such training programs run the gamut from introductory classes in traditional brainstorming to elaborate sessions that include games and horseplay. Obvious, but often overlooked, is training in the company's products, markets, competition, and technologies.

Activities to Encourage Creativity

Management should allow innovators freedom to associate with others in similar positions. This freedom extends to all functional areas and to outside the firm as well. Many firms permit innovators to visit customers, though this risks the disclosure of unfavorable data or experience. Many companies permit free time and/or flextime. Free time lets innovators decide what to do during a certain percentage of their working time, often as high as 20 percent. Innovators may work on their own pet projects during this time. Flextime for innovators is different from the traditional meaning of flextime. Rather than just permitting slightly varied workshifts, flextime for innovators means letting employees take work home or stay in the workplace and work all night if they wish. We must remember that newborn ideas are extremely fragile. If managers give innovators a hard time, show no appreciation for their ideas, and offer no encouragement, innovators are likely to drop their ideas, vowing never to waste their creative genius on those management clods again.

Removing Roadblocks to Creativity

We must not only encourage creativity, but also energetically remove all roadblocks to creativity. Managers often do more inhibiting than they realize as part of their routine efforts. Some examples are (1) putting more emphasis on procedures than outputs, (2) letting the boss hold sway over more knowledgeable people, (3) believing that more minds are better and making groups and meetings too large, and (4) letting financial concerns have too much influence at the idea generation stage.

Managers have even been known to set up more intentional roadblocks, such as:

- Setting up a *dummy* task group, with no authority, money, or goals, that is really a devious way of doing nothing.
- Setting up a *rigged* task group to prosecute only the manager's pet product idea and no other. No other ideas are welcome.

SEARCHING FOR NEW IDEAS

Interpreting Venture Strategy

In Chapter 2, we developed a venture strategy to support the corporate strategy. Before beginning our search, we should consult our venture strategy to obtain guidance for our search. For each planned venture the following information, which can be used to guide our search, should be available from the Venture Strategy:

- *Type of Venture.* The venture should be classified using the categories described in Chapter 2. If there is something unique about this particular venture, it should be pointed out.
- *Area of Focus.* For each proposed venture, there should be at least one clear technology dimension (such as a science, a material, or process skill) and one clear market dimension (such as user, a use, or an activity) that is expected to be the focus of development.
- *Product Concept.* Concepts are essentially descriptions of the envisioned product, market, or process in a form that can be readily understood and investigated by the people primarily responsible for development: high-level management, marketing, engineering, production, and customers. For example, a *product* concept should outline the **need**, **solution**, and **features** of a proposed product.
- *Estimated Time and Cost of Development.* These are "ball park" estimates that will be refined during the development process and the preparation of the venture plan.
- *Goals—Objectives.* Additional goals and objectives may be specified when appropriate.

Sources of Ideas

Conventional wisdom holds that new product development is performed primarily by manufacturers. Eric von Hippel challenges this assumption by demonstrating that innovation occurs in different places in different industries.[2] *Users* are the primary innovators in the scientific instrument, semiconductor, and pultrusion process industries, while *suppliers* are the primary innovators in the wire termination equipment industry. In only three of the nine types of industries (tractor shovel-related, engineering plastics, and plastics additives) are the manufacturers the major innovators. Arguing that innovation will take place where the greatest economic benefit from innovation occurs, von Hippel develops a theory that can be used to either predict or shift the source of innovation and to identify profitable modes of innovation sharing.

In the following paragraphs, we describe some of the more useful sources. To make the following description more useful, we have divided the sources into four categories: primary internal, secondary internal, primary external, and secondary external sources.

Primary Internal Sources

Marketing Personnel. The new product ideas that come from marketing personnel are primarily need-driven ideas. Given their grassroots experience and constant contact with customers, the sales force is an excellent source of new product ideas. They are constantly scanning and monitoring the market and thus are tuned in to changes in buyers' needs, wants, and behavior patterns as well as changes in competitive offerings. This is especially true for industrial products, where the salesperson is in direct contact with the actual end user. By observing trends and usage patterns and listening to customer complaints, the salesperson can formulate a new product idea or at least provide the direction for R & D to develop one.

Scientists and Engineers. Many new product ideas originate in the company's own research and development department. The new product ideas coming from scientists and engineers tend to be technology driven. One problem with this source is that many scientists and engineers may become too enamored with the technical aspects of a new product idea and pay too little attention to the market aspects. R & D personnel who appreciate both aspects will provide the most useful ideas.

Manufacturing Personnel. Manufacturing personnel are the primary source of new product ideas for reducing the cost of the product, particularly the cost to manufacture. Most of their ideas will be for improvements to existing products, rather than radically new products.

Secondary Internal Sources

High-Level Management. In addition to providing guidance to the new product development effort described in Chapter 2, high-level management can often provide specific new product ideas. They tend to have more of a future orientation than either marketing or engineering and can often provide seed ideas for radical new products in the future. They also have a broad view of the company's product line and can sometimes see gaps when others do not.

Other Employees. Employees from departments other than marketing, engineering, and operations can also be a good source of product ideas, if (1) they work closely with customers, such as field service, or (2) actually use the company's products themselves.

Primary External Sources

Customers. The greatest external source of new product ideas is the customer, although customers' ideas are usually for product modifications, occasionally for product differentiations, and almost never for product breakthroughs. Customers include both intermediate buyers (distributors, wholesalers, and retailers) and the ultimate buyer or consumer. Intermediate buyers can provide feedback from the marketplace or present suggestions of their own. They can also supply competitive product information that may prove helpful. Ultimate buyers, or consumers, constitute the best source of information because their reaction ultimately determines a new product's success. The most popular ways to gather consumer ideas are surveys, continuing panels, special focus groups, and the mail.

Suppliers. Suppliers can be valuable sources of ideas if they possess the technical expertise that enables them to make suggestions for new products for their customers. Virtually all producers of steel, aluminum, chemicals, metals, paper, plastic, glass, and wire have technical customer service departments with this capability. Forever competing to obtain or increase their share of a company's business, suppliers have every reason to propose product improvements to enhance their sales potential.

Competitors. Domestic competitors may be an indirect source for a leapfrog or add-on new products, but they are rarely sources of new product ideas except where benchmarking has been accepted as a strategy or there is government-mandated cross-licensing of ideas. *Foreign* competitors are a more productive source of ideas. By simply shopping abroad, one may obtain many useful ideas. While browsing in a West German supermarket, executives of Minnetonka found toothpaste in a pump dispenser. They contacted its manufacturer and introduced the first such product in America.

Inventors. Inventors can be a fertile source of new product ideas, especially since most of them do not have the financial resources to capitalize on their inventions. Locating the right inventor can be a difficult task because many of them lead a quiet life and work on their ideas at home. Some inventors take the initiative and contact firms they believe might be interested in their invention. Others exhibit their innovations at patent expositions, waiting for visitors to express an interest. Patent brokers or patent attorneys may act as go-betweens for some. To assist in overcoming this problem, Dvorkovits & Associates sponsors an annual international technology exposition, InstanTechEx, where attending individuals, firms, and governments display new product ideas they would like to sell. The shows are supermarkets of technology that go a long way toward solving the communications problem.

Resellers. Most mass merchandisers, such as Sears, have their own new products departments and invite manufacturers to bid on specifications. Many industrial representatives are skilled enough to be special advisers to their clients. Brokers, industrial distributors, and large jobbers are also good sources of ideas.

Consultants. Most management consulting firms do new products development, including idea generation, and some specialize in it (Booz, Allen & Hamilton and Arthur D. Little). Companies report many favorable experiences, but many horror stories also.

Secondary External Sources

Advertising Agents. Most advertising agencies have the creative talent and the product/market experience to generate new product concepts. They view themselves as marketing advisors to their clients, researching the market and putting their creative talent to work developing new product ideas. Some agencies have full-blown products departments and take their products all the way to market, including premarket testing.

Industrial Designers. Many industrial design engineers are extremely creative, and their firms are interested in capitalizing on their creativity by engaging in new product development. Industrial design departments of universities are sometimes assigned by government and other organizations to do original new product work.

Other Manufacturers. Most firms have potentially worthwhile new product ideas that they do not want because these ideas conflict with the firm's strategy. These ideas can usually be purchased for little cost, if they can be located. One firm, General Electric, went so far as to establish a "Business Opportunities Program" in the 1960s, in which it offered its spare technologies for sale. GE has expanded this service by listing the technologies of others in its monthly editions of *Selected Business Ventures* and in annual compilations of its *New Product New Business Digest.*

Research Laboratories. Most of the world's developed countries have at least one research laboratory that performs new product research on contract from sponsoring companies and may generate ideas on their own for sale. The fore most research laboratory is probably the Battelle Memorial Institute in Columbus, Ohio, but the Illinois Institute of Technology, Stanford Research Institute, and the National Engineering Laboratory in England are not far behind.

Governments. The U.S. government offers several services to assist companies in finding new product ideas.

- The Patent Office publishes the *Official Gazette* that provides a weekly listing of (1) all new patents issued, (2) condensed descriptions of patented items, and (3) patents that are for sale or license. Patent Office reports and services also make known what government patents and foreign patents are available.

- For a nominal fee, companies may obtain the latest government-sponsored research reports and patent information from the National Technical Information Service, which acts as a clearinghouse for all government technical information.

- New regulations can often be the source of new product ideas. Regulators are looking for companies that can solve such problems as unsafe and unhealthy products and working conditions that must be corrected per new regulations. For example, the Occupational Safety and Health Act encouraged and assisted several companies to develop new first aid kits.

Universities. Academia occasionally develops new product ideas, especially in schools of engineering, science, business, medicine, dentistry, and pharmacy. Research support for the university may grant the corporate sponsors certain rights to the new product ideas.

Literature. Technical, scientific, and trade journals in the area of technology pertinent to your company can be a source of new technology-oriented product ideas. Their usefulness is very much dependent upon the area of technology involved. There are some more general publications, such as *Newsweek*'s annual *New Products and Process*, *New Technology* (London) and the *Soviet Technology Bulletin*, that are useful to a wide range of industries as direct sources of new product ideas.

Precautions When Using External Sources

When receiving new product ideas from external sources, it is important that they be handled carefully to avoid later legal complications. The following procedure is recommended:

- If the idea is oral, have the suggester put it in writing.
- When a written idea is received, send it immediately to the legal department with no evaluation. If it is labeled externally as a idea, do not open it. If it is not labeled, reseal it as soon as you realize it is an idea and send it to the legal department.
- The legal department sends the suggester a form letter that expresses the firm's thanks, indicates the conditions under which the company considers outside ideas, and includes a waiver form for the suggester to sign and return. The waiver form stipulates, among other things, that the offer is made free of any obligation on the part of the firm, except as stated on the form.
- If the suggester returns the waiver form, the original suggestion is taken from its place of restricted storage and forwarded to the proper person/s for evaluation.
- The additional guidelines listed below should be followed during the process:

    —No acknowledgment of idea receipt is given by anyone but the legal department.

    —No one asks for more information from the suggester until a waiver form is received.

    —Even if the employee opening the suggestion thinks it is obviously not new or completely lacking in merit, the suggestion is still handled in the prescribed manner.

Search Procedures for New Product Ideas

If our search for new product ideas is to be productive, the search must be focused.[3] One approach to focusing the search is to focus on **change**. A situation that has changed recently often provides an excellent opportunity for a new product. By systematically examining our internal and external environment in a proactive and aggressive manner, we can identify changes that could lead to new products. In focusing on change, our problem is not the scarcity of changes but the overabundance. We must therefore narrow our search to those areas that are most productive. Listed below are eight types of change that have been found to be very productive.

1. Unexpected Success
2. Unexpected Failure
3. Unexpected Events

4. Changes in Industry and/or Market Structure
5. High-Growth Business Area
6. Demographic Changes
7. Emerging Technologies
8. Converging Technologies

Below are some questions that have been found useful in finding new product ideas from various types of change. By asking these questions about each of the eight types of change, you will be more apt to identify the consequences of these changes, whether they are yours or someone else's.

- What instances of (type of change) have you experienced recently?
- In which *geographic* areas have you experienced (type of change) recently?
- In which *market/industry* segments have you experienced (type of change) recently?
- What *customer* segments have experienced (type of change) recently?
- What instances of (type of change) have your *suppliers* experienced recently?
- What instances of (type of change) have your *competitors* experienced recently?
- Which of your *technologies* has experienced (type of change) recently?
- What *traditional customer/user* groups have experienced (type of change) recently?
- What *traditional market* segments have experienced (type of change) recently?

Once these questions have provided you with some raw material, the next question to ask is, "What specific product opportunities and ideas can be developed from this (type of change)?" The process is not completed simply by identifying instances of a particular type of change; we must seek opportunities that result from this type of change. The more specific and complete we can make these new product ideas, the better. However, we should not let making them specific interfere with finding more ideas. Each of these types of change is described more fully in the following paragraphs.

1. Unexpected Success. Unexpected successes can happen both to your own organization and to other organizations, including your competitors. Almost everyone analyzes their failures, but very few analyze their successes. Most people explain away unexpected successes as temporary aberrations and do not seek to find the cause.

2. Unexpected Failure. Unexpected failures may be a failure of your own organization or other organizations, including your competitors. In either case, we are looking for failures that we did not anticipate. We could say that all failures are unexpected; no one plans to fail. However, we are referring to those dramatic unexpected failures that occur when great success had been anticipated.

3. Unexpected Events. Unexpected events, like successes and failures, can be internal or external.

4. Changes in Industry and/or Market Structure. Industry and market structure changes, such as those in the telephone, cable television, and health care industries and in the internationalization of many businesses, are excellent sources of opportunities.

5. *High-Growth Business Areas.* High-growth areas are products, services, markets, industries, and so on, inside or outside the organization, that are growing faster than the gross national product or faster than the general population. High growth is one of the most overlooked of the search areas. One reason is that people are more attuned to looking for poor growth than to looking for high growth.

6. *Demographic Changes.* Demographic change can involve such things as the age or education of your users, their income, where they are living, the mix of users, and so forth. Demographic changes have long been used by direct mail advertisers, political analysts, and aggressive marketers. Such changes, however, can represent opportunity for *anyone*, irrespective of the business.

7. *Emerging Technologies.* Emerging technology is one of the more difficult areas to search, but it can be fruitful if searched correctly. In the first place, most technology is generated by private companies at considerable expense, and they go to great length not to disclose it. However, taking advantage of industrial shows, government research, technical journals, and conferences, one can obtain a good grasp of the state of technology.

8. *Converging Technologies.* Sometimes two or more technologies that singly do not represent an opportunity can represent a substantial opportunity when taken together. For example, the marriage of the computer with the videodisk has created an interactive learning combination that has provided several training companies with an excellent opportunity.

We have discussed the search areas in the order in which most companies find success in them. However, different industries and different companies find different areas most fruitful, so you must select the areas that are most fruitful for you. By systematically searching those areas, you will find considerable information to serve as the basis for new product ideas. However, this information is not initially in the form of new product ideas. To generate new product ideas you must ask the question, ''What specific product opportunities and ideas can be developed from this information?'' The process is not completed simply by identifying new information; you must seek new product ideas that result from this information. The techniques for creative synthesis, discussed later in this chapter, can be used to develop new product ideas from the information gained from your search.

GENERATING NEW IDEAS THROUGH CREATIVE SYNTHESIS

A number of procedures may be used to generate new product ideas. To make them more understandable and useful, we have divided them into three categories: (1) general procedures that can be used by everyone, (2) need-based procedures, which are used primarily by marketing-oriented personnel, and (3) technology-based procedures, which are used primarily by technical or engineering personnel. In one chapter, we cannot hope to describe all the idea generation procedures available. We will describe the more popular and productive procedures in each category and list the others at the end of the chapter, with references to where more information can be found.[4]

General Procedures for Creating New Product Ideas

A number of general procedures can be used to create new product ideas. In the following paragraphs, we discuss the most useful of these: brainstorming, checklists, and focus groups.

Brainstorming

Brainstorming is probably the best known and most widely used idea-generating technique. It is an unstructured process for generating—through spontaneous contributions by participants—all possible ideas for a new product in a particular product area. The technique can be used on an individual basis, but it is primarily a group process, providing organized idea generation. Because brainstorming is so well known, planning is often disregarded and groups just get together, often with disastrous results. For a good brainstorming session, a problem statement that is neither too broad (so as to diversify ideas too much) nor too narrow (so as to confine responses too much) should be carefully prepared.

After the problem statement is prepared, group members are chosen to represent a wide variety of knowledge. Group members should have a general knowledge of the product area under discussion, but they need not be experts. Some companies exclude experts because they tend to crimp the creativity of others. A group leader should be selected who has the capability of both stimulating discussion and controlling behavior. Individuals with supervisor-subordinate relationships should not be in the same group.

Brainstorming is based on two principles and four rules. The two principles are:

- *Deferral of judgment*. Participants should be free to express an idea that comes to mind without having to worry about criticism from others in the group. The judicial mind weighs evidence, but it discourages the free flowing of ideas.

- *Quantity breeds quality*. According to associationist psychology, our thoughts are structured hierarchically; the most dominant are the habitual thoughts with which we are most comfortable. To have really new ideas we must break through these conventional ideas. We can do this by generating a large number of ideas.

These two principles lead to the following four rules for conducting a brainstorming session:

- No criticism is allowed. Negative judgments must be withheld until later. Even chuckles or raised eyebrows are banned.

- Freewheeling is encouraged. The wilder the idea, the better; it is easier to tame down than to think up.

- Quantity is encouraged. The greater the number of ideas, the more likely the best idea has been identified.

- Combinations and improvements are sought. In addition to contributing ideas of their own, participants should suggest how ideas of others can be modified or improved to produce still another idea.

Using Checklists

The checklist method involves preparing a list of related questions that bring significant issues to the attention of the participants. Participants use the list to guide the direction but not necessarily the content of their ideas. The checklist primarily forces the user to concentrate in specific areas. Checklists may be specialized or generalized and may be of any length. Alex F. Osborn developed a general checklist using nine ways of changing an existing idea, as shown in Figure 6-1.[5]

If a more complete checklist is desired, Small's general checklist contains 112 questions in nine categories with examples for each.[6] These general checklists can be used to develop a more specific checklist that is exactly tailored to a company's products. An abbreviated example of such a tailored checklist is given in Figure 6-2.

Checklists produce a multitude of new product ideas. Since most of them are worthless, much time and effort are required to sort the wheat from the chaff. However, many of our new products have originated from a checklist effort,

Figure 6-1
Osborn's General Checklist

- Put to other uses? New ways to use as is? Other uses if modified?
- Adapt? What else is like this? What other ideas does this suggest? Does past offer a parallel? What could I copy? Whom could I emulate?
- Modify? New twist? Change meaning, color, motion, odor, form, shape? Other changes?
- Magnify? What to add? More time? Greater frequency? Stronger? Larger? Thicker? Extra value? Plus ingredient? Duplicate? Multiply? Exaggerate?
- Minify? What to substitute? Smaller? Condensed? Miniature? Lower? Shorter? Lighter? Omit? Streamline? Split up? Understated?
- Substitute? Who else instead? What else instead? Other ingredient? Other material? Other process? Other power? Other place? Other approach? Other tone of voice?
- Rearrange? Interchange components? Other pattern? Other layout? Other sequence? Transpose cause and effect? Change pace? Change schedule?
- Reverse? Transpose positive and negative? How about opposites? Turn it backwards? Turn it upside down? Reverse roles? Change shoes? Turn tables? Turn other cheek?
- Combine? How about a blend, an alloy, an assortment, an ensemble? Combine units? Combine purposes? Combine appeals? Combine ideas?

and users indicate they are well worth the effort. Some companies use a checkoff matrix, putting product types or brands on one dimension and the checklist questions on the other. This makes the checklist process somewhat more organized and efficient and helps find individual product deficiencies that can be capitalized on for particular product lines or market segments.

Focus Groups

Focus groups have been used frequently and successfully in marketing research. We discuss them here in regard to idea generation, but they can also be used for concept evaluation. A versatile organizational approach, the focus group involves leading a group of people, from outside the company, through an open, in-depth discussion of the company's product(s). In the focus group, the moderator focuses the discussion of the group on the new product area in either a directive or a nondirective manner. Either brainstorming or checklists or both may be used in a focus group. A session is usually conducted as a casual roundtable discussion with six to ten participants.

Recruits for a group session should be chosen from the product's target market on the basis of a *questionnaire*. They must possess relevant experience and be able to talk intelligently about the product area. The questionnaire should also obtain pertinent demographic information to facilitate forming meaningful groups. To entice recruits to attend the session they are usually offered an inducement in the form of a meal or cash.

The key figure in the focus group is the *moderator*, who introduces the topic and leads the discussion. The session gets underway with an introductory statement by the moderator in which he explains the purpose of the gathering as well as the "rules of the game." The setting should be relaxed and casual to encourage a free and uninhibited flow of ideas. It is normally better to hold the meetings external to the company, in hotel conference rooms or other specially designed facilities.

Figure 6-2
Checklist for Industrial Products at ABC Corp.

- Can we change the physical, thermal, electrical, chemical, and mechanical properties of the material?
- Are there new electrical, electronic, optical, hydraulic, mechanical, or magnetic ways of doing this?
- Are all functions really necessary?
- Can we construct a new model of this?
- Can we change the form of power to make it work better?
- Can standard components be substituted?
- What if the order of the process were changed?
- How might it be made more compact?
- What if it were heat-treated, hardened, alloyed, cured, frozen, or plated?
- Who else could use this operation or its output?
- Has every step been computerized as much as possible?

Need-Based Procedures for Creating New Ideas

Problem Analysis

Studying user problems has become a widely used technique for generating new product ideas. Problem analysis is much more than a simple compilation of user problems. The compilation is only the beginning; analysis is the key. For best results, a structured approach, such as described below, should be followed.

First, determine the appropriate *product* or *product category* for exploration. If the company has properly performed its strategic planning, this has already been done.

Second, identify a group of *heavy product users*. Heavy users are apt to have a better understanding of the problems, and they represent the bulk of the sales potential in most markets.

Third, gather from those heavy users or participants a *set of problems* associated with the category. Study the entire system of product use or activity. A good method of doing this is to ask respondents to rate (1) the benefits they want from a set of products and (2) the benefits they are getting. The differences indicate problems. Below we discuss a number of approaches that can be used in this problem-finding phase.

* *Focus groups.* Focus groups are designed to yield exploratory and in-depth discussions and are relatively inexpensive. To form the focus group, we should follow the guidelines provided above. To focus the effort of the group, we should pose questions similar to the following.

  —What is the real problem here? What if the product category did not exist?

  —What are the current attitudes and behaviors of the focus group members toward the product category?

  —What product attributes and benefits do the members of the focus group want?

  —What are their dissatisfactions, problems, and unfilled needs?

  —What changes occurring in their lifestyles are relevant to the product category?

* *User panels.* User panels or user groups are often a good source of problems. In particular, computer user groups have been very effective in identifying and seeking resolution of problems encountered by computer users. Also, the steel industry has an advisory panel of over 200 steel users that provides feedback to the steel industry on problems encountered.

* *Expert opinion.* Many problems can be gathered by simply canvassing the opinions of persons experienced in the category under study. These experts include sales personnel, retail and wholesale distribution personnel, and professionals who support the industry, such as architects, accountants, and the like.

* *Published sources.* Industry studies; the firm's own past studies on allied subjects; government reports; investigations by social, economic, and political critics; academic studies; and so on are frequently useful in identifying problems.

Fourth, sort and *rank the problems* according to their severity or importance. Various methods can be used for this, but a common one utilizes (1) the severity of the problem, (2) the frequency of its occurrence, and (3) the product of severity and frequency. Shown in Figure 6-3 is an example of this technique applied to pet owners' problems.

The output of the Problem Analysis technique becomes the input to the Problem Solving technique described in the next section. Close cooperation is required between marketing and engineering to make the Problem Analysis and Problem Solving techniques an integrated effort.

Perceptual Map Analysis

Perceptual map analysis is an approach that attempts to place a company's new product in a desirable location on the buyer's perceptual map, that is, to find a gap in the map. For every product category that customers buy, they compare, judge, and select from competing products in a process that can be illustrated through a two-dimensional model or map. The relative positions or locations of competing brands on the perceptual map can be identified by asking consumers to rate the different products according to a number of attributes.

To determine a desirable position on the map for a prospective new product, we must first ask buyers to rate currently available products on a number of relevant attributes. The average ratings for each brand are then entered into the map, where the two most important buying considerations form the two axes. The attributes mapped should be those that consumers consider to be most important and differentiating. For example, in the hypothetical map shown in Figure 6-4, consumers considered the attributes of crunchiness and nutritional value to be most important and differentiating. Snacks also have different shapes, colors, and textures, but these attributes were not as important in the eyes of the consumer.

After mapping all the existing products on our two-dimensional map, we then look for gaps—positions on the map with no products. In Figure 6-4 we see three gaps, identified by circles. These are candidates for new products.

Detecting gaps and positioning opportunities for new products has become increasingly popular for many companies. For example, Chrysler conducts periodic surveys asking owners of different makes "to rank their autos on a scale

Figure 6-3
A Technique for Scoring Pet Owners' Problems

	A Problem Occurs Frequently (%)	**B** Problem Is Bothersome (%)	**C** **A x B**
Need constant feeding	98	21	.21
Get fleas	78	53	.41
Shed hairs	70	46	.31
Make noise	66	25	.17
Have unwanted babies	44	48	.21

Figure 6-4
Perceptual Map for Snack Products

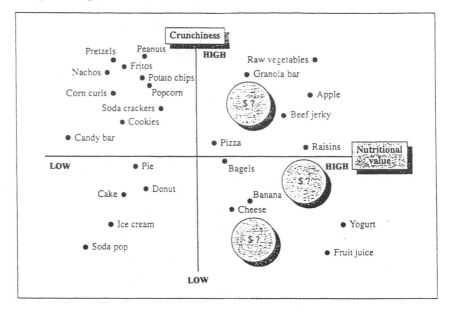

of one to 10 for such qualities as youthfulness, luxury, and practicality.'' An example of a perceptual map of the automobile market resulting from such a survey is shown in Figure 6-5. One of the deficiencies of the perceptual mapping technique is that it finds gaps, and not demand. We still must determine if the gap represents something that the people will buy.

Technology-Based Procedures for Creating New Ideas

Technology-based research can be divided into four categories:

- *Basic Research.* Original investigations for the advancement of scientific knowledge not having specific commercial objectives, although such investigations may be in a field of present or potential interest to the reporting company.

- *Applied Research.* Investigations directed to the discovery of new scientific knowledge having specific commercial objectives with respect to products or processes. This definition differs from that of basic research chiefly in terms of the objectives of the reporting company.

- *Technical Development.* Technical activities of a nonroutine nature concerned with translating research findings or other scientific knowledge into products or processes. Not included are routine technical services to customers.

- *Product Improvement.* Technical activities to modify the features of *existing* products to improve their performance, to reduce their cost, or for other purposes.

Figure 6-5
Perceptual Map for the Automobile Market

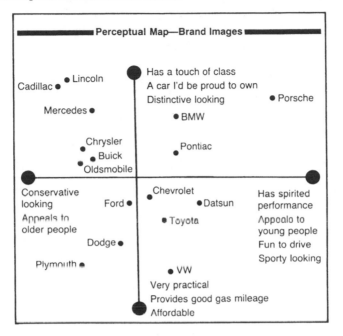

In this chapter, we are primarily concerned with *Product Improvement*. Technical development will be discussed in detail in Chapters 8 and 9. Product improvement is primarily oriented to making changes to existing products, rather than dreaming up new products. Of the many approaches to improving existing products, we will describe four of the most productive: (1) problem solving, (2) attribute analysis, (3) value analysis, and (4) reverse engineering.

Problem-Solving Technique

The output of the Problem Analysis technique described above is the primary input to the Problem-Solving technique. The approach of this technique is quite simple. From the output of the problem analysis effort, we first identify those problems that are amenable to solution by technology. This means we must eliminate all those problems caused by operator error, and so forth. The design engineer must then investigate alternative designs that might solve the identified problems. After the redesign is completed, either on paper or by computer, the proposed modification is incorporated into an existing product and tested both in-house and by users, to insure the modification truly solved the problem.

Attribute Analysis

Attribute analysis is an idea-generating technique requiring individuals to list the attributes of a product and then evaluate each attribute from a variety of viewpoints. Modification occurs in the process as each attribute suggests possible new uses to participants in the exercise. This may result in unrelated objects being brought together to form a new combination that better satisfies a need. Since deriving a list of attributes is not an easy undertaking, the technique works best when applied to specific or existing products, rather than to general or future ones.

Attributes are of three types: features, functions, and benefits. To illustrate, let's take a simple product such as toothpaste. The *features* of toothpaste include taste, texture, color, and container. Toothpaste performs the *functions* of cleaning a person's teeth and mouth. The *benefits* to the user are cleaner and healthier teeth, fewer cavities, cleaner mouth and breath, cleaner and healthier gums, and a prettier smile. The three attributes usually occur in sequence; a feature provides a certain function that in turn provides a benefit. For example, a shampoo may contain proteins (feature) that coat the hair during shampooing (function), which leads to shinier hair (benefit).

To demonstrate the use of attribute analysis, let us assume that a small company manufacturing pallets, used for shipping or moving products, wants to devise a better product. It lists the attributes that the existing pallets have, such as wood composition, rectangular runners, and accessibility from two sides by a forklift. It then examines each attribute for any possible changes that would improve the product. For example, the wood composition could be changed to plastic, resulting in a cheaper price. The rectangular wooden runner could be replaced by cups, make the pallets easier to store and allowing them to be accessed from all four sides for easier pickup. Though attribute listing, the small company develops an idea for a much improved product that can be successfully commercialized.

One should realize that attribute listing focuses on an existing product and is thus more useful for developing product improvement ideas than for generating new product ideas. The technique may even stifle imaginative thinking to some extent. Yet, as in the case of the pallet manufacturer, attribute analysis is often a useful method for developing product improvement ideas.

Value Analysis

The objective of value analysis is to achieve an equivalent or better performance of a product at a lower cost while retaining all functions desired by the customer. The value analysis team considers cheaper methods, materials, processes, and designs. Every element that adds cost but not value is a candidate for elimination. In addition to lower costs and higher profits, value analysis results in better products, improved product performance and reliability, improved quality, improved delivery through reduced lead times, and increased standardization that leads to improved maintenance and lower repair costs. Value analysis is very often an integral part of product and/or processs cost reduction ventures.

Value analysis programs are typically conducted by project teams consisting of design engineers, manufacturing engineers, purchasing specialists, financial analysts, and others who possess relevant skills. The team members familiarize themselves with the item under study using engineering drawings, operation sheets, specifications, and sample items. The team then follows a formalized analysis process that we will demonstrate using a radio transceiver. Value analysis examines first the basic objective (communicate), second the basic function (radio transceiver), and then secondary functions (modulate, transmit, receive, demodulate, etc.). The team looks at other ways to achieve the objective (letter, telephone) and then at alternate ways to achieve the basic function and secondary functions.

The value analysis approach may use checklist questions similar to the following:

- Does the item have any design features that are not necessary?
- Can two or more parts be combined into one?
- Can a less costly material be substituted?
- Are there any nonstandard parts that can be eliminated?

Reverse Engineering

Reverse engineering involves dissembling a competitor's product to see how it is made in order to consider imitation or improvement. In this process, a team of engineers systematically and painstakingly dissembles new models of a competitor's product to uncover new ideas that may be incorporated into their products. This technique has been used quite extensively by the American automobile industry and by various Japanese industries. Reverse engineering is at the heart of the product *imitation* venture.

Special Procedures for Generating New Ideas

In the preceding paragraphs, we have described the most popular and productive techniques for generating new product ideas. Space does not permit a full description of all possible techniques. In the following paragraphs we will list alphabetically a number of additional techniques and provide references for those desiring more information on them.

Blockbusting: James L. Adams, *Conceptual Blockbusting* (Addison-Wesley, 1986).

Delphi: Vincent Wayne Mitchell, "Using Delphi to Forecast in New Technology Industries," *Marketing Intelligence* (U.K.), no. 2, 1992, pp. 4–9.

Disciplines Panel: Robert A Mamis, "The Gang That Doesn't Think Straight," *Inc.* (October 1985), pp. 108–111.

Lateral Thinking: Edward de Bono, *Serious Creativity* (HarperBusiness, 1992).

Morphological Analysis: Fritz Zwicky, *Discovery, Invention, Research, Through the Morphological Approach* (Macmillan, 1969).

Scenario Analysis: Peter Schwartz, *The Art of the Long View* (Doubleday/Currency, 1991).

Synectics: W. J. J. Gordon, *Synectics: The Development of Creative Capacity* (Harper and Row, 1961).

Technological Forecasting: James R. Bright (ed.), *Technological Forecasting for Industry and Government* (Prentice-Hall, 1968).

IDEA GENERATION STAGE REVIEW

Before proceeding to the Concept Evaluation stage, the efforts of the Idea Generation stage should be reviewed by the executive committee to ensure that all actions for this stage have been adequately accomplished. Following are some questions that should be answered during the review.

- Have sufficient ideas been generated to warrant going into Concept Evaluation?
- Have the areas identified by the product strategy as being particularly important been adequately explored?
- Have all departments and all functions been actively involved?
- Have both need-driven and technology-driven efforts been appropriately pursued?
- Has an adequate search for ideas been conducted?
- Have appropriate sources been exploited?
- Have appropriate techniques been used to synthesize information into useful ideas?

NOTES

1. Ray Wise, "The Boom in Creativity Training," *Across the Board* (June 1991), pp. 38–42.

2. Eric von Hippel, *The Sources of Innovation* (Oxford University Press, 1988).

3. Adapted from Robert Michel and Alan Weiss, *The Innovation Formula* (Harper and Row, 1988).

4. A general reference where many of the other procedures may be found is Trevor Sowrey, *The Generation of Ideas for New Products* (London) (Logan Press, 1987).

5. Alex F. Osborn, *Applied Imagination* (Charles Scribner's Sons, 1957), p. 318.

6. Marvin Small, *How to Make More Money* (Pocket Books, 1959).

Chapter 7

Concept Evaluation; Finish Concept Development

THE CONCEPT EVALUATION PROCESS

Where the Idea Generation stage was creative, the Concept Evaluation stage is analytic. We purposely separated the creative effort from the analytical effort, since the analytic process tends to interfere with the effective functioning of the creative process. In the Idea Generation stage, a comprehensive and wide-ranging effort was undertaken to tap into the broadest possible gamut of idea sources to ensure that no promising idea was overlooked. Since the outcome of the Product Development Process can be no better than the input of product ideas, the Idea Generation stage should produce as many product ideas as possible.

For a number of reasons, most of these ideas are not worthy of further pursuit. Given the company's overall, marketing, and product objectives as well as internal and external constraints, only a very small number of ideas can and deserve to be turned into marketable products. These ideas must be identified and distilled from the accumulated pool through a process of successive elimination. We divide this successive elimination process into two steps: (1) initial screening of product *ideas* and (2) comprehensive evaluation of product *concepts*. When these two steps result in the selection of a product concept for further development, the venture team prepares the inputs for the Technical Development stage: (1) a product performance specification and (2) a venture plan.

The primary purpose of the initial screening step is to reduce the number of product ideas to a manageable number so that concept evaluation can be conducted efficiently. The purpose of the concept evaluation step is to select one (or a few) concepts that are worthy of technical development.

INITIAL SCREENING OF PRODUCT IDEAS

Informal Methods for Screening Product Ideas

In a high-tech company, technical screening is very often accomplished on an informal basis. Screening is performed by the innovators themselves, at the level of individual managers, scientists, and engineers. Repeated and interactive choice constitutes an initial screening, applied quite informally by the researchers or idea generators themselves. They decide what to work on. In the aggregate, their choices select and de-select. The *first criterion* then, is the level of excitement generated in the innovator by an idea. If it is promising and exciting enough, she or he will find or make time to work on it.

The next step involves getting others to "buy in" to the idea. This shift from an individual innovator to obtaining the approval and/or backing of several others, comprises the *second criterion*. Usually what happens is that somebody has an idea and talks to somebody else, and it sounds really good. If the idea is approved by or withstands the criticism of the other person, the originator then considers it worth further investigation. Personal credibility is involved in signing on, so both potential "supporters" and proposers judge carefully whether or not they should commit. The stakes go up as the venture proceeds. Personal credibility is on the line because to get an idea beyond its origin, the innovator must go public.

Formal Methods for Initial Screening of Product Ideas

Having gathered and created a large number of new product ideas in the Idea Generation stage, the corporation faces the challenge of separating the wheat from the chaff. It is simply not economically justifiable to evaluate comprehensively all proposed ideas. We therefore must develop some fast and inexpensive screening methods that will reduce the number of ideas that must be comprehensively evaluated. In using these quick and dirty screening methods, we are subject to two risks: *Good ideas may incorrectly be rejected, or poor ideas may be allowed to proceed.* Of the two, the mistaken rejection of a good idea is more serious, since poor ideas can still be rejected in later stages if incorrectly allowed to go through this stage. Good ideas are usually rejected at the screening stage for either of two reasons: inadequate information or management's reluctance to assume substantial risk in a new product venture. There are several safeguards we can take to reduce the risk of a wrong decision.

- Never let the same person generate and screen an idea. Objectivity is bound to suffer, and a person's talents will prove inadequate for mastering both tasks well.

- Assign the screening to a committee rather than a single individual. Several minds and diverse backgrounds are better than one for examining the consequences of an idea.

• Keep a file of rejected ideas and periodically review them. As a result, no idea is ever permanently eliminated from further consideration.

In the screening of product ideas, we will primarily utilize qualitative evaluation methods to avoid the time and cost of collecting quantitative data. There are a number of simple qualitative screening devices that can be employed. We describe two of the most popular of these: qualitative ranking and weighted multifactor scoring matrix.

Qualitative Ranking of Product Ideas

The **qualitative ranking** method is the quickest, but probably the least accurate method of screening. In this procedure, a small group of knowledgeable people are given a written list of numbered product ideas. The first phase of the procedure consists of making certain that each member of the group understands what each item on the list means. When everyone understands each idea to his or her satisfaction, the ranking can commence. Each member of the group is asked to select the top ten ideas from the list and assign a score of ten to the top idea and a score of one to the tenth idea. The ballots are then collected and tabulated. The results of the tabulation are made available to all members, followed by a discussion of the relative merits of the various product ideas. Another voting takes place, especially if there was no consensus on the first ballot. A number larger than ten could be used with a resultant small increase in accuracy, but the time required for voting and tabulating will be increased considerably.

One of the main deficiencies of the qualitative ranking is that each member of the group is using their own criteria or value system for determining which product idea is the best. This deficiency can be corrected somewhat by providing, or having the group develop, a common list of criteria, similar to the one shown in Figure 7-1. The criteria list is used only as a reference to improve ranking. It is not used to score the product ideas. That is left to the next procedure, the weighted multi-criteria matrix.

The Weighted Multi-Criteria Matrix

In using the Weighted Multi-Criteria Matrix shown in Figure 7-1, the following sequence of steps is recommended:

Develop the Screening Criteria. The screening criteria must be carefully chosen, so that they are consistent with the company's venture strategy and will therefore select the products of greatest benefit for the company. Normally the criteria and their weights are developed by a cross-functional group.

Determine the Weight of Each Screening Criterion. Normally it is best to *rank* the criteria first, before assigning weights. A weight can then be assigned to the highest-ranking criterion and corresponding weights assigned to lesser criteria. Weights need not equal one or some power of ten, since we can divide by the sum of the weights to obtain a "normalized score."

Determine the Scale for Each Criterion. A scale of "0 to 10" is usually

Figure 7-1
Weighted Multi-Criteria Matrix for Screening Product Ideas

| CRITERIA | | | Product A | | Product B |
| | | | Weighted | | Weighted |
Product Criteria	Weight	Score	Score	Score	Score
Product Uniqueness	1.5	10	15.0	7	10.5
Use of Existing Facilities	.3	6	1.8	7	2.1
Patent Position	.4	9	3.6	5	2.0
Servicing Requirements	.2	6	1.2	8	1.6
Technical Feasibility	1.0	9	9.0	7	7.0
Technical know-how	.8	8	6.4	6	4.8
Legal Considerations	.2	6	1.2	6	1.2
Availability of Raw Material	.4	7	2.8	8	3.2
Market Criteria					
Market size	1.0	5	5.0	8	8.0
Market growth potential	1.0	8	8.0	9	9.0
Valid Customer Need	1.5	8	12.0	8	12.0
Distribution requirements	.4	6	2.4	7	2.8
Market life	.5	5	2.5	6	3.0
Financial Criteria					
Cost of Entry	.7	6	4.2	7	4.9
Profit contribution	.8	7	5.6	8	6.4
Effect on cash flow	.4	6	2.4	4	1.6
Payback	.2	7	1.4	7	1.4
Return on Investment	.5	7	3.5	7	3.5
Total Weighted Scores	10.0		88.0		85.0
Normalized Scores			8.8		8.5

appropriate for criteria that are subjectively measured. A more refined scale can be used for criteria that can be measured objectively.

Score Each Product Idea against the Screening Criteria. This is where the real evaluation occurs. In most cases the scores are determined subjectively by the scorer. Thus the scorer must be knowledgeable in the product area, so that he or she can make an accurate evaluation. Normally, multiple scorers are utilized, with their scores appropriately combined.

Calculate Weighted Scores by Multiplying Scores Times the Weight of the Criterion. This is nothing but arithmetic, which can best be done by a computer. More specifically, it can be done by a computer *spreadsheet*.

Calculate the Total Weighted Score for Each Product Idea. More arithmetic to be done by the computer spreadsheet.

Compute Normalized Score by Dividing Weighted Scores by the Sum of the Weights. The largest weighted score represents the product that best meets the criteria. Normalizing the scores converts the scores to values we are accustomed to viewing, but does not change the relative ranking of the product concepts.

Selecting the Method for Screening Product Ideas

The method selected for screening product ideas depends primarily on the (1) number of ideas to screen, (2) time and talent available for screening, and (3) desired confidence in the results. The ranking method provides the most rapid screening with the least talent, but the confidence level in the results is quite low. The multi-criteria matrix provides the most valid results, but it is considerably more time consuming than the ranking method. Many companies use a combination of methods, starting with the simple ranking method to reduce the number of ideas by 50 percent or more and then using the matrix method to screen the remaining ideas with more confidence.

DEVELOPING PRODUCT SPECIFICATIONS

A product performance specification is a set of performance objectives that is written to guide the development of a product. It should be a precise description of what the product *should be able to do*. The development of product performance specifications, discussed in the next section, is conducted in parallel with Concept Evaluation.

When Are Specifications Established?

In the ideal world, the team would establish the product specifications once early in the development process and then proceed to design and engineer the product to meet these specifications exactly. For some products, such as soap or soup, this approach works quite well; the technologists on the team can reliably concoct a formula that satisfies almost any specifications. However, for technology-intensive products this is rarely possible. For such products, specifications are revised at least twice, and usually three times.[1]

Early in the concept evaluation stage, immediately after identifying the customer needs for the concept, the team prepares *concept performance specifications* for the most promising concepts. These specifications represent the best ideas of the team regarding what the product should be able to do, but they are established before the team knows what constraints the product technology will place on product performance. The team's efforts may fail to meet some of these specifications and may exceed others, depending on the product concept the team eventually selects.

For this reason, these concept specifications must be refined after a product concept has been evaluated and tentatively selected. The team revisits the concept specification after assessing the actual technological constraints and the expected production costs during concept evaluation. To prepare the resulting *product performance specifications*, the team must frequently make hard trade-offs among different desirable characteristics. The product performance specifications, sometimes called the product definition, along with the venture plan provides the primary justification for the concept going into technical development.

The *concept performance specifications* and the *product performance specifications* are **performance** specifications; they indicate what the new product is expected to *do*, what *benefits* it should deliver to the customer. They should not specify how it should be built or what features it should have. The specifications should be developed jointly between marketing, engineering, and production, with marketing taking the lead. These specifications should be *needs* documents and not *solutions* documents. They should specify what need the product is expected to satisfy, with little indication of how the need is to be satisfied.

Outlining the design requirements for the solution is the purpose of the *product* **design** *specification*, which is prepared early in design stage of technical development, to guide the design team in the design of the product. The design specification calls out the complete design requirements for the product so that the parallel work in all areas will be compatible. It will be described more completely in Chapter 8, and we will delay further discussion of it until then. In this chapter, we will concentrate on the two *performance* specifications.

Writing Specifications

Creating a specification should begin by focusing on the customer. Who is the target customer? What is that customer's problem? How will the product solve this problem? What benefits will it offer as compared to other solutions that are available to the customer? How will the customer value these benefits? On what basis will the customer judge the product?

Everyone involved in the development venture must understand who the customer is expected to be and what needs are to be satisfied. This understanding is essential, but not easily obtained. Most specifications provide merely a perfunctory one- or two-sentence statement of the need for the product. A much more detailed discussion is needed, though, to help those who will be making trade-off decisions later so that their decisions fit in with the purpose of the product.

A specification has to relate a product to the marketplace. There is no better way of doing this than by actually involving real customers or users in writing the specification. The most helpful users are usually the lead users, the innovators, who will be the first to use the new product. They are the most demanding and most aware of the shortcomings in competing solutions now on the market. Lead users are found by first identifying important, new, or leading trends in the appropriate marketplace. Then look for user groups that are on the leading edge of the trend.

Once a product's relationship to the marketplace is clear, the next step is to define its benefits. Too often, specification writers work with features rather than benefits—but customers buy benefits, not features. Two traps result from concentrating on features. One is that certain ones may be unnecessary to achieve product benefits, and imposing them only adds unnecessary design constraints. The other trap is that concentrating on features may obscure what the real need and purpose of the product are; one may become so enamored with the fancy features that the real need of the customer is neglected.

As a minimum, engineering, marketing, and manufacturing should be involved as a team in writing the specification. Depending on the product and how the company works, other functions such as purchasing, quality assurance, testing, or customer service may be brought in as well. The essence of a good specification is balance among the many design trade-offs that must be made as the product goes into development. Joint participation in writing the specification gets these trade-offs out in the open and starts the extensive interplay needed to resolve them in a way that will yield a competitive product. The trade-offs cannot all be resolved in writing the initial specification, and some design work must be done to provide more information for the refined specification.

If all the key players are involved in the discussion of the initial specification, they will be better able to reach consensus on the direction of concept evaluation and will be capable of making consistent trade-off decisions. A perhaps more important outcome from involving all key players in writing the initial specifications is that of "buying in" to the venture. This buy-in is essential to getting the venture completed quickly and effectively. When a person actually contributes to writing the specification, they are more committed to developing a product that meets the specification.

Content of the Product Performance Specification (PPS)

The PPS provides the basis for the product's design and serves as the primary objective statement for the product. Since the PPS provides the basis for Technical Development, it is important that it be complete and accurate.[2] The recommended content of the PPS in four critical product areas is described below:

Performance. Critical performance items, from a user's point of view, are to be defined, particularly for the human interface. This is important because design requirements, such as microprocessor and memory needs, will depend on how performance requirements are defined. Dimensions of performance that generally must be specified include response time, throughput, capacity, task complexity, and system load.

Capabilities. All capabilities needed by the product to enable it to perform properly should be included in the PPS. Maintenance capabilities should be identified. Products with embedded software, for example, may require security, audit, diagnostic, or recovery capabilities. Required interfaces to other systems should be identified. If the software component receives information from an external data source, the form and integrity of the external data must be defined. If the integrity of externally supplied data cannot be ensured, data validation and error-handling features must be included in the PPS.

Product Quality Objectives. Product reliability requirements in appropriate units of measure should be established. For the hardware, mean time to failure or its reciprocal failure/time are meaningful measurements of reliability. Another meaningful measurement is "uptime," the time that the machine is available for use. For software, the reliability also might be expressed as mean time to failure.

Modularity. Modularity capabilities enable hardware and software to be used in derivative products. In particular, software should generally be specified for *reusability* in derivative products, *portability* to other processor platforms in product upgrades, and *maintainability* for ease in modification. Generally, hardware subsystems should also be modular, unless space or weight requirements prevent it.

COMPREHENSIVE EVALUATION OF PRODUCT CONCEPTS

Developing Product Concepts

What emerges from the screening phase are raw ideas that have survived a qualitative review based on limited and subjective information. They hold sufficient promise, though, to warrant a more thorough evaluation. To accomplish this, these ideas must be thought out more carefully and completely and expressed in a more substantive testable form. In other words, the surviving ideas must be transformed into **product concepts**. Product concepts are essentially descriptions of the envisioned product in a form that can be investigated and tested by the functions primarily responsible for concept evaluation: high-level management, marketing, engineering, operations, and customers.

When transforming an idea into a concept, we must first ask, what problem (*need*) is this product intended to solve and for whom (the market)? Second, we must define *how* the product proposes to *solve* the problem or address the need. And third, we must spell out the *relevant features* the product will possess. The relevant features provide details relating to the composition of the product, its size, capacity, speed, or other operational features.

Ideally, the product offers a solution to a problem that has remained unsolved or a need that is being satisfied inadequately. To appeal to the customer, the solution should take an innovative approach that customers are likely to perceive as significant. For engineering and production personnel, the solution must be definitive enough to enable them to determine development and production feasibility and costs. In summary, the product concept should outline the **need**, **solution**, and **features** of a proposed product.

A product concept is a statement about anticipated product features that will yield selected customer benefits relative to other products or problems solutions already available. The concept statement should make the new product's differences absolutely clear, point out attributes that make a difference in the buying decision, be completely credible and realistic, and be as short as possible. This information is presented to potential buyers in one or a combination of four formats:

• Narrative (verbal)
• Drawing, diagram, or sketch (visual)

- Model or prototype
- Virtual reality

Typically containing both verbal and visual elements, a concept statement will usually read like an advertisement. It describes and praises the innovation in several paragraphs of text and in an accompanying drawing or mock-up. The drawing, showing how the product is used, should be kept simple. Unnecessary detail is likely to distract from the core message and should be avoided. The drawing should support and illustrate the text and should not assume a life of its own.

Prototypes or models are a more expensive form of concept statement, because many decisions have to be made about the new product to get it into a prototype. Whoever builds an early prototype makes many decisions about the new product that should be kept open at this early date. Virtual reality can capture the advantages of the prototype without incurring the disadvantages. It allows the developer to "build" three-dimensional virtual images of the new product by means of software that the customer can view and manipulate from all angles.

Product Concept Evaluation

The purpose of the Concept Evaluation stage is to determine which product concepts have sufficient merit to warrant a full-scale Technical Development effort. In the first phase, we reduced the myriad of ideas to a small number of concepts. In this second phase, we will conduct a comprehensive and in-depth analysis of the retained concepts to ensure we select the best one for technical development. Concept evaluation endeavors to answer the following five questions in a definitive, quantitative, and complete manner. At first glance, these five questions may appear disarmingly simple. However, a company that endeavors to answer them completely must undertake an exhaustive analysis.

- Does it fit the company?
- Is it sufficiently different from our competitor's product(s)?
- Does it fit the customers in the target market?
- Can we develop it in a reasonable time and cost?
- Can we produce and sell it at a reasonable profit for a reasonable time?

Does It Fit the Company?

New product development should not be the result of unbridled enthusiasm spinning off into every direction at once. Rather, it should be an organized, purposeful, and focused effort to improve the organization's products to enhance achievement of the company's *mission* and *strategic objectives*.

In order to evaluate whether a concept fits the company, the company's mission and strategic objectives must be well known and accepted throughout the company. We are suggesting that the concept should fit the firm's future strategic objectives, and not its current directions. In order to survive and grow, companies must change to some extent—-penetrate new industries, gain new knowledge, and enter new markets. If company fit were interpreted to mean perfect fit with the company as it is today, that company would be doomed to inevitable decline.

Is It Sufficiently Different from Our Competitors' Products?

We will attempt to answer this question by performing a competitive (benchmarking) analysis, which is the process of measuring one's products, services, and practices against one's toughest competitors or those recognized as world leaders. The steps in competitive benchmarking are (1) identifying the competing firms, (2) identifying the competing products, and (3) benchmarking the products.

Identifying the competing firms. The first, and fairly obvious, step is to identify the firm's key competitors. How many firms compete in this product area? Who are they? Given the increasingly global nature of competition, both national and foreign firms should be investigated. The competitive strengths and weaknesses of key competitors are assessed to look for potential barriers to success and to identify opportunities. What proprietary technologies, patents, or technical skills are held by other firms that would make them difficult to compete against?

Identifying the competing products. Products that are expected to compete directly against the proposed product also need to be identified. Both domestic and foreign products should be considered. While currently available products are much more obvious and much easier to assess, the team should also consider what new products will arise during the new product's life.

Benchmarking the product. Once appropriate competitive products are identified, they are compared to the proposed product. How do features, performance, and other customer-identified features of the proposed product compare to these alternatives? Both market information (such as competitor's marketing brochures) and physical product testing are important sources of information about competitive offerings. Often, these results can be compiled into a cross-reference table for simpler analysis.

A useful technique is to dissemble and ''reverse engineer'' competitive products to understand how they operate, what technologies they employ, and what materials they use. The manufacturing cost of the product can often be estimated quite accurately using this approach. Also, a historical assessment of competing products can help identify major product trends. How have technologies, features, speed, and so forth changed from the older products to the newer products? How could they be expected to change in the future?

Beyond Benchmarking. Benchmarking alone is not sufficient to determine the requirements for our new product. If a firm designs a product to meet the requirements determined by benchmarking, it can be assured it will be at least one product development cycle behind. While we are designing to meet *current* requirements, some other firm will be designing to meet *future* requirements. Our new products must address the future needs of our future customers, and not the current needs. To determine the requirements for our new product, we must go beyond the current benchmarked capabilities of our competitors.

Does It Fit the Customers in the Target Market?

We will try to answer this question by employing *product concept testing*, which involves testing the concept with representative customers in the target market to determine the acceptability of the concept. More specifically, the procedure for product concept testing is as follows:

1. Select the strongest concepts from a pool of alternative concepts.
2. Eliminate weak concepts that find little favor with the target market.
3. Identify key consumer concerns and evaluation criteria in the product category.
4. Determine desired product features.

The first and second purposes coincide in that they serve to narrow the field further and concentrate resources on the most promising concepts. *Intention-to-buy* scales or *preference rankings* can be used for this sorting task. An *intention-to-buy* instrument asks consumers to indicate the intensity of their feelings, using a scale of 1 to 5 as shown below:

1. Definitely will buy the product
2. Probably will buy the product
3. Undecided—may or may not buy
4. Probably will not buy the product
5. Definitely will not buy the product

Although an intention-to-buy measure is quite tentative, because the product exists only in concept form, experience has shown that only those concepts receiving a rating of 1 or 2 stand a chance to succeed in the marketplace. This early indicator, therefore, has considerable validity in predicting future buyer behavior. *Preference rankings* simply ask the respondents which of the six or seven concepts they like best, second best, and so on. Concepts that consistently rank at the bottom of the list are discarded.

The third function of concept testing—identifying key consumer concerns and evaluation criteria in the product category—provides an essential learning experience for management. One of the things management has to learn is how consumers think and talk about such products. The last function of concept testing—determining desired product features—is the most freewheeling. Prospective consumers will be invited to design or redesign the product based on the broad outline contained in the concept statement. They will be asked which of the features should remain, which should be added, and which should be dropped to bring the concept more in line with what the consumer needs and desires. Reconfiguring the product at this point is inexpensive because no money has been spent on technical development.

The technique used frequently in conducting concept testing is the *focus group interviews*. A versatile organizational approach, the focus group involves leading a group of people, from outside the company, through an open, in-depth discussion of the company's product concepts. Recruits for a group session should be chosen from the product's target market on the basis of a *questionnaire*. They must possess relevant experience and be able to talk intelligently about the product area. The questionnaire should also obtain pertinent demographic information to facilitate forming meaningful groups. To entice recruits to attend the session, they are usually offered an inducement in the form of a meal or cash. A session is usually conducted as a casual roundtable discussion with six to ten participants. The setting should be relaxed and casual to encourage a free and uninhibited flow of ideas. It is normally better to hold the meetings external to the company, in hotel conference rooms or other specially designed facilities.

The key figure in the focus group is the *moderator*, who focuses the discussion of the group. The session gets underway with an introductory statement by the moderator, in which he explains the purpose of the gathering as well as the "rules of the game." The moderator first ensures that all members of the group understand the concept under discussion. With everyone understanding the concept, the moderator will seek other reactions, such as:

• Uniqueness of the concept
• Extent to which the concept solves a problem or satisfies a need
• Importance of the problem being addressed
• Extent to which the concept is realistic, practical, and useful
• How likely they would be to buy the product
• What problems they foresee in using the product

Concept testing interviews with prospective customers may also be conducted individually in their homes, in a shopping mall, or in other suitable locations. In general, individual interviews are less effective and more costly than group interviews.

Can We Develop and Launch It in a Reasonable Time, Quality, and Cost?

In evaluating product concepts, the company must consider whether it is in a position to provide the technical and engineering expertise required to develop the product. The ideal product concept is one for which the firm already possesses exactly the mix of special knowledge and experience required for product development. If the company lacks the required technical and engineering expertise, this can be solved by intelligent hiring or even through alliances, joint ventures, and so on. However, this should be considered in the decision to start development and in the plans for development.

One required success factor, often overlooked, is knowledge and experience in the proposed industry (unless you are starting a new industry). Unless the firm has or can employ knowledgeable people or can acquire a foothold firm to provide the knowledge and experience, the opportunity should be dropped—or delayed until the firm can learn something about the business through a small-scale entry or acquisition.

Can We Produce and Sell It at a Reasonable Profit for a Reasonable Time?

What Functions Are Required for the Product's Success? The company must understand what functions are needed to develop the new product and the relative importance of the various functions involved (marketing, R&D, manufacturing, finance, human resources, etc.). For example, for most consumer products marketing and distribution are primary. For the majority of industrial products, engineering and manufacturing are important. It would be disastrous for a manufacturer of industrial products to move into consumer products without a major revamping of the marketing department. An organization new to an industry would be well advised to study the leading companies in the target industry to identify what accounts for their success.

Can We Produce and Sell It at a Reasonable Profit? At this point in product development, this is a difficult question to answer. For guidelines, we turn to the venture capital industry, in which the economic characteristics of successful ventures reportedly include the following[3]:

* A break-even time of less than 36 months
* Stable gross margins of 20 percent to 50 percent
* After-tax profit potential of 10 percent to 15 percent
* Multiple rather than one-shot investments
* For industrial customers, payback in 18 months or less
* Low asset intensity
* Differentiation on the basis of product rather than price

The venture capital guidelines stated above are applicable to medium-sized corporations that cannot take large investment risks as well as to large corporations that use a conservative approach to venturing.

How Long Will the Product Live? Identifying the factors responsible for an opportunity enables an organization to make some meaningful judgments about how long those factors are likely to last. For example, a drop in interest rates might provide an opportunity for a new product related to the building industry.

In evaluating such an opportunity, a firm would have to consider how long those lower rates could be expected to continue, which would greatly affect whether to make the entry and how quickly to enter and exit. In contrast, environmental legislation is here to stay; and as a source of opportunity, that factor can be regarded as fairly durable.

Although rigorous probing for the factors producing an opportunity is a necessary part of the evaluation process, this does not mean a product should be automatically rejected if one or more of the underlying factors proves to be temporary. It will, however, affect such issues as speed, scale, and aggressiveness of entry, investment level, and financial return requirements.

In Conclusion

During this analysis we should also be looking for ways that we could improve the product concepts under investigation; it should not be purely an evaluation effort. The results of this analysis will form the basis for writing the *venture plan*, which is the formal document on which high-level management will base their decision regarding whether or not to go into Technical Development.

PREPARE INPUT FOR TECHNICAL DEVELOPMENT JUSTIFICATION

Once a product concept has been selected, the next step is to prepare a product performance specification and a venture plan. The venture plan has two purposes: (1) to provide the justification to higher-level management for going into the technical development stage and (2) to provide a plan of action for all concerned for the entire product development process. Taking a product concept into technical development means making a sizable investment at considerable risk. Before high-level management will make this investment, they must be convinced that a viable product concept exists that will eventually become a profitable business.

Prepare a Venture Plan

The venture plan must illustrate current status, expected needs, and projected results of the proposed product venture. Every aspect of the development needs to be described—the organization, marketing, research and development, production, critical risks, finances, and milestones. A description of all of these facets of the proposed venture is necessary to demonstrate a clear picture of what that venture is, where it is projected to go, and how the company proposes it will get there. It is important that the venture plan show a clear line of action in realistic terms from the product concept to the commercial product.

The venture plan is normally first prepared to justify the decision for going into Technical Development. It is later updated and expanded to justify the decision to launch the product. In the initial version it is neither necessary nor

Figure 7-2
Outline of Venture Plan

I. EXECUTIVE SUMMARY -- Several pages summarizing the complete plan.
II. VENTURE DEFINITION
      *A.   Product Concept Statement
      *B.   Product Performance Specification
      +C.   Product Family
      +D.   Business Concept Statement
      *E.   Corporate Fit
      *F.   Competitive Analysis
      *G.   Overall Business Analysis
III. MARKETING PLAN
      A.   Research and Analysis Results
           *1.   Results of Market Testing
           +2.   Target market (customers) description
           +3.   Market size and trends
      B.   Marketing Strategy
           1.   Sales and distribution strategy
           2.   Pricing strategy
           3.   Advertising and promotion strategy
IV. RESEARCH, DEVELOPMENT, AND ENGINEERING PLAN
      *A.   Technical Feasibility Analysis
      *B.   Technical research results
      *C,   Technical development and design plans
      D.   Engineering needs: personnel, facilities, and equipment
      E.   Estimated cost of technical development
V. PRODUCTION PLAN
      *A.   Production system concept
      +B.   Production system development and design plans
      C.   Production needs: personnel, facilities, and equipment
      D.   Production support needs: suppliers, transportation, etc.
VI. ORGANIZATION AND MANAGEMENT PLAN
      *A.   Organization for technical development (team or other)
      +B.   Management Plan for Technical Development
      C.   Organization for commercial operations
      D.   Plan for transition from a development to a commercial product
VII. RISK MANAGEMENT PLAN
      A.   Marketing Risks
      +B.   Technological Risks
      +C.   Financial Risks
      D.   Other Risks
VIII. FINANCIAL PLAN
      +A.   Financial Statements
      +B.   Budgets
      +C.   Cost Controls
IX. MILESTONE SCHEDULES
      +A.   Timing and Objectives
      +B.   Deadlines and milestones
      +C.   Network chart of events with milestones

expected that all the elements of the plan, as shown in Figure 7-2, be completed. Those elements considered absolutely essential are indicated by an asterisk (*). Those that are strongly advised are indicated by a plus sign (+). The decision as to exactly what elements to include and how complete they should be must be made by each firm based on the size, cost, importance, visibility, and other factors of the product concept under consideration.

Description of the Elements of a Venture Plan

A venture plan usually has about ten sections, and the length usually runs about 30–40 pages, although it can range from 10 to over 100 pages. The remainder of this section describes the salient elements of a typical plan, following the outline shown in Figure 7-2.

Executive Summary

The summary should be no longer than three pages and should be written only after the entire plan has been completed. In this way the salient features of each segment can be identified for inclusion in the summary. Since the summary is the first, and sometimes the only, part of a plan that is read, particularly by high-level management, it must present the essence of the entire plan.

Venture Definition

The **product concept statement** developed at the beginning of the Concept Evaluation phase should be reviewed and updated based on the results of Concept Evaluation.

The **product performance specification** indicates to the engineering designer what the new product is expected to *do* (i.e., what *benefits* it should deliver to the customer). It should not specify how it should be built or what features it should have. The specification should be developed jointly among marketing, engineering, and production, with marketing taking the lead. The specification should be a *needs* document and not a *solutions* document. It should specify what need the product is expected to satisfy, with no indication of how the need is to be satisfied. That is the purpose of the next stage of technical development. The specification should be written in a manner that will be most useful to the scientific and engineering personnel designing the prototype.

The concept of a **product family** (the development of a platform product followed at later dates by a series of derivative products) allows a major product development pitfall to be avoided. In virtually every venture, good ideas about product features and functions arise after the product design is well under way. To add these ideas to the platform product would delay the product's introduction to market. However, if derivative products have been planned, these new ideas can be applied to the most appropriate derivative product without delaying the introduction of the platform product. This aspect of the venture definition can be expected to grow as the ventures proceeds.

The **business concept statement** going into Technical Development may be quite general, but the following factors should be described as completely as possible, realizing that their description will become more specific as the venture proceeds:

- what markets will be served
- what distribution channels will be utilized

- how the product will be produced (in-house or how)
- who will be our principal suppliers
- who will be our main competitors
- expected organization of the business
- strategic relationship between new business and parent firm
- expected growth rate, size, and profitability of the business

Corporate Fit refers to how the planned product will fit into the firm's venture strategy and product line and how the planned business will fit into the overall corporation. This should not be construed to mean that the new product and new business should be exactly like the existing ones but rather that the company should recognize any differences at the outset and develop appropriate plans to ensure that they can work together.

Competitive Analysis. An attempt should be made to assess the strengths and weaknesses of the competing products or services. Include a comparison of competing products or services on the basis of price, performance, service, warranties, and other pertinent features. There should be a short discussion of the current advantages and disadvantages of competing products and services and why they are not meeting customer needs. Any knowledge of competitors' actions that could lead to new or improved products and an advantageous position should also be presented.

Overall Business Analysis. This element summarizes our analysis in response to our earlier question, *"Can we produce and sell it at a reasonable profit for a reasonable time?"* While profitability is fundamental to each product development venture, it should not be used as the only basis for decision making. A given product development venture may enable the firm to win new customers, to gain substantial market share, to keep its present customers during a transition period, or enable the firm to earn a leadership position in its industry. Under certain conditions, it may be desirable for a firm to introduce a product with minimal profit potential in order to build the strategic technology and manufacturing base needed to launch a variety of related products.

Marketing Plan

The marketing section of the plan must convince the reader that there *is* a market, that sales projections *can be achieved*, and that the competition *can be beaten*. Going into the Technical Development Stage, the Research and Analysis portion is probably more important than the Marketing Strategy portion. Upgrading the Marketing Plan at least annually will be required.

Target Market Description. For new products, the target market can often be identified as a *niche market*, which is a homogeneous group of customers with common characteristics, that is, all the customers who have a need for the newly proposed product. To properly describe this niche market, we should address the bases of customer purchase decisions: price, quality, service, personal contacts, or some combination of these factors.

Market Size and Trends. On the basis of advantage of the product or service, the market size and trends, the customers, and the sales trends in prior years, we should estimate market share and sales in units and dollars for each of the next three years. The growth of the company's sales and its estimated market share should be related to the growth of the industry and the customer base.

Sales and Distribution Strategy. This section should include a discussion of (1) the kinds of customer groups that will be targeted for initial intensive selling, (2) the customer groups that will be targeted for later selling efforts, (3) methods of identifying and contacting potential customers in these groups, (4) the features of the product or service (quality, price, delivery, warranty, etc.) that will be emphasized, (5) distribution channels that will be utilized, and (6) any innovative or unusual marketing concepts that will enhance customer acceptance.

Pricing Strategy. In this discussion a number of pricing strategies should be examined and then one should be convincingly presented. This pricing policy should be compared with the policies of the major competitors.

Advertising and Promotion Strategy. A discussion of the advertising and promotional campaign that is contemplated to introduce the product and the kind of sales aids that will be provided to dealers should be set forth. The planned use of promotional literature, trade show participation, trade magazine advertisements, direct mailings, and the use of advertising agencies should be presented.

Research, Development, and Engineering Plan

This section should include a summary of the results of technical research conducted to date. The most important part of this section is the description of the proposed plans for designing, building, and technically testing the prototype(s). The discussion should include a delineation of the technical resources needed to complete technical development—-personnel, facilities, and equipment. And last it should provide an estimated cost for technical development.

Production Plan

This primary part of this plan is a *production system concept statement*, which should provide basic information on the proposed production system, including: (1) whether the production system now exists, must be modified, or is completely new; (2) the type of production process envisaged (project, job shop, repetitive line, continuous line, etc.); (3) type of production control system anticipated (project management, material requirements planning, just-in-time, etc.); (4) general layout of the production system; and (5) the anticipated location of the production plant. Production needs should be discussed in terms of the *personnel* needed to design, install, operate, and maintain the new system; *facilities* required to produce the new product such as plant, warehouse, and offices; and *equipment* that must be acquired such as machines, tooling, computers, and vehicles.

Organization and Management Plan

This section should outline the organization and management plan for the venture development process. Most companies utilize the venture team organization and management approach described in Chapters 5 and 8. At this time we should indicate what the organization will be when the product becomes fully operational and outline the timing and plan for shifting from one organization to another.

Risk Management Plan

In planning for venture development we must make a number of forecasts or assumptions on which we base our planning. Although these assumptions are made by highly competent personnel using the latest and most accurate techniques, they are still predictions and are prone to error. These risky assumptions must be identified now so that they can be monitored throughout the development, in order that timely corrective action can be taken if our initial assumptions prove to be incorrect.

Financial Plan

The financial section of the plan must demonstrate the financial viability of the venture. To start, four basic financial statements must be prepared: revenue (sales) forecast, balance sheet, income statement, and the cash flow statement. This is followed by a break-even analysis to determine if and when the venture will become profitable. The second part contains detailed expense budgets for marketing, engineering, production, and all other activities involved in the venture. The third part describes the cost control methods that will be used to ensure that all activities stay within their budget.

CONDUCT STAGE REVIEW: READY FOR TECHNICAL DEVELOPMENT?

Before proceeding to Technical Development, the results of the Concept Evaluation stage and especially the venture plan should be reviewed by the executive committee to ensure that all actions for the stage have been adequately accomplished. Following are some questions that should be answered during the review.

• Has the Venture Plan been satisfactorily completed (especially Part II)?
• Has the Concept Evaluation of the Proposed Product been satisfactorily completed?
• Does the Proposed Product meet the following criteria?
  —Does it fit the company?

—Is it sufficiently different from our competitor's product(s)?

—Does it fit the customers in the target market?

—Can we develop it in a reasonable time and cost?

—Can we produce and sell it at a reasonable profit for a reasonable time?

• Does the proposed product concept represent a viable candidate for Technical Development?

NOTES

1. Karl T. Ulrich and Steven D. Eppinger, *Product Design and Development* (McGraw-Hill, 1995), p. 54.

2. Clement C. Wilson, Michael E. Kennedy, and Carmen J. Trammell, *Superior Product Development* (Blackwell, 1996), pp. 101–103.

3. J. A. Timmons, D. F. Muzyka, H. H. Stevenson, and W. D. Bygrave, "Opportunity Recognition: The Cores of Entrepreneurship," in J. A. Timmons (ed.), *Frontiers of Entrepreneurship Research* (Babson College, 1987), pp. 109–121.

Chapter 8

Start Technical Development; Preliminary Design and Review

INTRODUCTION TO TECHNICAL DEVELOPMENT

The Technical Development Process (often called the Design, Build, and Test Process), as shown in Figure 8-1, proceeds in a counterclockwise direction through eleven phases. In this chapter we are concerned with the shaded top-down *design* phases on the left-hand side of Figure 8-1. After Forming the Venture Team, conducting a QFD study, and developing the Product Design Specification, top-down design proceeds through System Architecture, Subsystem Design, and Part Design and ends with Internal Design Review. In Chapter 9, we will complete Technical Development by completing the *build and test* phases shown on the right-hand side of Figure 8-1.

From Figure 8-1 and from the description in this chapter, it may appear that the Technical Development Process is a one-pass linear process with no backward loops or repetitions. Nothing could be further from the truth. To make the process easier to understand and comprehend, we have drawn and explained it in a linear fashion. However, in the real world there are normally several iterations of the process, with considerable doubling back within an iteration. During each design, build, and test iteration, we also normally considering several alternative designs.

Specifically, once the developer has framed the design problem by preparing the Product Design Specification, the first step in the *design* phase is to generate several alternative designs. In an early iteration, the purpose of the alternative designs may be to explore the relationship between design parameters and specific customer needs. In a later iteration, the purpose of the alternative designs may be to refine an established concept.

In the *build* phase, the developer builds working models of the design alter-

Figure 8-1
Technical Development (Product Design, Build, and Test) Process

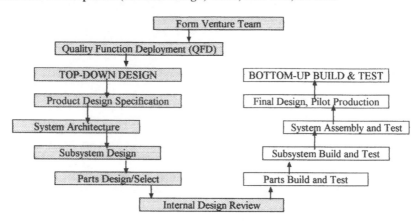

natives. The purpose of this phase is to put alternative designs into a form that will allow testing. Depending upon what a developer is trying to learn, the working models may take several forms. While computer simulation may provide sufficient information to arrive at effective early solutions, later-stage testing and development may require prototypes more nearly like the actual product. In the *test* phase of the process, working models, prototypes, or computer-generated images are tested. Depending upon the purposes of the particular iteration, the tests may focus on a particular dimension or may involve full-scale evaluation.

A single design-build-test cycle generates insight and information about the connections between specific design parameters and customer needs. That information becomes the basis for the next design-build-test cycle, and the process continues until developers arrive at a solution—a design that meets the requirements. It is important is that individual activities in the process—design of alternatives, building of prototypes, and conducting tests—be carried out effectively. However, performance in the design-build-test process depends more on establishing effective connections between these activities. For example, if the tests conducted are not planned with a clear understanding of design objectives, the information generated may not be useful to the designers. If the prototypes do not accurately reflect the design intent, they may also fail to deliver useful information.

In this chapter, we will primarily discuss the *design* portion of the design-build-test process (the left-hand portion of Figure 8-1). In Chapter 9, we will primarily discuss the *build and test* portion of the technical development process (the right-hand portion of Figure 8-1). However, as you well know, the technical development process is an iterative process that cannot cleanly be divided into two halves.

FORMING THE VENTURE TEAM

Before doing anything else in Technical Development, we must form the venture team. The venture team should be formed no later than the beginning of Technical Development for all types of ventures. Forming the venture team should be one of the first actions of high-level management after they have approved the venture plan for the concept. Leading the venture through technical development definitely requires the efforts of a fully formed full-time core venture team. For ventures of large scope and visibility it may be advisable to establish the venture team much earlier during the Concept Development phase, perhaps when the venture concept is firmly identified.

Composition of the Venture Team

The *full* venture team is composed of two components: the *core* venture team and the *virtual* venture team. The *core* venture team consists of three to ten members who are assigned *full time*. The *virtual* venture team consists of an unlimited number of people who contribute to the venture on a *part-time* or *as-needed* basis. The core team is the permanent nucleus of the team, while the virtual team is the ever-changing outer layer.

Members of the Core Team

An ideal core team would be staffed with ten or fewer members, with three being perhaps the minimum. The team should have one representative each from marketing, engineering, and production. Additional representatives from the three primary functions and members from purchasing, quality control, personnel, finance, and other functions may also be appropriate, depending on the nature and size of the venture. Ventures big enough to require more than ten people should be organized into several teams of ten or less. Full-time participation and the small size of the core team are crucial to building a level of commitment that will get the development completed quickly and effectively. Part-time players lack the concentration and commitment needed to be effective.

Members of the Virtual Team

Members of the virtual team include all those personnel outside the core team who work for or contribute to the venture on a part-time basis. Most of the members of the virtual team are in the functional departments of the parent organization, primarily marketing, engineering, production, procurement, finance, personnel, accounting, legal, and others. However, there may be some members from outside the parent organization, such as suppliers, customers, government personnel, and others.

Although virtual team members do not work full time for the venture, they continuously report to and receive information from the venture office for coordination and motivation purposes. By being included in all general meetings and being kept updated on schedules and other information, they are made to feel that they are definitely an important part of the team.

Responsibilities and Qualifications of Core Team Members

General Qualifications of the Core Team

The more of the following criteria the members of a core team can satisfy, the more effective the core team will be.

- There are ten or fewer members on the core team.
- Members are assigned to the core team full time.
- Members volunteer to serve on the core team.
- Members stay on the core team until the product is in production.
- Members report solely to the core team leader.
- The key functions, including at least marketing, engineering and production, are represented on the core team.
- Members are located within conversational distance of each other.

In reality, it is rare to have all team members meet all these criteria, but the more they can meet, the better. The expected market, technology, production methods, resources available, and the scope of the development effort must be taken into consideration when determining the composition of the core team.

Responsibilities and Qualifications of the Core Team Leader

At the center of the core team is the core team leader. This individual has the responsibility and accountability for ensuring that the product meets its goals for quality, schedule, and cost. A team leader is more than an excellent engineer or fine administrator. He or she must be more than technically outstanding and a charismatic leader.

In seeking out the core team leader we are looking for a future general manager, an individual who views the product development venture as a business endeavor, not simply as a technical or marketing problem. Failing to appoint such an individual implicitly makes the team rely upon a general manager somewhere higher in the organization to be the actual venture leader. When this happens, decision making becomes diffuse and unclear, and the venture is invariably slowed. The chosen leader must have a broad enough base of skills that management will feel comfortable having him or her alone lead the whole venture, and not just a functional portion of it.

Responsibilities and Qualifications of Core Team Members

Core team members should be able to handle all the functional responsibilities of the venture. The core team should have at least one member for each of the primary functions of marketing, engineering, and production. Core team members perform and coordinate venture activities for their particular functions.

Core team members manage the virtual team members working in the function for which they have responsibility. For example, the electronic design engineering core team member manages virtual team members working on processor, communication, and interface boards, as well as those working on backplanes and power systems. Members of the virtual team work on the new product at specific points in time, checking in with the appropriate core member when they start work and checking out when it is completed.

Core team members (via appropriate members of the virtual team) act as conduits for transmitting requests to the functional departments of the parent organization and then receiving and interpreting the responses to these requests. It is neither expected nor desired that all the necessary expertise, information, and resources reside in the core team. The core team members must take maximum advantage of the expertise, information, and resources that are available from virtual members and the rest of the parent organization.

Responsibilities and Qualifications of the Virtual Team

Purpose of the Virtual Team

The purpose of the virtual team is to provide a mechanism for the venture team to better tap the expertise, information, and other resources of the parent organization and certain other activities. The core venture team is performing a function that is new and different and very foreign to most members of the parent organization. Too many people neither understand nor appreciate the importance of providing information, taking actions, and providing other resources required for product development in an expeditious and accurate manner. The virtual team provides a badly needed conduit between the core team and the functional components of the parent organization.

Specific Virtual Team Roles

The members of a firm's virtual team are highly dependent on the nature and scope of the venture. However, there are several roles that one can expect to find in almost every virtual team.[1] Personnel occupying these roles should be kept well informed about what the venture is doing and what it intends to do.

CEO of Parent Organization. The CEO is the person who is ultimately in charge of the venture. If you can keep the CEO interested in your venture and on your side, this can be a big help.

Executive Reported to. This person is obviously interested in the success of your venture. However, one should make him or her your ally instead of an enemy. Peak his or her interest by asking for advice, even if you never use it.

Executive Champion. A high-level person in the parent company who acts as buffer, protector, and modifier of rules and policies and who helps the venture obtain the needed resources. He is a powerful person who is well respected by all members of the high-level management team and who knows his way through and around the company bureaucracy.

Product Champion. Any individual or group that promoted the progress of the venture during its early stages, particularly up to the point of officially establishing a venture team. Very often an individual product champion is included in the core team, but not always.

Functional Gateways. The core team should endeavor to establish key people in each functional department of the parent organization (especially marketing, engineering, and production). All communications to and from the function should be routed through the functional gateways.

Technical Experts. Often technical experts are too narrowly focused to make good members of the core team. However, the core team should identify and keep in touch with the true technical experts in the parent organization so that their expertise can be tapped when needed.

Specialty Suppliers. In some situations the necessary technical expertise does not reside in parent organization, but must be obtained from a specialty supplier. To ensure full trust and cooperation from essential suppliers, it is sometimes advisable to include them in the virtual team.

Operation of the Venture Team

Managing the Team's Work

Molding the *team's work* into effective *teamwork* is not an accident, nor does it come easily or automatically. Management of the team is a major and continuing task. The integration of persons from functions critical to successful product development (including hardware and software engineering, production, and marketing) into an effective team is the most fundamental requirement for success. Technical skills must match the technical task to be done. With highly skilled people in each area, the team can function effectively with only a few people. Evaluation methods used to assess the performance of team members must not divide the team or demoralize them; for this reason team-based performance measures are used increasingly.

Managing the Team Culture

Team members come from different organizational subcultures that may be based on functions, divisions, or geography. Members of each subculture bring their own behaviors, values, beliefs, and ways of thinking to the team and usually assume that their language, styles, and meanings are shared. When these undiscovered differences are not worked through, people leave meetings and conversations assuming they understand and have been understood. When they discover otherwise, confusion and anger often result, much time may have been lost, and other damage may have resulted.

A team environment must be developed in which all team members feel free to air their differences in perceptions and understanding. They should be encouraged to talk about any and all problems that endanger the venture's success and to take actions to assure success. Communications must occur so that all team members share the same vision for the new product and become motivated toward its success. Team members must be proud to be a member of the venture team and must take ownership of all the tasks to be accomplished and all the problems to be solved.

Assembling the Venture Team

Appointing the Team Leader

Of all the decisions that high-level management makes in managing the venture, none is more crucial than the choice of the venture team leader. A strong leader will be able to overcome many shortcomings of imperfect management decisions, but a mediocre one will be stymied even by small obstacles. It is important to pick a leader carefully and announce the choice publicly. Everyone should know exactly who is responsible for successful completion of the venture.

The most obvious choice for venture leader is often the product champion— the person who vigorously promoted the venture idea to the point of approval. It's hard to ignore the enthusiasm and drive of product champions, but putting them in charge of the venture has some potential risks. The product champion may unnecessarily increase the company's losses by encouraging prolonged efforts to revive moribund ventures rather than killing them in a timely manner.

Experience has shown that better results are obtained by selecting venture leaders who have a proven capability for planning and visioning, strong leadership skills, experience in project management and well-rounded technical capabilities. A person satisfying these qualifications combined with high energy and resourcefulness will make an outstanding venture leader.

Recruiting Members

Members should be recruited to enable the core team to handle all the functions required by the venture, especially marketing, engineering, and production. The only way to obtain the required level of commitment to the venture is for all participants to make a conscious decision to be fully involved—they must volunteer. However, if a desired member does not initially volunteer, the benefits of being on the team must be explained. The recruiter must identify each prospect's motivations and present the virtues of team membership forcefully but honestly.

QUALITY FUNCTION DEPLOYMENT (QFD)

Quality Function Deployment (QFD) is a disciplined methodology that ensures that customer wants are understood, documented, and converted into appropriate product and service requirements. QFD helps managers bring together all the elements needed to define the product requirements that will satisfy and delight the customer and to develop the means to provide that satisfaction. Part of the power of QFD is its ability to integrate management, engineering, manufacturing, and marketing in the development of revolutionary products, where both the product and customers are new.

The abbreviated discussion of QFD that follows will give you a feel for what QFD can do and help you decide whether or not to use QFD. However, there is certainly not enough detail here to actually conduct QFD if you so decide. To conduct a QFD study, you are referred to the references on QFD at the end of the chapter.[2]

QFD is extremely effective because it provides a common language and framework with which design engineers and marketers may fruitfully interact. The House of Quality makes the interrelationship and inherent design choices explicit. It gives precision to the conversations and discussions that go on in identifying design objectives and critical design parameters. By clarifying a very complex and ambiguous situation, the House of Quality facilitates early consideration of difficult issues and helps to identify gaps in engineering and marketing knowledge. QFD, and the House of Quality in particular, is a tool to be used with focus and flexibility. It needs to be adapted to fit the circumstances of particular products, processes, and firms; it needs to be used where it will have the most value.

In particular, the use of QFD should be based upon the type of product being developed. If an evolutionary type of product (cost reduction, modification, consolidation, or imitation) is being developed, the use of QFD is questionable. For these types of product developments, the customers and their needs are fairly well known (or should be), since we are developing similar products for essentially the same customers. QFD is considerably more appropriate for a revolutionary type of product (differentiation, diversification, breakthrough, or platform). For these types of product ventures, both the product and market are new, and QFD could be very useful in matching the new customers' wants with the new product's capabilities. If there are strong time constraints on the development, we must recognize that a thorough QFD effort cannot be completed in less than three or four months. Also, QFD does not explicitly develop a Product Design Specification (discussed in the next section). This has to be done in parallel with or upon completion of the QFD.

Once an organization has developed some experience with QFD as a process, it becomes apparent that the formal methodology—the specific matrices and the filling in of cells, columns, and rows—is less important than the underlying philosophy and framework for analysis, discussion, and experimentation. Moreover, QFD can be a way to build and store knowledge crucial to the design and development of particular products or processes. Thus, to have its most significant impact, QFD needs to be managed as a framework for communications and analysis and as a methodology for building and summarizing knowledge about the linkages between design parameters and customer wants.

Yet even where QFD is understood and used effectively, outstanding firms do not rely on the formal procedures or mechanisms by themselves. QFD is a useful framework, but there really is no substitute for engineers who understand customers or for marketing personnel who understand the basic technology of the product. Thus, while formal methods like QFD have important roles to play, they are at their most powerful when used in an organization where engineers interact directly with customers and have experience in dealing with issues of marketing and where marketing specialists are comfortable with the technology and have experience interacting with engineers on technical problems. In this, as in so much of development, there is no substitute for competence and for understanding the territory of one's functional counterpart.

THE PRODUCT DESIGN SPECIFICATION

The Product Design Specification is the complete description of the requirements for the product and the environment in which it is required to operate. A comprehensive yet concise PDS provides everyone with a common reference for the full spectrum of product requirements. This document should be prepared at the beginning of Technical Development to guide the venture throughout Technical Development. The PDS should contain the following information.[3]

- *Product characteristics*: features, performance, product cost target, quality and reliability targets, aesthetics, ergonomics, size, weight, and modularization
- *Product life*: the product's life span, lives for replaceable parts or modules, warranty periods, and storage or shelf life
- *Customer use*: installation procedures, documentation, maintenance, and disposal
- *Product development considerations*: development time (time risks), use environment, materials used (hazards), standards and safety, testing, company constraints (resources), and patents and legal
- *Manufacturing and product delivery considerations*: process selection, production volumes, product packaging, and product shipment
- *Market definition and plan*: customer identification, competitive assessment, market window (price, place, and promotion), and market share and size

The PDS specifies the complete requirements for the product to the product development team so that the parallel work in all the different areas will be compatible. The PDS is used by all involved in developing the product. It defines a framework for the work of the team. Since it affects all parts of the product development process, all relevant functions should participate in developing the PDS. While it is important to have a comprehensive PDS, it equally important to have a concise one. If there is no limitation of the length of this document, it becomes so unwieldy that it is unusable. The best results come from having only the necessary information, as indicated above, in a very concise form.

In developing the content of the PDS, one should be sure to:

• Define quantifiable targets for critical variables (or estimated values if unknown);
• Define the relative importance of or trade-off criteria for items that might conflict with each other;
• Resolve specification conflicts immediately, either by adjusting targets or by defining tradeoffs;
• Make sure that specification priorities agree with the customer benefits defined in the Product Performance Specification in the Venture Plan.

DEVELOPING THE PRODUCT ARCHITECTURE

Product architecture is the top-level design of a product—the arrangement of the functional elements of a product into physical blocks. A product's architecture begins to emerge during concept development. This happens informally—in the sketches, function diagrams, and proof-of-concept prototypes of the concept development phase. However, the architectural decisions should be formalized after the product concept has been selected and before the detailed design of the product begins. This occurs during the system-level phase of preliminary design. The purpose of the product architecture is to define the basic physical building blocks of the product in terms of what they do and what their interfaces are with the rest of the product. Architectural decisions allow the detailed design and test of these building blocks to be assigned to teams, individuals, and/or suppliers, such that the development of different portions of the product can be carried out simultaneously.

Procedure for Developing the Product Architecture

Because the product architecture will have profound implications for subsequent product development activities as well as for the manufacturing and marketing of the completed product, it should be developed by a cross-functional team effort. The end result of this activity is an approximate geometric layout of the product, descriptions of the major modules, and documentation of the key interactions among the modules. A product architecture can be developed by utilizing the following five steps:

- Create a schematic of the product.
- Cluster the elements of the schematic.
- Create a rough geometric layout.
- Identify the fundamental and incidental interactions.
- Iterate for improvement.

Create a Schematic of the Product

A schematic is a diagram representing the team's understanding of the elements of a product. It should reflect the team's best understanding of the product, but it does not have to contain every imaginable detail. A good rule of thumb is to aim for fewer than thirty elements in the schematic, for the purposes of establishing the product architecture. If the product is complex, involving hundreds of functional elements, then it is useful to omit some of the minor ones and to group some of the others into higher-level functions to be decomposed later.

Cluster the Elements of the Schematic

The challenge of this step is to assign each of the elements of the schematic to a module. At one extreme, each element could be assigned to its own module. At the other extreme, all elements could be placed in one module. The consideration of all possible clusterings of elements would yield thousands of alternatives. One procedure for managing the complexity of the alternatives is to begin with the assumption that each element of the schematic will be assigned to its own module and then make logical combinations.

Create a Rough Geometric Layout

A geometric layout can be created in two or three dimensions, using drawings or models (of cardboard or foam, for example). Creating a geometric layout forces the team to consider whether the geometric interfaces among the modules are feasible. In this step, as in the previous step, the team benefits from generating several alternative layouts and selecting the best one. Layout decision criteria are closely related to the clustering factors discussed above. In some cases, the team may discover that the clustering is not geometrically feasible, and some of the elements may have to be reassigned to other modules.

Identify the Fundamental and Incidental Interactions

Most likely each module will be designed by a different person or group. Because the modules interact with one another in both planned and unintended ways, the different groups will have to coordinate their activities and exchange information. In order to better manage this coordination process, the team should identify the known interactions between modules.

There are two categories of interactions between modules. First, *fundamental* interactions are those corresponding to the lines on the schematic. Second, *in-*

cidental interactions are those that arise because the particular physical implementation of functional elements or because of the geometric of the modules. We can use the mapping of the interactions between modules to provide guidance for structuring and managing the remaining development activities. Modules with important interactions should be designed by groups with strong communication and coordination between them. Conversely, modules with little interaction can be designed by groups with less coordination.

Iterate for Improvement

The development of the product architecture is an iterative process that requires considerable discipline. Experienced engineers deliberately create multiple configurations and compare them over a period of time. Several configuration concepts are developed from the Product Design Specification, each of which undergoes the first four steps of this procedure. The competing concepts are then compared, using a structured process. The strongest designs are selected for additional development in the next iteration. This controlled iteration continues until the requirements are adequately met. The result is a product architecture that is significantly better than the initial concept.

When the architecture design process is completed, the following information is available: (1) the primary system configuration with physical groupings and module definitions, (2) a product family definition with upgrade plans for expansion from a single product, and (3) the subsystem configuration with the module interfaces defined.

Guidelines for Decision Making during Product Architecture

Experience suggests that the success of a product is often determined by the decisions made during the short but important product architecture design phase. If it is done well, it creates the perfect foundation upon which to build the rest of the design. However, if it is done poorly there will be almost no chance of recovery. Especially, certain architectural choices provide more opportunities than others for using time-saving techniques such as concurrent design. Three key architectural decisions must be made in developing the product architecture:

• To what degree should modularity be used?
• How much reserve performance should be put in each module?
• What type of interfaces should be used between modules?

Determining the Degree of Modularity

One key decision in establishing product architecture is whether the functionality of the product will be allocated among a number of modules or left in a single location. This can be viewed as a decision on the degree of modularity to incorporate into the product.

Modularity Speeds Development. Increased modularity generally enables sub-dividing the design task, permits simultaneous work on different subsystems, and enables a shorter development process. If we can divide a system into well-defined modules, we can start work on these modules immediately. Additionally, modular construction allows individual modules to be tested separately from the system, reused in derivative products, and used as "field replaceable units."

However, these benefits are not free; modularity is likely to impose several disadvantages. First, it adds cost, because more parts must be used and because modules must be interfaced with one another. The modules usually require electronic as well as mechanical interfaces. Second, modularity can reduce performance. Both the mechanical and the electronic interfaces tend to be weak links in the product.

Hardware and Software Trade-Offs in Modular Design. Well-conceived modular products that integrate hardware and software capabilities can greatly improve the ability of the project to be completed using a rapid development schedule. The design team must make appropriate trade-off decisions and divide functions between *hardware* and *software* controls. Putting the critical system variables under software control, for example, may make it easier to accommodate change during the development process.

Module Performance Margins

A key design decision is the amount of reserve performance to put into each module. Putting in too much costs money, and too little results in inadequate performance. Normally, we strive to put in just the right amount of reserve, and if necessary to err slightly on the side of extra performance. However, this may not make sense when trying to develop products quickly. Trying to put the precise amount of performance into a module requires understanding overall system needs exactly and requires a complete understanding of all the subsystems with which it will interact. The information needed to do the precise design does not become available until many of the other subsystems have been designed, which delays the design. The overall effect of being stingy with performance margins is to slow the design process. Allowing generous design margins on all subsystems achieves a shorter development cycle.

Interface Design

Having stable interfaces is vital because interfaces are the key external constraint of the module designer. If an interface changes, the module designer may need to redesign the module. Such a redesign could range from a relatively minor task to one in which the entire current design would have to be discarded. Since the objective is to design as many modules concurrently as possible, interfaces must be defined early in the process and prevented from changing. Doing so allows the module design to work within a stable framework.

The most powerful approach for ensuring stable interfaces is to make them robust. Robust interfaces are desirable for the same reason as are generous margins in subsystems. Standard interfaces should be used whenever possible. Standard interfaces have a number of important advantages; designers and suppliers already understand them, and their quirks have already been discovered.

DESIGNING THE PRODUCTION PROCESS

With the product designed, it is now time to design the *production process.*[4] The effort needed for the process design varies widely, depending upon the type of product. If the product is a new platform product requiring new production facilities, much planning and implementation will be needed. If the product is a close derivative of one already in production, a much smaller effort is needed to convert the manufacturing facility so that it can produce the new product.

We discuss manufacturing system design in the two areas of process and layout design and detailed design. For process and layout design, we first describe a number of design alternatives that are available. With the design options described, we identify the pertinent factors that must be diagnosed to decide which alternative should be selected. In the section on detailed design we present a procedure for matching the tolerance capability of the process to the tolerance requirements of the product. We close with a discussion of the necessity of integrating product and process design.

Description of Process and Layout Options

One of the most important decisions in the design of a manufacturing system is the selection of the basic transformation process and layout to be used in the factory. In this section we discuss the three alternatives available to the designer: project process with fixed layout, job shop with process layout, and line process with product layout. We have further divided line process into three types, all of which utilize the product layout: small batch (or interrupted) line flow, large batch (or repetitive) line flow, and continuous line flow. Finally, we discuss two relatively new process types, the Flexible Manufacturing System (FMS) and the Agile Manufacturing System (AMS).

Project (No Product Flow) with Fixed Layout

In a **project**, the materials, tools, and personnel are brought to the location where the product is being fabricated or the service is being provided. Strictly speaking, there is no product flow for a project, but there is still a sequence of operations. The project form of operations is used when there is a great need for creativity and uniqueness. Projects tend to have high costs and are difficult to plan and control, because projects can be hard to define initially and can be subject to a high degree of change and innovation.

In a **fixed** layout, the product is stationary while resources (people, equipment, and materials) are brought to it. This is often done for large, complex products that are built from the ground up and are not suitable for movement. With a fixed layout, there are usually only a small number of units processed. Since congestion can develop, the scheduling of operations at the fixed site is a major consideration. This layout is used when size, fragility, weight, cost, and other factors render it undesirable or impractical to move the product through a system.

Job Shop (Jumbled Flow) with Process Layout

In a Job Shop or Jumbled Flow Process, products are manufactured in batches at intermittent intervals. Job shops organize equipment and labor into work centers by type (e.g., all lathes in a work center, all grinders in another work center). Jobs flow only to those work centers that they require, resulting in a jumbled flow pattern. Because they use general-purpose equipment and highly skilled labor, job shop operations are extremely flexible in responding to changes in product design or volume, but they are also rather inefficient. The jumbled flow pattern and product variety lead to severe problems in controlling inventories, schedules, and quality.

A **process** layout (sometimes called a functional or job shop layout) results in machines, equipment, and processes of the same functional type being grouped together. It is employed when the same facilities must be used to fabricate and assemble a wide variety of products. With the process layout, the facilities and equipment are flexible so that they can be used on numerous products. The central problem of process layout design is the relative location of work centers. It is desirable to locate those work centers with the most interaction close to each other. This reduces the transportation of materials from work center to work center. For organizations producing a physical product, adjacency lowers materials handling costs. For organizations producing a service, adjacency reduces process time in the system.

Line Flow with Product Layout

A **line flow** processing system arranges the work stations in the sequence of operations that make the product. Line flow is sometimes called product flow because the product always follows the same sequential steps of production. All products require the same tasks, and all follow a standard flow pattern. The automotive assembly line is a good example of a line flow process. There are three types of line flow: small batch (interrupted), large batch (repetitive), and continuous. They all use the product, or line, layout.

A **product** layout (sometimes called a line layout) has equipment arranged according to the sequence of operations to be performed on the product. Operations are often routine and highly repetitive, so wage rates are comparatively low and the jobs are not appealing to all workers. With a product layout, the best configuration of tasks assigned to work stations (or work zones) are obtained by balancing the line. Balance refers to the equality of output of each successive work station along the line. Tasks are assigned to work stations so that ideally each work station takes the same amount of time to complete its work effort. All three types of line flow use the product layout.

Small Batch (or Interrupted) Line Flow

Small batch line flow has all the characteristics of line flow, but it does not process the same product continuously. Rather, it processes several products in small batches, with setups normally required between batches. Small batch flow is used when the cost of a line process is justified, even though the items are not produced continuously. Relatively low-demand parts, assemblies, and non-discrete items (e.g., pharmaceuticals) are often produced using interrupted or batch flow production.

Large Batch (or Repetitive) Line Flow

Large batch or repetitive line flow refers to the production of discrete products in large volumes. A large batch flow line produces only a few products on the line with long runs (large batches) of each product, with setups between batches. A repetitive flow line produces only one product in large volume, but the line does not operate continuously (e.g., automobile assembly line). Although the large batch and repetitive lines are slightly different, they are sufficiently similar for our purposes that we can lump them together.

Continuous Line Flow

Continuous line flow refers to the continuous production or processing of fluids, powders, basic metals, and other continuous products. Continuous line flow is used extensively in the process industries to process commodities such as petroleum, sugar, paper, and other fluids, powders, and basic metals.

Flexible Manufacturing Systems (FMS)

An FMS is totally automated, with a computer-integrated group of computer-controlled machines or workstations linked together by an automated materials handling system. It provides completely automatic processing of various product parts or the assembly of parts into different units. The FMS is designed to respond accurately and rapidly to the needs of the customer regarding changes in product design, product volume, or product services. The flexibility and efficiency of FMSs are driving batch manufacturing toward cost-effective lot sizes of one.

Agile Manufacturing System (AMS)

The AMS enables a company to achieve many of the benefits provided by a FMS, without using extensive automation. AMS is more a philosophy than a specific set of hardware. In one industry, an AMS will use Just in Time (JIT) as the shop floor execution vehicle because JIT, with its manual but highly efficient material flow, is by far the most appropriate. In another industry, an AMS will use an automated system on the shop floor because the technology is available and cost-effective. The hallmark of an AMS is its ability to support ruthless time-based competition, emphasizing quick response, flexibility, and efficiency.

In Conclusion

We emphasize that the process types discussed in the preceding sections are the pure forms of what are likely to be observed in practice. Few organizations use any one of the transformation processes in its pure form for all its operations; most combine two or more forms. For example, in manufacturing computer keyboards, some parts and subassemblies are produced in a job shop, but they feed into an assembly line where batches of the final product are assembled. However, in order to diagnose what process is best for a particular company, we start with the pure forms and then combine them as necessary to represent reality.

Selecting the Manufacturing Process and Layout

Introduction to the Product-Process Matrix

In the **product-process matrix**, the product and process life cycles can be viewed as two sides of a matrix as shown in Figure 8-2. Across the top of the matrix the product life cycle goes from low-volume, one-of-a-kind products through high-volume standard commodity products, ending with Totally Flexible Products. As a product matures, it usually moves from the left side of the matrix to the right side (but occasionally products become stuck in one particular column).

The rows of the matrix contain the type of process, ranging from a project (no product flow) through a continuous flow process and ending with Agile-Flexible Manufacturing Systems. The process can go through a life cycle just as the product does. The process moves from a fluid and flexible process (but not very efficient or standardized) in the first row of the matrix to an efficient and highly standardized (but much less fluid and flexible) continuous line process in the next to last row. It ends with a process that is both flexible and efficient (the AMS-FMS Process).

As this matrix demonstrates, the type of manufacturing process a firm should select depends greatly on the nature of its products. To be most effective and efficient, a firm should select the manufacturing system that most closely matches its products, that is, lies on the diagonal of Figure 8-2. If the product and process are not matched (are not on the diagonal), the firm's competitiveness will probably suffer.

Using the Product-Process Matrix for Process Design

To use the product-process matrix, manufacturing system designers must carefully determine the nature of their products. With the nature of their products

Figure 8-2
Manufacturing Product-Process Matrix

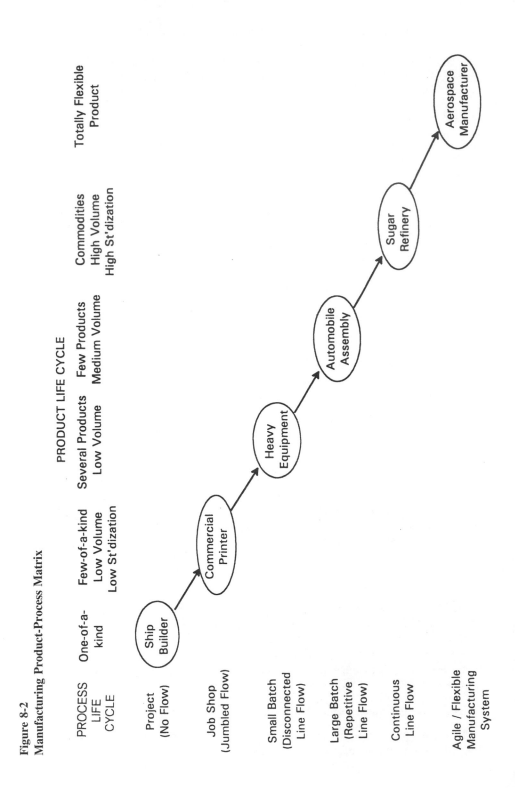

PRODUCT LIFE CYCLE

PROCESS LIFE CYCLE	One-of-a-kind	Few-of-a-kind Low Volume Low St'dization	Several Products Low Volume	Few Products Medium Volume	Commodities High Volume High St'dization	Totally Flexible Product
Project (No Flow)	Ship Builder					
Job Shop (Jumbled Flow)		Commercial Printer				
Small Batch (Disconnected Line Flow)			Heavy Equipment			
Large Batch (Repetitive Line Flow)				Automobile Assembly		
Continuous Line Flow					Sugar Refinery	
Agile / Flexible Manufacturing System						Aerospace Manufacturer

known, they can enter the product-process matrix to determine the correct process. Only by being on the diagonal do processes properly match the products. Being off the diagonal results in a mismatch with undesirable results. Assume a company tries to manufacture low volumes of many different products using a repetitive line flow. This match is below the diagonal and clearly inappropriate. The line process would have to be interrupted constantly and retooled to permit the kind of flexibility needed to produce low-volume, high-variety products. Not only is the match inappropriate, but it is expensive to boot. The purchase prices of automated machines and the cost of product changeovers would be staggering, involving a great deal of out-of-pocket expense.

Being above the diagonal brings on costs of a different kind. For example, suppose a very standard product made in great volume were manufactured using a job shop process. Here again the match is clearly inappropriate, though not because too many dollars will go out-of-pocket to buy expensive machinery. Rather, operating costs (mainly labor costs) are much higher than they should be, which means that the profit margin on each unit of the product is much lower than it should be. By not substituting specific, special-purpose machinery for high labor input and general purpose equipment, the company forgoes profits that it would otherwise earn.

However, a business may consciously seek a position away from the diagonal in order to differentiate itself from its competitors. For a given product structure, a company whose competitive strategy is based on offering customized products or features and rapid response to market shifts would tend to choose a much more flexible production technology than would a competitor that has the same product structure but follows a low-cost strategy. The former approach positions the company above the matrix diagonal; the latter positions it somewhere below the diagonal.

Detailed Design Procedures for the Production Process

In this section we describe a detailed design procedure that can be used to eliminate many of the major problems causing much of the rework observed in American factories. The goal of this design procedure is to select and construct cost-effective, capable production processes for parts fabrication and assembly. The key to achieving this goal is to select production processes based upon their process capability.

In particular, we need to relate the critical variable controlling the performance of the *product* to the critical variable that controls the *production process*. In other words, we relate the product's *engineering tolerance* to the *capability* of the production process. Using this technique to select and control the production process will prevent many of the problems that plague American producers. Firms who compete successfully in the world market pay a great deal of attention to the match between detailed product requirements and process capability. The details of this process design procedure are contained in the following five steps:

1. Ascertain the product's critical requirements. What are the features, performance, and quality attributes that contribute significantly to the product's value? The Product Design Specification provides a good overall guide for understanding which requirements are critical.

2. Determine the process steps that control the critical variables. Once the critical features (critical dimensions, surface finishes, and so forth) of the parts or subassemblies are understood, the team then determines which step or steps in the production process are responsible for the creation of that feature.

3. Determine the process capability to meet the product's critical requirements. Determining the process capability required to meet the product's critical requirements is the most difficult step of this process. Many design engineers educated in the United States never received any instruction in process capability as part of their education. When they design parts, they set tolerances on those parts without knowing whether the production process can meet these tolerances or not.

4. Determine whether the selected process meets design needs. Once the process capability is determined, the team must decide whether the process is appropriate for this particular part or assembly. Some very aggressive firms require that their process capability indexes equal or exceed 2.0. Processes that attain this very high level of capability make it possible for the process mean to move as much as three standard deviations either way before the limit is reached. Some companies are contending that a capability index of 5/3 is adequate for the production processes for mechanical parts.

5. Critical manufacturing and assembly processes are performed in-house. The parts and assemblies critical to the product should be specially designed and manufactured in-house to provide the firm with a distinct competitive advantage. Preferably, the critical manufacturing processes are developed in-house and kept proprietary to maintain the highest competitive advantage. If in-house development is not possible, very close partnership with specialty suppliers is the next best approach.

INTEGRATING PRODUCT AND PROCESS DESIGN

One of the reasons for forming an integrated team at the beginning of technical development was to enable the company's product design and associated production process design to be performed in an integrated manner. Much of the early work in integrating product and process design was driven by considerations of product cost and quality. Later efforts were driven primarily by the desire to reduce development time. Regardless of the motive, people have discovered that the best way to make significant improvements is to start at the very beginning of the product's preliminary design stage. That is where the basic product design choices are made that will influence the production processes and therefore the product's time, cost, and quality.

The initial process decisions also have a profound impact on development schedules. From a speed perspective it is an issue of doing things right or doing them over. If the proper process decisions are not made at the first opportunity, the product design nevertheless takes form and solidifies around the wrong process alternatives. The later this mistake is discovered, the more costly and difficult it is to correct. Once it has been discovered, we have two options. One is to live with the poor decision, which will have product cost and quality ramifications over the product's life. The other is to go back and correct the initial mistake, which is likely to require substantial redesign and lost time, both being schedule issues.

The essence of early production involvement is that it enables a process engineer to interact closely with a product engineer during the product design phase, especially during its formative systems portion. This is easier said than done, unfortunately. What typically happens is that the process engineer is busy at the start of a project cleaning up the details on the last project. It does not seem critical to have the process person there during the first few weeks because there is apparently nothing to be reviewed. So the organization compromises and allows the process engineer just to attend team meetings while the team is starting.

This is simply not adequate. For one thing, design details usually are not discussed in team meetings, so the process engineer will not be exposed to the design concepts that are beginning to evolve. Moreover, his or her creative energies are still being consumed by problem solving on the last project. Rather than creatively thinking about how the product design might effect the process design and vice versa, the process engineer is worrying about how to solve the urgent problems on the production floor, even while attending the development team meeting.

CONDUCT STAGE REVIEW: INTERNAL DESIGN REVIEW

An internal product and process design review is held at the conclusion of the preliminary design. If there are more than one iteration of preliminary design, there will normally be an internal design review at the completion of each iteration. Other engineers from within the organization bring experience from previous projects to bear on this project. The defense of the design can help clarify the design. The purpose of the review is to catch any weaknesses in the design before prototypes of the product and process are built.

Following are some key items that should be examined during the *product* design review:

• The control or functional layout
• The basic configuration for minimum complexity and adequate precision

- The suitability and fit of parts
- A check of critical variables and dimensions to see if they are known and documented
- A design that stays within the operating space of critical variables
- A check of critical interfaces of software and hardware
- A check of critical tolerances, functions, and manufacturing capabilities to implement the critical dimensions
- A check of critical time of hardware and software (functional timing diagram)
- Memory and microprocessor speed calculations for throughput requirements
- A software architecture review a review of the plan for controlled iterations of tests
- The coordination of schedules for software and hardware

Following are some key items that should be examined during the *process design review*:

- Is the process properly matched with the product?
- Does the process design use proven design concepts?
- How well does the new process fit into the existing production system?
- Can the planned equipment be procured from certified suppliers?
- Can the planned equipment readily achieve the required tolerances?

NOTES

1. Zenas Block and Ian C. MacMillan, *Corporate Venturing* (Harvard Business School Press, 1995), pp. 115–116.

2. Yoji Akoa, *Integrating Customer Requirements into Product Design* (Productivity Press, 1990); James Bossart, *Quality Function Deployment: A Practitioner's Approach* (ASQC Press, 1991); William Barnard and Douglas Daetz, *Building Competitive Advantage Using QFD: A Comprehensive Guide for Leaders* (Oliver Wight Publications, 1994); William Barnard and Thomas F. Wallace, *The Innovation Edge: Creating Strategic Breakthroughs Using the Voice of the Customer* (Oliver Wight Publications, 1994); Bob King, *Better Designs in Half the Time—Implement QFD in America* (Goal/QPC, 1987).

3. Clement C. Wilson, Michael E. Kennedy, and Carmen J. Trammell, *Superior Product Development* (Blackwell, 1996), pp. 129–131.

4. Howard W. Oden, G. A. Langenwalter, and R. A. Lucier, *Handbook of Material and Capacity Requirements Planning* (McGraw-Hill, 1993).

Chapter 9

Prototype Build and Test; Final Design and Pilot Production

In Chapter 8, we discussed the *design* portion of the design-build-test process (the left-hand portion of Figure 8-1, repeated as Figure 9-1). In this chapter, we will discuss the *build and test* portion of the technical development process (the shaded right-hand portion of Figure 9-1). In our discussions, we will be referring to Chapter 8 frequently, since the technical development process is an iterative process that cannot cleanly be divided into two halves.

INITIAL BUILD AND TEST OF THE PRODUCT

Building and Procuring Parts

Upon completion of the design review, which is the last step in the design phase, our first act in the build and test phase is to build or order the parts. We will expedite the building or ordering of parts by having either an internal prototype manufacturing capability or by having preselected suppliers make the parts. Having the normal purchasing organization procure the parts using their business-as-usual three-bid process, which takes upward of twelve weeks, is false economy. Moving the purchasing function into the product development team will cut the procurement time by at least one-half. To minimize development time, the development team should directly control the making and buying of parts and should not be dependent on outside functions.

Initial Build and Test of Parts and Subsystems

Checking Parts against Drawings. The first level of testing is the checking of parts. The critical dimensions of these parts are checked against the drawings prior to starting the build of the prototype subsystems.

Figure 9-1
Technical Development (Product Design, Build, and Test) Process

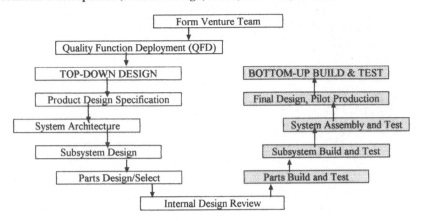

Build and Test Subsystems for Parts Fit. Building the subsystem modules is the second level of testing for parts fit. The engineer assembles the unit or observes a technician doing it and takes notes on all assembly difficulties. Experienced engineers pay attention to solving fit problems immediately through firsthand knowledge of the problems encountered. Any interferences or very close fits call for a detailed tolerance study to ensure parts interchangeability of all subassemblies.

Initial Function Tests. The subassemblies or modules get the first level of functional testing if the subassemblies are truly independent. Often additional support in terms of special test rigs is required in order to demonstrate their function. These test fixtures are designed to allow critical functional tests to be run on the subassembly.

Wear and Life Tests. In addition to the initial functional tests, many life and wear studies are done at the module level using special test rigs developed just for that purpose. Extra units are built and tested in parallel. One should not order extra units for wear or life testing until the configuration is stable from the initial functional tests. Experienced engineers manage this part of the project very carefully in order to get critical life and wear test information early in the build and test process. By getting this information early from module tests, weak areas may be identified and corrected prior to discovery of the problems during systems testing.

Build and Test the Total System

The third phase is the building and testing of the total system. Often the first system build is not of the total system but of the main engine only. It is important that the main engine function be demonstrated to work properly prior to the evaluation of ancillary functions. Thus the preliminary evaluation can proceed in an orderly fashion from the simplest system to the more complex system as the initial assembly problems are uncovered and solved.

For completely new products, it is not unusual for a corrective action cycle of redesign and rebuild based upon the solution of the initial test problems be required. If the modules of the system have too many initial functional problems, comprehensive testing is futile. Correction of initial function failures will be needed before proceeding with the comprehensive testing program.

PROTOTYPES AND PROTOTYPING

A *prototype* is defined as an approximation of the product along one or more dimensions of interest. Under this definition, any entity that exhibits some aspect of the product that is of interest to the development team can be viewed as a prototype. This definition is purposely broad and includes prototypes ranging from concept sketches to fully functional artifacts. *Prototyping* is the process of developing such approximations to a product.

Need for Prototypes and Prototyping

The increasing global competition has imposed severe demands on product development. World-class products must be completed in minimum time and provide the greatest possible value to customers. Companies who want to lead the way must get up to full speed quickly and cannot afford any missteps. In order to compete in this manner, a development team has to learn rapidly. The best development ventures now rely on the integration of many functions. In these integrated efforts, prototypes are the key to increased learning, reduced mistakes, and increased system integrity.

Prototypes are one of the most powerful tools a development team can use to resolve important questions quickly and unambiguously. In addition, they provide a common understanding and integrating force for all members of the team, regardless of the members' differences in function and culture. Yet, far too often, companies do not create enough prototypes, nor do they create them early enough to resolve important uncertainties. Furthermore, those that are made are often inadequate to prove out performance in production, compounding rather than solving problems. *The traditional approach to prototyping is not effective.*

A new approach must be taken. Prototyping is no longer done only to answer questions at stage review time; it is done to allow the team to progress swiftly and intelligently through the incremental steps of development. Prototypes are no longer the exclusive domain of the engineer. They are the common language that knits together the development team, the company that supports the team, and the team's eventual customers.

Types of Prototypes

Prototypes can be usefully classified along two dimensions. The first dimension is the degree to which a prototype is *physical* as opposed to *analytical*. Physical prototypes are tangible artifacts created to approximate the product. Aspects of the product of interest to the development team are actually built for testing and experimentation. Analytical prototypes represent the product in a nontangible, usually mathematical, manner. Interesting aspects of the product are analyzed, rather than built.

The second dimension is the degree to which a prototype is *comprehensive* as opposed to *focused*. Comprehensive prototypes implement most, if not all, of the attributes of a product. A comprehensive prototype is a full-scale, fully operational version of the product. In contrast to comprehensive prototypes, focused prototypes implement one or a few of the attributes of a product. A common practice is to use two focused prototypes together to investigate the overall performance of a product. One of these prototypes is often a ''looks like'' prototype, while the other is a ''works like'' prototype. By building two focused prototypes, the team may be able to answer its questions faster and cheaper than with one comprehensive prototype.

Principles of Prototypes and Prototyping

Several principles are useful in guiding decisions about prototypes during product development.[1] These principles assist decision making about what type of prototype to build and how to use them in development.

Analytical Prototypes Are Generally More Flexible than Physical Prototypes. Because an analytical prototype is a mathematical approximation of the product, it will generally contain parameters that can be varied in order to represent design alternatives. In most cases, changing a parameter in an analytical prototype is easier than changing an attribute in a physical prototype. For this reason, an analytical prototype frequently precedes a physical prototype. The analytical prototype is used to narrow the range of feasible parameters, and then the physical prototype is used to fine-tune or confirm the design.

Physical Prototypes Are Required to Detect Unanticipated Phenomena. A physical prototype often exhibits unanticipated phenomena completely unrelated to the original objective of the prototype. Some of these incidental properties of physical prototypes will also manifest themselves in the final product. In these cases, a physical prototype can serve as a tool for detecting unanticipated detrimental phenomena that may arise in the final product. Analytical prototypes, in contrast, can never reveal phenomena that are not part of the underlying analytical model on which the prototype is based. For this reason, at least one physical prototype is almost always built in a product development effort.

A Prototype May Reduce the Risk of Costly Iterations. If building and testing a prototype substantially increases the likelihood that the subsequent activities will proceed without iteration (for example, from 60 percent to 95 percent), the prototype may be justified. The anticipated benefits of a prototype in reducing risk must be weighed against the time and money required to build and test the prototype. Products that are high risk due to high costs of failure, new technology, or the revolutionary nature of the product will benefit from prototypes. On the other hand, products for which failure costs are low and the technology is well known do not derive as much risk-reduction benefit from prototyping.

A Prototype May Expedite Other Development Steps. Sometimes the addition of a short prototyping phase may allow a subsequent activity to be completed more quickly than if the prototype were not built. If the required time for the prototype phase is less than the savings in duration of the subsequent activity, then this strategy is appropriate.

Using Prototypes to Reduce Cost, Time, and Risk

Early learning decreases uncertainty; thus the effectiveness of prototyping depends on the *timing* of prototypes throughout the development program. Effective early prototyping reduces the cost of products, reduces the development time, and reduces the development risk.

Minimizing Cost by Minimizing Late Design Changes

The process of development is by its nature a process of change. But when extensive design changes are introduced late in the development cycle they can undermine even the best of product plans. Late design changes invariably upset the optimum balance between the features, cost, and quality required of the product. In the long term, the negative consequences of late changes can only lead to costly, inferior products and can permanently pervade a company by creating a demoralized work force, poor productivity, and severely delayed schedules.

An effective approach to design changes is one in which early prototyping is used to flush out problems. The approach emphasizes quick turnaround—which requires early prototypes to check out important ideas quickly to avoid problems in the later stages that would necessitate a redesign. Early problem detection is achieved by early and frequent analytical and physical prototypes that are characterized by a reasonably high authenticity of the parts and processes. The intent of such early prototyping is not to seek perfection but to gain essential knowledge.

To make early prototyping possible, development teams must be fully integrated from the beginning. Especially, manufacturing people should be integrated so that the earliest prototypes will reflect the realities of production procedures. Early prototyping will require that management invest more money up front. To implement this strategy, the team must enjoy priority access to prototyping resources such as simulation software, an extensive database, and shop facilities.

The Timing of Prototypes

Time plays an absolutely critical role in the development of new products. The design latitude essential to creating the best balance between the fundamental cost of a product, its competitive features, and its quality is only attainable in the early stage of development. The real window of opportunity is the period prior to the completion of the preliminary design. After that decision point, the changes that are possible can only have a marginal effect on the basic product. Most product development managers will agree that about 85 percent of the ultimate cost of a product is determined during the first 15 percent of the development time. Hence rapid learning and the ability to make critical decisions early are essential for product success. Early prototypes provide one of the most effective means for achieving the learning essential to sound decisions.

Because substantial learning accompanies each prototype stage, it follows that early prototyping with subsequent updates at important junctures can provide several major benefits. These include a reduction in total development time, a reduction in the risk introduced by innovation, and the early detection of problems, which leads to the avoidance of expensive, late design changes.

Limiting Risk with Early Prototypes

In competitive product lines, significant innovation is vital and must be achieved with very tight time schedules. Innovation runs the risk of extended development time or even failure, which always come with ventures into unfamiliar territory. Because of time pressures and reduced design flexibility, problems that crop up late in the development cycles have serious consequences. Ferreting out problems early, with a strategy of early prototyping, allows for corrections at the time of greatest venture adaptability, thereby reducing risk.

Using Prototypes to Improve Quality and Manufacturability

Even if early prototyping is used to get the project off to a strong start, the use of system prototypes near the end of the development cycle is critical. There is a strong relationship between the quality of the full system prototype and the final quality of the end product. The number of problems that can be solved between the system prototype and production is very limited. The greater the number of problems remaining in the final system prototype, the greater the likelihood that problems will persist when production begins. Even with a frantic effort at the end, products that require major design changes after final systems prototyping will probably be significantly deficient at product launch.

Matching Prototypes with Stage of Product Development

Very often, the most effective way to obtain the array of development information needed is to use a spectrum of prototypes. The precise nature of the

Figure 9-2
Matching Prototypes with Product Development Stage

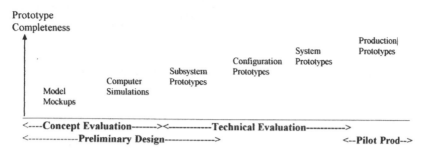

Prototype
Completeness

| | | | | | System | Production\|
| | | | | Configuration | Prototypes | Prototypes |

Subsystem   Configuration
Computer   Prototypes   Prototypes
Model   Simulations
Mockups

<----Concept Evaluation-------><------------Technical Evaluation----------->
<-------------Preliminary Design--------------->   <--Pilot Prod-->

prototype varies widely according to the questions it is intended to answer. The best results are achieved when venture teams use prototypes that are best suited for a particular stage of development, as shown in Figure 9-2.[2]

All prototypes play important but different roles in the resolution of crucial development questions. Most early prototypes are fashioned as models, mock-ups, or computer simulations and are useful in scoping out basic product characteristics in the Concept Evaluation Stage even though their completeness is low. As the venture proceeds, subsystems and configuration prototypes that more closely represent the product are used in the Preliminary Design Stage. As production ramp-up approaches, the full-system prototypes and the production prototypes are called into action as a final check of systems integration.

These different forms of prototypes are discussed in more detail in the following paragraphs.

Models and Mock-ups

Models and mock-ups constitute inexpensive and knowingly incomplete physical representations that are useful for focusing attention on a limited number of key features. They avoid the distractions and complexities of a complete system prototype. In automotive development, for example, clay models are the substantive medium for designing and quantitatively defining the body styling.

Computer Simulations

With the advances in computer capabilities, electronic models today can provide attractive alternatives to physical prototypes. Computer models can often be used to provide accurate visualizations of design concepts and yield accurate simulations of complex aspects of system performance. Although such computer software is often costly to construct, once available in generic form, it can be applied to a range of development projects with benefits that accrue on a continuing basis.

Subsystem Prototypes

The identification of system-level interactions and interdependencies permits more efficient utilization of resources and a reduction in overall development time. The division of a product into sets of stand-alone subsystems also makes it possible to contain the risk posed by major innovations. As long as full-system checks are made at appropriate stages, the refinement of the product and detailed definition of part design are best carried out with subsystem prototypes.

Configuration Prototypes

The primary purpose of the configuration prototype is to ensure that the parts fit into the subsystems and that the subsystems fit into the overall system both mechanically and electronically. The configuration prototype can be partially mock-up or all mock-up. However, the more actual hardware that can be used the better. If made of actual hardware, it can be used for performance testing after configuration testing is completed.

System Prototypes

Systems prototypes are primarily for performance testing and not configuration testing. Early prototyping of the full system is a significant factor in product development. When it is done effectively, it contributes to ultimate success. When done haphazardly or too late in the cycle, it allows significant system problem to go undetected. When the total initial focus is on the feasibility of subsystems and full-system prototyping is left to the very end, serious complications often arise.

Production Prototype

The production prototype is the version of the product that is produced during pilot production (described later in this chapter). It would be desirable if the production prototype were exactly the same as the final product, but it very seldom is. Usually some problems are detected during pilot production that will require correcting before full-scale production.

TESTING OF PRODUCT AND PROCESS PROTOTYPES

Engineering Testing of the Product Prototype

Upon the successful completion of the initial build and test effort, we are ready to start the comprehensive testing of the product.[3] The purpose of the testing during the initial stage of Technical Development was primarily to determine *whether or not* the product would work. The purpose of comprehensive testing the second phase of Technical Development is to determine *how well* the product works and especially how well it meets the requirements of the Product Design Specification.

The first step is the preparation of a comprehensive test plan using the Product Design Specification as a guide. The comprehensive test plan includes tests being conducted in succession at the parts, subsystem, and system levels. For example, a four-month schedule of system testing may have planned updates at the end of each of the first three months, followed by the final tests for success in the last month. Planning and executing such a comprehensive test plan takes a great deal of cooperation within the team to ensure that the problems are identified and solved.

Within the comprehensive testing effort, four major types of testing are performed:

- *Testing for Success*, testing to specification to assure that everything works right within the operating environment specified;
- *Testing for Failure*, stress testing, to provoke failures and determine design margins;
- *Operating Space Verification*, to ensure that the critical variables are controlled within necessary limits; and
- *Life Testing*, to understand and plan the replacement of any life-limited parts.

Testing for Success

Testing for Success primarily tests whether or not the product meets the requirements of the PDS or not. Testing for Success will eventually reveal the problems that need to be solved, but only after a very long testing period. In testing for success, one never knows just how close failures are to the test region. Thus a product may be tested successfully in a laboratory but may fail in the factory or customer environment that is only slightly out of the laboratory test range.

Testing for Failure

Testing for failure is a stress testing method used to provoke failures. Once revealed, the engineering investigation proceeds to the root cause of the failures and corrects them in a redesign process. It is critical to analyze the product's potential failure modes and the conditions that will cause the worst effect of the failure. These failure modes must be tested. Stress testing requires considerable judgment and experience, especially when determining what to stress test and which failures should be corrected.

Operating Space Verification

The stress testing method is also used to find the operating space of the critical variables that control the product. By discovering the limits of the operating space and redesigning to enlarge it, the engineer builds design margin or robustness into the product. Designing experiments that simultaneously vary several critical variables beyond their normal limits will assist in determining the operating space. These tests are similar to those conducted during the Concept Evaluation stage, but now we are performing them on near-production hardware.

Life Testing

Life testing is conducted early in the design and evaluation process to get critical life and wear test information early in the process. By getting this information early, weak areas may be identified and corrected prior to discovery of the problems during system testing.

Market Testing of the Product Prototype

Although not as busy as the engineering and production members of the venture team during the technical development stage, the marketing members are still quite busy. First, they are preparing the marketing plans that will be implemented when the product is launched, which we will discuss in Chapter 10. Second, they will be conducting a number of market tests on the product, which we discuss in this chapter.

The output of the technical development stage is a product that has been fully tested (technically) by engineering. However, an extremely critical hurdle for a new product is market acceptance (or rejection). For an innovation to become a commercial success, market reaction to its introduction has to be carefully and thoroughly tested by marketing.

Consumers are complex and at times paradoxical creatures. Bored with the endless repetition of their product purchases and looking for the excitement of change, they nevertheless frequently shy away from the uncertainty and risk associated with new products. A product should offer something new, but not too new. This is why improvements of existing products usually fare quite well. But when an innovation represents a significant departure from past offerings, market response becomes more difficult to predict. No amount of concept testing, however extensive it may be, will ever be a true substitute for actual field experience with the real product in the hands of consumers.

This essential live market feedback can be generated through various types of market tests: *consumer product testing*, *premarket testing*, and *test marketing*. Premarket testing and test marketing are conducted using the pilot production product and will be discussed at the end of this chapter. Consumer product testing utilizes the product prototype and will be discussed in the following paragraphs.

Consumer Product Testing

Even though the new product has been thoroughly tested technically for performance during the earlier stages of product technical development, it still needs to be evaluated by consumers in two areas, to measure their satisfaction with the product's performance and their degree of interest in purchasing it. These two areas can be evaluated through consumer product testing, where a representative sample of consumers uses the product under normal conditions.

Consumer product testing can be used continually, not only to test a new product before it is launched but also to evaluate the product while in the market to determine when there is a need for improvements.

Consumer Product Testing Methods

There are a wide variety of options available for consumer product testing. The first decision involves whether to use company employees or other consumers. Using company employees who fit the demography of the target market provides a high degree of secrecy, expediency, and cost efficiency compared to using consumers. Many different types of businesses use their employees to test new products and continually to evaluate product performance of established brands.

Two problems arise in using employees to test new products: the representativeness of the sample and the validity of the responses. For the information to be meaningful, employees have to be statistically representative of the target market along the relevant variables of shopping behavior, usage, and demographic characteristics. Even when representative, employee panels may give results that are overly positive. Management must establish a climate in which employees in the test panel will feel comfortable reporting their actual experience in product usage, not holding back any criticism.

Although a significant amount of information can be obtained from employees, frequently companies feel they need more information from consumers who are not part of the company. In consumer product testing the consumers use the product in their own homes as they would if they actually purchased the product. The consumers in the panel are recruited by telephone or personal contact and given a sample of the product to use. The product usually carries no brand identification. When two versions of the product are to be tested, half the panel tests one version and the other half tests the second version. If time is available it is usually better to have both versions tested by everyone. Usually this type of testing minimizes any distortion in the marketplace caused by the test procedure. Asking each panel to rate the relative merits of two products options generally produces the most accurate information because the method does not put a strain on the panel members in choosing among several alternatives.

There are several alternatives to "in home" consumer testing: *mall testing*, establishing an ongoing *consumer panel*, or using an *established group* or club. **Mall testing** is widely used in the United States to test various aspects of new consumer products. Many marketing research companies rent storefront space in malls for intercepting and recruiting shoppers to come in and try the new product or evaluate aspects of it. The testing procedures usually follow a fairly established pattern. The shopper is given an explanation of what is taking place and tries the new product or evaluates some aspect of it using the blind paired comparison method. He/she then participates in a brief interview that frequently includes standard demographic questions, product usage questions, and the product selection process.

An alternative, which is frequently adopted by companies who introduce new products on a regular basis, is to establish an ongoing **consumer panel**. These panels can be run by an outside agency or by the company itself, which eliminates the need to select a panel each time a new product needs testing. Of course, the critical issue is the selection and rotation of panel members. Generally, the characteristics of panel members need to satisfy the objective of the test and often disproportionately favor heavy users of the product category.

Another alternative to in-home testing is to use church or civic groups or some other already **established group**. Although the degree of representation of the group is usually lower than any other method, the costs are also much lower, usually involving a modest donation to the club or organization. The degree of interaction among group members causes some concern because it could affect the independence of individual testers. Combining several groups can reduce the interaction problem and also improve representation.

Often companies use a combination of in-home testing and mall intercepts before introducing the new consumer product. In-home testing provides valuable information on the performance characteristics of the innovation, and mall intercepts produce information on consumer preferences on many product attributes such as color, style, package, brand name, advertising, and logo. Better results are achieved when the participants are presented with alternative products instead of a single product. In comparison tests, participants should be given at least four but not more than six paired comparison tests, because people usually cannot discriminate effectively among more than six alternatives.

Limitations of Consumer Product Testing

Consumer product testing using employees, consumers, or both provides useful information, but it does not ensure successful new product introduction because it does not involve a purchase decision by the consumer. A product test does not evaluate some of the other critical elements of the market mix that significantly affect the successful introduction of a new product. Consumer product testing isolates and investigates only part of the total picture. A product test can show that the concept motivates; a use test can verify that the product works or tastes good; a package test can indicate that the package appeals. But, we don't know how these factors—concept, use, package, and so on—work in combination. The intention-to-buy scales (used to determine consumer intent to purchase) give interesting information that is difficult to use in forecasting new product sales. Indeed, resulting forecasts are questionable because the data were not obtained under competitive market conditions and the consumers did not have to buy the product.

Manufacturing Testing of the Process Prototype

Manufacturing testing of the process prototype tends to be somewhat less organized than engineering or market testing of the product prototype. This results from several reasons. First, major process development efforts—those that require significant investment in people, equipment, and procedures—typically occur less frequently but are larger in magnitude than most product development efforts when they do occur. Second, many of the critical tasks in a process effort are *subcontracted* to equipment suppliers, so that success depends on more than one organization. Not only does this make coordination more difficult, but it requires close communication and trust between organizations and individuals who may not have worked together previously.

In dealing with equipment subcontractors, most manufacturers believe that the equipment supplier is the expert and therefore should be delegated complete responsibility for design and testing of the equipment. Nothing could be further from the truth. While it is true that the equipment supplier is the expert in designing the equipment, the user is the expert in knowing what it should do. Users may not know or care too much *how* the equipment operates, but they should definitely know and be able *to test what it does.*

CONDUCT STAGE REVIEW: READINESS FOR FINAL DESIGN AND PILOT PRODUCTION

When the testing of the product and process prototype indicates that they meet the requirements of the Product Design Specification and there are no serious problems, then moving to the final stage of Technical Development is warranted. Following are some key items that should be examined by the executive committee during the final stage review:

• Has engineering testing of the product prototype been completed with satisfactory results?

• Has marketing testing of the product prototype been completed with satisfactory results?

• Has production testing of the process prototype been completed with satisfactory results?

• Will the design of the final product be essentially the same as the last product prototype?

• Will the design of the final production system be essentially the same as the last production system prototype?

• Have the results of market testing been incorporated in the design of the product?

FINAL DESIGN, PILOT PRODUCTION, AND TEST MARKETING

This is the final stage of the technical development process that occurs just prior to the business development stage.

Final Product and Process Design

The economic success of a product depends on the profit margin earned on each sale and the volume of sales. Profit margin is the difference between the manufacturer's selling price and the cost of making the product. The number of units sold and the sales price are to a large degree determined by the overall quality of the product. A successful final design therefore involves ensuring a high product quality while minimizing manufacturing cost. Thus, manufacturing cost is a key determinant of the economic success of the final design.

To minimize manufacturing costs we must implement a special approach to design, often called Design for Manufacturability (DFM). DFM should be considered throughout technical development, but it must receive special attention during the final design phase. During the early phases of technical development, design attention is correctly focused on satisfying customer needs, meeting performance specifications, and laying out the product architecture. However, during the final design phase of technical development the design emphasis shifts to Design for Manufacturability.

Using Design Rules to Implement Design for Manufacturability

Design rules are often used to implement Design for Manufacturability. The intent of design rules is to establish an envelope within which the manufacturing process is capable of meeting design and cost requirements. Through the design rules the manufacturing engineers are sending a message to the product designer saying, "If you design within this envelope, our manufacturing process can meet the firm's requirements for cost, quality, volume, and product performance." In the following paragraphs we will describe some of the design rules used by a number of companies.

Use modular design where feasible. A modular design permits a firm to assemble customized products from standardized modules, thereby meeting the unique needs of particular customers at a lower cost.

Minimize the number of parts in a design. Minimizing the number of parts will simplify assembly, reduce direct labor, reduce material handling, and reduce inventory costs.

Minimize the number of part numbers (standardize components). Reduces the material handling and inventory cost and improves the economies of scale (increase volume through commonality).

Design for robustness. Lowers sensitivity to component variability. Less degradation of performance with time.

Make assembly easy and foolproof. Parts cannot be assembled wrong. Obvious when parts are missing. Parts are self-securing.

Design for efficient and adequate testing. Reduces the cost of testing. Less mistaking good products for bad, and vice versa.

Eliminate adjustments. Reducing adjustments reduces assembly errors, allows automation, and increases capacity throughput.

Eliminate fasteners. This will simplify assembly, reduce direct labor costs, reduce squeaks and rattles, improve durability, and allow automation.

Eliminate jigs and fixtures. Reducing jigs and fixtures will reduce line change-over cost and lower required investment.

Understand process capabilities and constraints. Some component parts may be costly simply because the designer did not understand the capabilities of the production process. For example, a designer may specify a small internal corner radius on a machined part without realizing that expensive EDM equipment is required to achieve it.

Redesign components to eliminate processing steps. Careful scrutiny of the proposed design may lead to suggestions for redesign that can result in simplification of the production process. Reducing the number of steps in the part fabrication process generally results in reduced costs.

Adhere to the "black box" component specification. The team provides a supplier with only a "black box" specification of the component, a description of what the component should do, not how to make it. This kind of specification leaves the vendor with the widest possible latitude in designing for minimum cost.

The above abbreviated discussion of design rules for DFM will give you a feel for what DFM can do and help you decide whether or not to use it. However, there is much more to DFM than we have been able to cover here. For more information, and especially if you decide to actually conduct DFM, you are referred to the books on DFM at the end of the chapter.[4]

Concurrency of Product and Process Design

One should not view design for manufacturability procedures described above as a static one-way process in which design engineers take the existing manufacturing process as a given and design around those constraints. Such an approach might be appropriate for evolutionary products (such as cost reductions, modifications, and consolidations), but it is definitely not appropriate for revolutionary products (such as differentiations, diversifications, breakthroughs, and platforms). Using such a one-way approach for revolutionary products would miss many opportunities to change the manufacturing process to enhance the performance of both the product and the manufacturing system. *The final design process for the product and manufacturing has to be an interactive concurrent process in which product and process engineers create a joint product and process design.*

Pilot Production

The purpose of *pilot production* is to demonstrate the ability to manufacture, assemble, and deliver a quality product in a cost-effective manner consistent with the actual customer demand for the product. Only when the firm is able to manufacture and deliver a product that pleases customers with its performance and satisfies their needs can there be a successful completion of the product development process. Products produced during pilot production are very often used for Test Marketing, which is described in the following section.

During pilot production, process control methods are used in the critical processes to continuously measure manufacturing process variation and to ensure product reliability and quality. Processes are continuously improved—not just measured and maintained—by the manufacturing members of the venture team. Product delivery is provided in a timely fashion as promised and without damaging the product. The quality of the delivered product is evaluated, and rapid remedial action is take to correct any product or process problems that occur.

In the pilot production, a limited number of products are produced using the actual production process, and then the process is stopped. Both the processes and the products are evaluated. Corrective action is taken on all process and product problems that must be corrected before product launch.

Controlling In-house Effort during Pilot Production

Although the in-house effort is highly dependent on the nature of the product and the firm, there are some general guidelines that are applicable to all products and firms.

Venture Team Should be Completely Responsible for Pilot Production. The venture team should be responsible for not only product design and testing but also process design and testing, of which Pilot Production is the last stage. This should be well known at the start of the venture, when the team is formed. The team's goals should be aimed at successful product manufacture and not at the traditional "release to manufacture."

Ensure All Manufacturing Processes Have Been Verified. All processes must be verified to be operating properly before pilot production begins. To be verifiable, each process must have measures that tell you whether it operating properly or not. Next, no mystery processes are permitted; that is, all key performance attributes of the process must be causally related to known and measurable variables. Also, processes must be "engineering-free"; that is, processes must function without excessive engineering support. Obviously, process verification is highly dependent upon the quality of process design.

Ensure Adequate Product Testing before Shipping. Short-duration functional tests demonstrate only one-time nominal operation and provide no indication of the product's operation over a range of conditions. Products that pass factory functional tests may be shipped to customers, only to fail as soon as the product experiences a slight variation in operating conditions. To solve this problem, manufacturing stress testing can be used in selected instances to verify that the functional operating space of the product was not compromised during assembly.

Controlling Suppliers during Pilot Production

One important aspect of Pilot Production that is too often overlooked, with disastrous results, is the control of suppliers that provide parts for the new product. It is imperative that the new suppliers supply the new parts on time with high quality if pilot production is to be successful. To ensure that this happens the following actions are recommended:

Venture Team Responsible for Supplier Selection and Parts Ordering. Supplier selection and parts ordering should be controlled completely by the venture team and not by the normal procurement organization. This is usually accomplished by having procurement personnel assigned to and located with the venture team. This approach requires a change in management practices so that the team controls the firm's procurement practices for the new product, rather than the normal procurement organization. Decisions regarding suppliers should be based on ensuring a continuous flow of quality parts and assemblies with minimum of scrap, rework, and service costs.

Minimization of the Number of Suppliers. Minimizing the number of suppliers and establishing certification programs for the parts manufacturing processes of the selected suppliers will reduce parts quality problems. Whenever legal and feasible, single sourcing the parts for the new product is recommended.

Requiring Process Control at the Supplier. Process control at the point of manufacture will ensure the receipt of high-quality parts. By offering single-source long-term contracts, almost any supplier can be convinced to establish statistical process control to ensure continuous high quality. Also, the long-term contractual partnership provides an incentive for continual quality improvement by the supplier.

Test Marketing

Premarket Testing

Because of the time and costs of test marketing, some companies elect to perform premarket testing instead, to overcome some of the limitations of consumer product testing. The two most-used types of premarket testing are **in-home shopping** and **simulated stores**.

In-home shopping is a simulation of the purchase decision-making process in a competitive setting. It differs from consumer product testing in several important ways:

- The product bears its brand name.
- It is fully labeled and identified.
- It is packaged the same way as that planned for national introduction.
- The innovation is priced as in a store environment.

A sample advertisement or some direct mail promotional piece accompanies the product. In order to duplicate the actual store purchase situation as closely as possible in the home environment, several fully identified competitive products are included in the test. Consumers are given a fixed amount to spend in the in-home pseudo store on the products of their choice within the product category being investigated. Each participant is repeatedly asked to make a selection from varying combinations of major brands and alternative new products being tested. Thus, many of the ingredients of the true store environment are there, except that the decision is made at consumers' homes.

Because in-home shopping is conducted over an extended period of time, repeat purchase patterns will emerge. Participants will repeatedly purchase from the interviewer the brands of their choice at discount prices that they are actually paying. In-home shopping has the added advantage that no public disclosure occurs because the new product is not yet advertised in the mass media or available in regular stores.

Another scheme uses **simulated stores** run either by companies themselves or by marketing research organizations. Procter and Gamble, for example, runs a simulated store in its headquarters, which displays the company's products as well as competitive products. The only difference between this store and a regular one is the limited assortment of merchandise and the smaller size. Regardless of who operates the simulated store, the testing procedure is basically the same. The product being tested employs its normal brand name, label, packaging, and price and is placed on the store shelf with competitive products. Consumers are given a fixed amount to spend and can choose among the products offered. Usually an exit interview is performed to elicit demographic information and purchase motivations.

Although it provides more information than consumer product testing, pre-market testing still cannot provide all the information available from a test market. The test market is the only way, short of actual product introduction, to obtain actual sales information in a true sales environment.

Test Marketing

Test marketing consists of offering the new product for sale in a select group of cities, using the intended introductory marketing mix. Products used for Test Marketing are very often produced during the Pilot Production stage (described in the previous section). Test marketing the new product has two primary objectives: (1) to provide a "real-world laboratory" and (2) to forecast national sales through projecting sales occurring in the test market areas. The "real-world laboratory" enables the company to experiment with various options of the new product and its mix, determine any problems with the product, and obtain feedback vital to successful new product launching. Test marketing is differentiated from consumer product testing by the following characteristics:

• Users are not selected by random sample. Thus, at best, the test cities are representative of the national market, but the actual distribution of test market buyers may be quite distorted in comparison with the later national patterns because of uncontrollable influences.

• The purchasers of the new product have to take the buying initiative themselves.

- The buyers have to pay the regular (introductory) price and receive no special benefits.
- The new product competes head-on with existing products and brands in the authentic sales environment of the chosen store and is thus typically just one among many products serving the same purpose.

Benefits of Test Marketing. Consumer product testing may well yield favorable responses because the participants enjoy products for which they do not have to pay. For this reason, their indication of buying intentions can not be trusted. In test marketing, the consumer must actually buy and pay for the product in a competitive situation, which provides a much more valid picture of consumer buying intentions. It is the authenticity of the sales environment and the direct confrontation of the new product with the full range of competitive forces that makes for the uniqueness and importance of test marketing.

Consumer satisfaction with the emerging product was tested at various points, principally in concept testing and consumer product testing. In test marketing, satisfaction is tested by the most critical measure: the repurchase rate. It is relatively easy to sell someone a new product for the first time. Curiosity and excitement of change, or trying something different, propel people to buy. The proof of the pudding, however, lies in repeat purchases that indicate how many converts have been made. People will only buy a new product again and again if they are satisfied with its performance and consider it worth the price. It is the measuring of purchasing and repurchasing of the product that makes test marketing so important.

As the new product enters the final stages of development, management may not be sure about one or more elements of the marketing mix and may still be considering several alternatives, such as different price levels, different packages, or different promotional approaches. These alternatives can now be tried out simultaneously in separate test cities to determine the most successful one. The consumer is exposed to these alternatives, has to find and select the product over a broad array of competitive choices, and has to pay for it. Thus test marketing can assist in finding the best marketing mix for the new product.

Deciding to Test Market. Four main factors should be evaluated before deciding whether to test market or not. First, the company should compare the costs and risks of product failure with the profits and probability of success. If the costs and risks of product failure are low, commercialization and launching can proceed without a test market. Second, if market testing requires roughly the same investment as launching the product, the company has a good reason to proceed directly to launch. However, if a larger investment is required for a launch, test marketing is usually warranted. The investment risk must be weighed against the loss of profit that could otherwise be made through national sales while the new product is being tested. Third, the extra time that the competition has to develop a similar product must be assessed in terms of the benefits of the test market. The competition will usually monitor the test while simultaneously developing their version of the product. If the competition can bypass a test market of their newly developed product, a test probably should *not* be conducted. Finally, all other aspects of the new product must be examined. Advertising expenditures, effort by the sales force, and possible negative impact on the firm's reputation if the new product fails must be carefully weighed before making a decision on whether or not to schedule a test market.

Selecting the Test Market. Test markets should be similar to national norms in such areas as advertising, competition, distribution, and product usage. A detailed national marketing plan that covers media selection, sales effort, and promotional budget should be prepared before the test market begins. The test market provides an evaluation of alternative marketing strategies that can be used in the national marketing plan. The first decision to be made is whether to test in a metropolitan or nonmetropolitan area or in a district or regional market. Once this decision is made, the exact cities or regions can be selected. Although some unique attribute of a particular city or region may mandate its inclusion, a test market should generally be selected based on applying the following criteria:

- Average income near the national average
- Not dependent on a single industry
- Not dominated by one ethnic or racial group
- Suitable size (central city with at least 200,000 inhabitants)
- Self-contained with no dependence on neighboring areas
- Adequate media coverage
- Not excessively used for testing by other companies

NOTES

1. Karl T. Ulrich and Steven D. Eppinger, *Product Design and Development* (Mc-Graw-Hill, 1995), pp. 223–226.

2. H. Kent Bowen, Kim B. Clark, Charles A. Holloway, and Steven C. Wheelwright (eds.), *The Perpetual Enterprise Machine* (Oxford University Press, 1994), pp. 219–222.

3. Clement C. Wilson, Michael E. Kennedy, and Carmen J. Trammell, *Superior Product Development* (Blackwell, 1996), pp. 145–151.

4. Geoffrey Boothroyd and Peter Dewhurst, *Product Design for Assembly* (Wakefield, RI: Boothroyd Dewhurst, Inc., 1989); Geoffrey Boothroyd, *Assembly and Product Design* (Marcel Dekker, 1992); Geoffrey Boothroyd, Peter Dewhurst, and Winston A. Knight, *Product Design for Manufacturing* (Marcel Dekker, 1994); James G. Bralla (ed.), *Handbook of Product Design for Manufacturing: A Practical Guide to Low-Cost Production* (McGraw-Hill, 1986); John Corbett, Mike Dooner, John Meleka, and Christopher Pym, *Design for Manufacture* (Addison-Wesley, 1991); H. E. Trucks, *Designing for Economical Production*, 2d ed. (Society of Manufacturing Engineers, 1987); William H. Cubberly and Ramon Bakerjian, *Tools and Manufacturing Engineers Handbook* (Society of Manufacturing Engineers, 1989).

Chapter 10

Developing New Business; Launching the New Product

The new business development stage represents the high point to which every prior stage of the venturing process has been building—the full-scale market introduction of the new product. Before launching the product, the nature, scale, and timing of the launch must be determined. Selecting and implementing the optimum introductory marketing program is extremely important and represents the principal task of marketing during this stage. Although manufacturing has been involved in the technical development process from early on, it is during this stage that they really come under the gun to ramp-up production to meet demand. Because of limited capacity, the new product introduction may be divided into an initial regional introduction, followed by a nationwide rollout as capacity expands. Although this stage constitutes the culmination of the Corporate Venturing process, it also marks the beginning or introductory phase of the product's life cycle. Procedures must be developed to monitor the results of the product launch and to correct any problems during introduction.

DETERMINING NATURE, SCALE, AND TIMING OF LAUNCH

The full-scale launch of a new product is the stage of new product development that requires the largest commitment of money and managerial resources.[1] No matter how well the product is designed and tested, the launch presents risks. Marketing and production must be well coordinated, and the time of the launch must be planned carefully. Without such planning, profits are jeopardized. In this section, we will determine the nature, scale, and timing of the launch.

Nature of Launch Dependent upon Type of Product

The nature of the launch will depend to a large extent on the type of new product being introduced. The two types of new products that we will consider are *revolutionary* products and *evolutionary* products. As discussed in Chapter 2, the revolutionary products consist of differentiation, diversification, breakthrough, and platform products. The evolutionary products include the repositioned, modification, consolidation, and imitation products. In general the revolutionary products are products that are relatively new to both the customer and the producer and require high learning by both before the product can be used effectively. The evolutionary products are relatively simple updates to existing products and will require little learning by either the customer or the producer.

Launching Revolutionary Products

If the new product is a revolutionary one, it is likely that the firm will need to commit extensive resources for a successful launch. The marketing strategy will be based on a prolonged marketing development effort during which management will need to give special attention to sales and distribution as well as any known product design weaknesses. The marketing strategy for the launch of a revolutionary product must reflect the likelihood of consumers' lack of understanding of the product. Because of this, management should also expect that the introduction stage will be much longer than for an evolutionary product.

A number of important marketing mix issues occur during the launch of a revolutionary product. Typically the price will be high so that the producer can meet demand with existing capabilities, distribution will require trade incentives to penetrate retailers, and advertising will focus on consumer education until awareness has been achieved. The firm will need to induce consumer trials during the introduction stage so that repeat buying and sales growth will occur. During the launch, management must develop strategies to enhance the adoption process. For a revolutionary product it is also important for management to minimize the number of models available; this minimizes the required learning.

Launching Evolutionary Products

The launching of an evolutionary product will require different strategies. Management will recognize that because of the ease of imitation and likely ease of market entry, every attempt should be made to establish a strong position early with distributors and end-users. The introduction stage for an evolutionary product will be much shorter than for revolutionary products and will rapidly blend into the growth stage.

In the launch stage, the firm will need to develop a competitive advantage even if the competition has not yet introduced their products. A more aggressive marketing effort is necessitated in promotion, distribution, and pricing. In promotion, extensive use of the media helps reach the strong brand awareness necessary. This also helps in distribution, since high awareness with trade incentives and good service will enhance the participation of retailers. With an evolutionary product, management will try to set price at a very competitive level, since market volume and share will be more important for this type of product.

Determining Scale of the Launch

The firm must determine before launching the new product whether to (1) enter the *national* market immediately, (2) *roll out* the product from one geographic area to another, or (3) enter specific *segments* of the market and then expand to other segments. The choice among the strategies is a function of type of new product (revolutionary or evolutionary), expected life of the product, ease of entry for competition, the existing production and distribution capabilities, and expected demand for the product.

Entering the national market by making the product available in every state in the United States is not easy and sometimes results in timing problems. Basically all the major distribution centers would receive shipments of the new product and would be responsible for distribution to the retail trade. In the case of evolutionary products, national entry may be necessary to protect market share and fend off any competitive threats. National entry for a revolutionary product is neither necessary nor recommended. There are usually no threatening competitors, and national entry will bring unnecessary complexity to the launch.

In some markets, because of the capital requirements or skills needed, it is difficult for competitors to enter. As a result, the firm can take a more gradual approach to the launch of the product. The same case can be made when the firm does not have production or distribution capabilities. In these cases the firm can select the *roll out* strategy. In the roll out strategy, the product is first introduced in one geographic area, say, the Northeast, and then gradually rolled out to each geographic area until the entire United States is covered.

If the demand is expected to exist in only certain segments of the market, the firm should use the *segment* approach. For example, if demand is expected in only metropolitan areas, the firm could start with the largest cities of Boston, New York, Atlanta, Los Angeles, and Dallas-Fort Worth. The next segment could be metropolitan areas of slightly smaller cities such as San Francisco, Denver, Phoenix, St. Louis, New Orleans, Miami, Philadelphia, and Washington.

Determining Time of the Launch

The time of market entry marks the formal starting point for new product introduction. It depends not only on the organization's development time but also on the firm's strategy and on existing market conditions. Not only is the seasonality of the product a factor, but the firm must decide whether it wants to be conservative and follow others into the market or to be aggressive and be the first one in the market. Thus, a firm may select one of the following basic timing strategies: (1) first to market, (2) among early entries, or (3) among late entries. Each of these strategies is directly related to the mission of the firm, the firm's innovation strategy, resources available, and competitive environment.

First to Market. Being first to market provides a clear competitive advantage. The first firm in the market has an opportunity to build barriers to defend against competitors. If the entry is a product that satisfies an unmet need, potential buyers would be highly receptive to information about the new product and be quick to try it and develop loyalty. Building an early and loyal base of customers, who might also favorably influence other potential buyers, is an important step in building a strong market position.

Among Early Entries. This timing strategy involves introducing a new product very soon after the first-in-market firm enters. This strategy is used in the situation where being first does not provide a big advantage but being late results in a serious disadvantage. The firm must be in the market early enough to prevent the first-in-market firm from developing a strong brand loyalty for its product.

Among Late Entries. A major advantage of delaying entry is waiting for a market opportunity to grow to an attractive size. Also, this strategy enables the firm to learn from the early entrants' experience. The learning can translate to lower cost of innovation, design, marketing research, and production, particularly if the firm uses reverse engineering to develop an *imitative* new product.

PRELAUNCH PREPARATIONS

Marketing Preparations for Launch

Marketing actually starts planning for launch early in the Technical Development phase. However, they must put the final touches on their plans after the completion of Pilot Production and Test Marketing. For clarity and conciseness we have placed the entire discussion of marketing preparations at this point in the book.

Superior product design is not a sufficient condition for product success. Customers must be made aware of the product and then must be provided with some method for purchasing and obtaining the product. These are the functions that marketing performs.

Defining Target Market

The target market was initially defined in the Venture plan, which justified the product for Technical Development. At this point in time we need to define the target market more accurately. We must decide among three basic options: (1) make one product and sell it to everyone (*undifferentiated market*); (2) make one product for each of the various segments and sell them as a line (*differen-*

tiated markets); and (3) concentrate on only one segment and go all out for that one (*niche market*).

Competition forces the overwhelming majority of companies to use either niche or differentiated marketing, so companies must usually market new items to specific market *segments*. Market segments can be divided into the follow five types:

1. *End use.* Running shoes are made for and sold to runners.
2. *Geographic.* Snow skis and water skis are targeted for two different geographic areas.
3. *Demographic.* MacDonald's "Arch" sandwich was targeted for senior citizens.
4. *Behavioral.* Bullet-proof vests are made for police and others who get in the way of bullets.
5. *Psychographic.* Many products are targeted to lifestyles—clothing, cars, hotels.

The more clearly we can define the target market the better we can define the product's facilitating goods and services and the price, distribution, and promotion that will best sell the product.

Defining the Complete Commercial Product

As we discussed in Chapter 1, the complete commercial product consists of the core product plus the facilitating goods and facilitating services that provide additional benefits and value to the customer. Customers purchase products for their benefits, not for their features. For many products, benefits and value can be greatly enhanced by providing supporting goods and services. In technical development, we designed and built the *core product*. Now we must define, design, and provide the supporting goods and services that will supplement the core product to provide the *complete commercial product*.

Figure 10-1 displays some examples of the facilitating goods and services that can be provided. Because of their importance and the fact they are provided for nearly all new consumer products, we will discuss two of the facilitating goods and services in some detail: *branding* and *packaging*.

Figure 10-1
Examples of Facilitating Goods and Services

Examples of Facilitating Goods	**Examples of Facilitating Services**
• **Packaging**	• **Branding**
• Repair parts	• Warranty
• Complete, easy-to-use, documentation	• Service plan
• Built-in tutorial or operating instructions	• Free installation
• Added Features	• Free maintenance
	• Toll-free ordering
	• On-site training
	• Free technical support
	• Customization assistance

Branding the New Product. A key decision, particularly for consumer products in a large undifferentiated market, is the branding of the new product. A *brand* is a number, symbol, or design that is intended to identify the products of the seller and to differentiate them from those of competitors. Any distinctive means of identification and differentiation can serve as a brand. Best known and subsequently discussed in this section is the brand name.

Branding is the activity of a seller to establish a means of identification for its products. To the seller, this presents an opportunity to imbue the products with distinctive personalities and aggressively stimulate demand for them. Unless a new product is branded, a prospective customer has no meaningful way of singling out the item that this particular seller is offering. Only branded merchandise can successfully be advertised and distinguished from competitive entries. Accordingly, branding enables a buyer to develop loyalty and make repeat purchases. A brand further identifies the firm behind the product and offers a guarantee of consistent quality.

The use of a brand name assures its owner that it can make all crucial marketing decisions, such as packaging, advertising, pricing, and channel selection and thereby keep close control over the market. Because branding can create a difference in buyers' minds, even between chemically and physically identical products, price differentials can be maintained. This is evident in the price differentials between generic and brand name drugs.

In choosing a brand name for a new product, the firm has two basic options: *family* branding and *individual* branding. In family branding, a company places the same brand name (usually the corporate name) on all products in a product family or even its entire product line, distinguishing individual products simply by their generic description. Campbell, for instance, uses its name on its entire family of soups, supplemented by a generic identification, such as Campbell's tomato soup. In *individual* branding, each new product is assigned its own unique brand name with little association with the selling firm.

Family branding enjoys the distinct advantage of instant recognition, benefiting from the "halo effect" of the brand's established reputation. A new product using the family brand name thus gains instant credibility and visibility. On the other hand, problems with a new product can affect the salability of all items bearing the same name. The danger of *individually* branded new products affecting the salability of older products is much less.

However, individual branding requires the firm to create a brand name for each product from scratch. When first presented to the public, the new name has no meaning to the consumer and bears no association with any other products. Heavy advertising is necessary to imprint the product's image in the buyer's mind and generate demand for the product. However, individual brands do have the advantage that they can be introduced and withdrawn without affecting the firm's reputation or established products.

Considering the magnitude of registered trademarks, it has become increasingly difficult to develop unique brand names. For this reason, computers are frequently used to develop short, distinctive, and easy-to-remember letter combinations for possible brand names. Users are then interviewed to get their reaction to these possible brand names. The following guidelines can be used in selecting a brand name:

Is It Easy to Use and Remember? The brand name should be short, easy to spell, easy to pronounce, easy to understand, and especially easy to recall.

Is the Message Clear and Relevant? Product characteristics should come forth loud and clear. Pick Die-Hard over Delco, Budget over Avis, and Sprint over MCI.

Does the Brand Insult or Irritate Any Particular Market Group? This is particularly important for global products. The brand name may mean something completely different in a foreign language than it does in English.

Will This Product be a Bridgehead to a Family of Products? If so, the name should not limit the nature of future products. We now accept *Frigid*aire stoves and *Hot*point refrigerators, but it was difficult at first.

Do You Expect a Long-Term Position in the Market? If so, a more general and less dramatic name is preferable. If not, something like Screaming Yellow Zonkers can, and did, work well.

Packaging the New Product. Traditionally the function of packaging was to protect goods. In some industries, this is still considered the primary function. However, in many industries the package has become a promotional tool and image builder for the new product, enhancing its success in the market. In those cases where the consumer must choose from several alternatives on a shelf, the package becomes a point-of-sale display. The venture team must weigh four factors in selecting a packaging design: marketing considerations, product protection, economic factors, and environmental factors.

Marketing Considerations. The package designer must consider the marketing implications of the package on the manufacturer, the retailer (or other middlemen), and the consumer. The retailer's major concern is to get the product on the shelf with a minimum of difficulty and to prevent pilferage of high-priced small items. The consumer, on the other hand, is most concerned with such factors as convenience and information provided on the package.

The manufacturer must consider the ease of recognition and image conveyed by the package design. Packaging offers the manufacturer an important promotional medium, particularly when many of the products in the marketplace are similar and difficult for consumers to differentiate. Packaging may be the dominant force in the consumer's choice when there is little product information available and the size and price are perceived as similar. The importance of the promotional impact of packaging is reflected in the battle by manufacturers to obtain shelf space in retail stores.

Product Protection. Manufacturers are particularly concerned with physical damage if the product is fragile and expensive. Typical hazards are physical (shock, vibration, static electricity, compression), climatic (heat, cold, moisture, oxidation, pollution), and biological (infestation, bacteria, decay). Because losses due to physical damage of the product are generally the responsibility of the manufacturer, the package must be carefully designed to prevent damage.

Economic Factors. Because financial losses due to breakage or spoilage can be significant, meeting certain product-protection criteria can minimize cost to the manufacturer. The manufacturer must also consider the actual packaging cost for the new product. For high-value products, the cost of an expensive package is relatively unimportant, since it is such a small percentage of the value of the product. However, for many consumer products the cost of the package is significant—especially when competition allows only a small profit margin.

Environmental Factors. Without question one of the most significant trends in our society is the consumer's concern with pollution, particularly from discarded packaging. As a result, most states have passed legislation to restrict the sale of throw-away containers. Currently many manufacturers are packaging their products in reusable containers as a means of recycling the package materials. In addition, research is being performed to develop new packaging materials that are biodegradable or that minimize pollution.

Price Determination

Within the framework of new product development, price determination is a strategic factor of prime importance that strongly affects the sales and profit performance of the new product. Price determination is important for a number of reasons. First, a company can employ pricing policy in such a way as to discourage competition from entering the market if this threat is present. Second, in accordance with different demand elasticities throughout a market, pricing determines the kind and number of market segments that can be penetrated. Third, a new product's price shapes its image in terms of quality and thus its acceptability to certain customers. Fourth, price directly influences the profit margin and profit contribution of a new product.

Pricing Methods. Actual price determination can be either cost based, market based, or a combination of the two.

Cost-Based Pricing. Cost-based pricing is in some way related to the cost of the product. In its most frequent method, *cost-plus pricing*, a company computes its cost of making or acquiring an item and marks up this figure by a standard percentage. This markup may be straight profit (before taxes), or it may contain an allowance for operating cost. Although easy to administer, cost-plus ignores demand and competitive consideration altogether.

Market-Based Pricing. Market-based pricing uses market considerations and valuations in setting the price of a product. Instead of being guided by what it costs to make/buy and sell an item, this approach is psychologically oriented toward consumer perception. The most popular version, *demand-oriented pricing*, selects a price in accordance with the value that prospective buyers place on the product and is colloquially known as "charging what the traffic will bear."

New Product Pricing Strategies. In setting prices for new products, a firm has a variety of factors to consider and number of options from which to choose. It will typically combine cost-based and market-based considerations by adopting a cost-plus price as the minimum level and examining whether market forces permit charging more. Conversely, if market conditions predetermine the new product's price, a reverse computation can help management decide how much it can afford to pay for the item's ingredients and manufacture.

A firm may select from two basic pricing strategies for new products: *skimming* and *penetration. Skimming* uses a relatively high initial price, followed by subsequent price reductions to tap successively more price elastic market segments. *Penetration* uses a relatively low introductory price to create and maintain mass market appeal.

Skimming Price Strategy. A skimming price strategy is particular well suited to the introduction of revolutionary products, those products that are dramatically different and create entirely new markets, such as electric cars and personal computers. Under such circumstances, demand is usually fairly inelastic with respect to price, simply because consumers have no meaningful idea as to what such a product is worth. A substantial change in consumer behavior is required, so market resistance is high, and only a very limited number of people are willing to assume the risk involved in an untried product. This affluent group can well afford the product and may actually be attracted by a high price because of its implied exclusivity. Because the new product does not yet have real rivals, its vulnerability to competitive prices is low. As the product becomes better known and more widely accepted, competition appears on the scene and consumer responsiveness to price incentives increases significantly.

In light of the uncertainties associated with the launching of a new product in the marketplace, skimming is the safer pricing strategy. The idea behind setting introductory prices high is to recover the cost of development and introduction before the competitors enter and initiate competition based on cost. It is always easier to reduce a price that is too high (to generate sufficient volume) than to increase a price that is too low (to provide a satisfactory profit). A company can afford to use skimming if it is likely to be the sole supplier of a new product for some time into the future. This may be due to advanced technology, a patent or license, or simply a wait-and-see attitude on the part of potential competitors.

Penetration Price Strategy. A firm using penetration pricing enters the market with a deliberately modest price to obtain substantial volume from the beginning. It is an appropriate pricing approach if demand is price elastic—a condition that is likely to be present for evolutionary products that provide only small improvements over existing products. This strategy is also advantageous if the threat of potential competition exists. The low price reduces the profit potential of would-be competitors and may prevent them from entering the market altogether. Manufacturers of products that cannot be patented and are easy to imitate (food, services, etc.) will typically set prices that enable them to penetrate a significant portion of the market before their competition can react.

A penetration strategy is meaningful if a sufficiently large market volume can be expected. A penetration strategy will build a strong position in the marketplace while discouraging competitors at the same time. A policy of fairly low, stable prices is much more likely to create brand loyalty than are high initial prices. It also erects entry barriers by requiring competitors to make large-scale investments to meet or undercut the price of the pioneer. Based on a philosophy of "profit through volume," penetration pricing keeps the profit per unit low and relies on quantity to raise total profit to a satisfactory level.

Additional Pricing Considerations. We must remember that the product does not necessarily have to be sold at one price only. If the product uses multiple sales or distribution channels, it may be appropriate for the product to be sold at different prices in different channels. Preferred customers might be offered preferred pricing programs. Standard orders might be priced lower than a product combinations that requires customization. Combinations of factors may be used to set prices—airlines charge different fares, for example, depending on the class of service, whether or not the ticket is purchased in advance, and the demand for the flight.

Complete products (core products with facilitating goods and services) can be bundled in several ways and combined with differential pricing. For example, personal computers can be sold with different-size hard disks and with or without certain software or services. Usually the larger the number of items sold in the product bundle, the larger the price break given on each item. Modular products (computer, automobiles, and such) are especially amenable to developing a multitude of product bundle and price combinations.

A leasing option may be appropriate for high-priced products that require customers to make significant investments. A leasing option reduces the customer's initial cost, making it easier for the customer to afford the product. Examples of products that are commonly leased are cars, computers, copiers, buildings, and land. Alternatively, the firm may arrange to sell the product to leasing companies, who then assume the responsibility (and risk) involved in leasing.

Distribution

Distribution Channels. A *distribution channel* is the route that the title of a product takes from the producer to the ultimate buyer. It is distinct from physical distribution, which refers to the physical movement of tangible goods. The distribution channel describes the process of how and where the customer purchases the product and how ownership travels from the firm to the customer. The chain of ownership transfers involved in a channel of distribution can be either direct or indirect. In *direct distribution*, title to the product is transferred directly from the producer to the ultimate user. In *indirect distribution*, the product's ownership changes hands several times, involving independent intermediaries.

New Product Channel Selection. Often a firm will find itself constrained by its own past patterns or prevailing industry practice in choosing the channel(s) for a new product. Current intermediaries handling the company's established products will want to benefit from the appeal of a new product. Also, the company will want to leverage this immensely valuable asset in trade relations. The most likely solution to the channel selection issue is to use existing channels. This is especially appropriate if the new product is closely related to the present product mix and is likely to be bought as an alternative to, or in conjunction with, other company products.

Occasionally, a company will find itself in unfamiliar territory without the option of using or buying an established distribution network. When this happens, the firm faces the challenge of building a new channel from the ground up. Typically, this will mean either hiring a sales force or going the indirect route by calling on wholesalers, who in turn promote the new product to their associated retailers. Revolutionary new products often require completely new distribution channels. The success of revolutionary products is often dependent upon the timely development of appropriate new distribution channels.

Promotion

The market success of a new product depends substantially on the firm's ability to communicate its features and benefits to the intended target market. Promotion is the element of the marketing mix that informs the target audience about the new product and persuades customers to buy it. Promotion consists of three major components: personal selling, advertising, and sales promotion. *Personal selling* is the person-to-person effort of a salesperson to obtain an order from and build a continuing relationship with a customer. *Advertising* is the paid presentation of promotional messages through the mass media. *Sales promotion,* in contrast, involves the short-term stimulation of demand by various means. Sales promotions encompass all those promotional activities that are neither advertising nor personal selling.

A critical factor in developing product promotion is to ensure that it is consistent with definitions of the *target market* and the *complete commercial product* discussed earlier in this chapter. Promotion should be squarely aimed at the product's target customers, using the product's "points of difference" as the key element of the campaign. For example, if the product will have superior ergonomic features, promotional materials should highlight this feature.

Advertising. In new product introduction, *advertising* is used as the major instrument for demand creation and sales support. It plays a key role in communicating the product's existence and benefits to potential buyers. The creative challenge is formidable: communicating uniqueness, creating a product identity, and preselling the new product. Most venture managers prefer to address this challenge by seeking professional help from an advertising agency. This agency may be one that the company is currently employing, or it may be specifically recruited and selected for this particular purpose. If a new agency is needed, the following steps are suggested to recruit one: (1) familiarization with services offered by agencies, (2) identification of firm's advertising needs and selection criteria, (3) evaluation of agency candidates, and (4) selection and agreement.

If a separate agency is retained for the venture, it is important that venture management maintain positive control over the actions of the agency. In working with the agency on a daily basis, venture management should make proper use of the agency's resources and talents but also offer constructive criticism of its output. The venture manager should not become so friendly with agency personnel as to cloud objective judgment but should engage in a healthy, ongoing dialogue with the agency team.

Sales Promotion for New Products. Sales promotion consists of a variety of tactical tools used for short-term sales stimulation. In new product introduction, the extra inducement that a sales promotion tool often represents may be crucial to overcoming initial buyer resistance. Even firms that do not usually employ sales promotion programs in their existing marketing effort (such as industrial marketers) will often use them during the launch of a new product.

In designing a sales promotion program, the venture manager can choose from alternatives aimed at three different targets: (1) at the company's own sales force, (2) at intermediaries, or (3) at ultimate buyers. A *sales force program* is aimed at giving the company's salespeople a special reason to exert themselves during the introductory period. A *trade promotion* is directed at wholesalers and/or retailers (distributors, dealers, or agents), attempting to enlist their cooperation in carrying and promoting the new product. A *consumer promotion* is a tool used in a strategy to create demand, traffic, and purchasing action at the retail level.

The resourceful venture manager can choose from a gamut of sales promotion tools: samples, coupons, trial sizes, cents-off deals, premiums, contests, point-of-purchase promotions, trade promotions, and trade shows. All of these aim to add incentives to the purchasing decision during a limited time period and thus expedite new product trial and acceptance.

Personal Selling. The personal selling effort for a new product is one of the most critical factors affecting its success in the marketplace. It begins with organizing the new product sales force according to some relevant principle—geography, product classification, or customer category. New product sales planning is an important responsibility that begins by determining which of several sales force options will be chosen. Venture managers can select from four alternatives: (1) using the existing sales force, (2) hiring a new sales force, (3) employing a temporary salesforce, or (4) utilizing manufacturer's representatives. The new product sales objectives, which typically consists of obtaining and maintaining predetermined levels of sales volume, are used to guide the remainder of the sales planning process.

In order to carry out the new product sales plan successfully, the sales force has to be adequately trained to possess sufficient product-related knowledge, skills, and attitudes. In executing their challenging task, new product salespeople are greatly assisted by specially designed sales manuals and other audiovisual aids.

Integrating the Elements of New Product Promotion. New product promotion will work best if its elements are used in concert, reinforcing and building on each other rather than being designed and implemented independently. Advertising alone cannot meaningfully assume the entire burden of communications and persuasion. It creates an initial burst of awareness and excitement for the new product, giving it visibility, identity, recognizability, and a first lease on market life. However, advertising is too expensive to be carried on continuously.

New product sales promotion builds on advertising. It can stir up excitement at the point of sale, possibly featuring the presenter who appeared in the advertising for the new product. Advertising is also often used to announce a particular sales promotion program such as a contest or sweepstakes. Sales promotion also interacts with personal selling in various ways. For one, salespeople will often deliver sales promotion materials to dealers or stores, frequently even setting up and stocking special displays. For another, sales promotion programs provide sales personnel with a selling point in persuading intermediaries to take on and feature the new product.

Production Preparations for Launch

Achieving Production Ramp-up. The principal task of production during the period between the completion of pilot production and the product launch date is to achieve the production capability (commonly called *ramp-up*) necessary to meet the projected sales volume. At the same time, production must successfully meet the new product's targets for unit cost, conform to performance specifications, and satisfy other measures of quality, including customer satisfaction.

Action must be taken to ensure that all necessary equipment, tooling, and other resources will be available at the right levels to provide the required capacity. In the ramp-up phase, the work force must be adequately trained and supervised as they begin to produce the new product at commercial levels. Successful ramp-up also requires ongoing supplier management to ensure the quality and timeliness of incoming material and parts. Suppliers must be selected and trained in total quality methods. Efficient physical distribution systems must be established.

In some industries special effort is required to ensure that the production process itself is operating as designed. This often requires the pursuit of improved product quality and cost by reducing the variability of the production processes. Skills in optimizing production process plans and learning from ongoing production experience are particularly critical at this time.

During the ramp-up stage, key members of the venture team are still involved in production. Their skills are primarily needed to optimize the coordination between marketing and production. Also, they will be involved in initiating product redesign to correct cost and quality problems, if needed. Full responsibility for production normally shifts to the production department only after product launch.

Coordination of Marketing and Production. The marketing and production preparations for launch must be closely coordinated. One important aspect of launch coordination is the timing of production startup. A startup that is too early may create large, expensive inventories and result in product deterioration. If the startup is too late, there may not be enough produced to meet the growing demand and large back orders. Insufficient supplies cause opportunities to be missed and cause goodwill to be lost with consumers and channel members.

To prevent these problems a joint plan must be developed for marketing and production, which should include the relative timing of production, launch, and the marketing mix. For example, marketing managers may delay advertising or promotion to avoid too much demand too soon, or production managers may build up a sizable inventory to be prepared for large advertising and promotion efforts planned in the future.

Engineering Preparations for Launch

The successful launching of a new product often depends on its early reputation for reliability and dependability. The engineering challenge for new product introductions is to avoid failures by taking very careful preventive measures. Proper design is the best way to prevent failures, but the establishment of a *Rapid Failure Detection and Correction* (RFDC) program will enable the company to detect and correct failures before they affect the sales of the new product.

The RFDC program is started by establishing an RFDC group as a part of the virtual venture team. The primary purpose of the RFDC group is to rapidly analyze all failure reports and take immediate corrective action. Field service personnel would be instructed to report all product failures and customer comments to the RFDC group by the fastest possible means: telephone, facsimile, or E-mail. All failed parts and modules would be returned to the RFDC group by the fastest possible means for failure analysis. The RFDC group would establish a hotline over which customers could report all failures, product problems, and questions.

The RFDC group would also initiate an aggressive tracking program that would enable the firm to determine and improve the reliability of parts and modules. A certain number of products would be fully tracked in the field, and all their failures, maintenance actions, and problems would be recorded. The RFDC group would establish a Problem List that defines (1) the observed problem, (2) the root cause of the problem, (3) the corrective action taken, (4) the person responsible for ensuring that the corrective actions are completed, and (5) the target completion date for all actions. They would also track the product's actual failure rate versus the predicted reliability for the product and take corrective action until the actual reliability reaches the goal.

The quick gathering of information by a group dedicated to identifying and solving problems through rapid remedial action will make a big difference in the success of the product launch. Having the Rapid Failure Detection and Correction program as an integral part of the product launch program enables unexpected problems to be caught and corrected early enough to avoid customer exposure to these problems.

CONDUCT STAGE REVIEW: READINESS FOR LAUNCH

Before authorizing launch of a product, the executive committee should ensure that final design, pilot production, and test marketing have been satisfactorily completed; that marketing, production, and engineering pre-launch preparations have been completed; and that a business analysis indicates the advisability of launching the product. The following questions should be answered in the affirmative before product launch is authorized:

- Has the venture plan been satisfactorily *updated*? (See Chapter 7 for details)
- Have the results of the pilot production been satisfactory?
- Has the design of the product been satisfactory through pilot production?
- Has test marketing been completed with satisfactory results?
- Has marketing satisfactorily completed its pre-launch preparations?
  —Commercial product completely defined and ready?
  —Pricing strategy and price determined?
  —Distribution channels selected and activated?
  —Promotion plans ready?
- Is production prepared for ramp-up of capacity?
- Is engineering prepared to initiate product failure detection and correction program?

LAUNCHING THE NEW PRODUCT

Organizing for the Launch

As the new product moves toward introduction, some reorganization of the venture team is indicated. In technical development, the design and testing work has been handled by a venture team consisting primarily of technical specialists. In the launch stage, different skills are needed to plan and coordinate the detailed activities of the launch. The launch will require the coordination of a large amount of marketing and production resources.[2]

For the launch stage, we need a manager who has experience in launching new products or in managing large numbers of marketing and production people in some other capacity. If the current venture manager does not have this experience, he or she must be replaced by, or the team must be augmented by, someone who does. Probably, the best alternative is to augment the team, since that would preserve the continuity and accountability of the venture. Adding an experienced manager with the necessary skills and experience to the core team, who would assist in managing the additional marketing and production members of the virtual team, would be one way of accomplishing the needed change.

Managing the Launch

To achieve the target dates for launch and to generate time-cost tradeoffs, venture management must enumerate and schedule all the details of the launch. This can best be done by using some method of *network planning*, which structures a sequence of activities and identifies those that are most critical. There are two well-known methods of network planning: program evaluation and review technique (PERT) and critical path method (CPM).

While the details may vary between these two methods of network planning, the basic concepts are the same. Related tasks are laid out in paths according to the order in which they are to be completed. The time to complete each task is determined; then these times are summed to give the total time for each path. The longest path is called the "critical path." To launch the product earlier, resources must be directed at shortening the critical path. A PERT diagram of a new-product launch is shown in Figure 10-2.

Network planning enables the venture team to (1) define the activities and show the interrelationships between tasks, (2) evaluate alternatives for getting to market faster, (3) establish responsibilities of various functional units, (4)

Figure 10-2
PERT Diagram of Product Launch

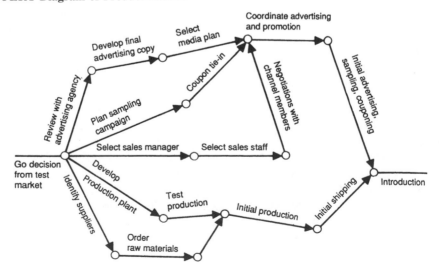

check progress at intermediate times against original schedules, (5) forecast bottlenecks, and (6) replan and redesign to avoid bottlenecks and delays.

POSTLAUNCH CONTROL OF NEW PRODUCT

Once the product is launched, some may feel that the responsibilities of the venture team have been completed. However, the team is responsible for launching a *winning* product, not just a product. Thus, the venture team must exercise managerial control over the new product until it is officially turned over to the marketing and production departments.[3] In performing postlaunch control of the new target the following steps are recommended:

- *Spot potential problems.* The first step is to identify all potential weak spots or potential troubles for the new product. These problems occur either in the firm's actions (such as poor advertising) or in the outside environment (such as competitive retaliation). As one manager said, "I look for things that will really hurt if they happen or don't happen."
- *Select problems for control.* Each potential problem is analyzed to determine its expected impact. Naturally, only problems that would hurt us are on the list, but some problems are more likely than others. The expected impact (expected damage multiplied by probability of occurring) is used to rank the problems and select those that will be monitored.
- *Develop contingency plans for the problems.* Contingency plans are what, if anything, will be done if the problems actually occur. The degree of completeness in this planning varies, but the best contingency plans are ready for *immediate* action.
- *Design the tracking system.* The tracking system must send back usable data fast. We must have some experience to evaluate the data. Trigger points in the data should be determined that will trigger our contingency plans into actions.

On the following pages, we will look into each of these four steps in more detail.

Spotting Potential Problems

Three approaches can be used to develop the list of potential problems. First, many potential problems can be identified by analyzing the *Venture Plan*, initially prepared at the end of the Concept Evaluation stage and updated in preparation for Launch. The Risk Management Plan, Marketing Plan, and Production Plan should be the most fruitful parts of the Venture Plan. A second approach is to role-play what competitors will do after they have heard of the new product. Vigorous devil's advocate sessions can turn up scary options that competitors may exercise—they usually have more options than we think of at first glance. Third, look back over all of the data accumulated in the venture team's files. Start with the concept test reports, then the prototype engineering tests, the prototype marketing tests, and finally the pilot production data and the results of the test market, if conducted. These records contain lots of potential troubles, some of which we have ignored to keep the development on schedule.

Selecting Problems for Control

No one can managerially control the scores of potential problems that come from the analysis in the first step. So the venture manager's judgment must cut the list down to a number the team can handle. The judgment used to reduce the list of problems is usually based on the potential damage and the likelihood of occurrence. Those problems with little harm and little probability of occurring can safely be ignored. However, problems that would be devastating with a high probability of occurring must be monitored continuously. The worst should be taken care of now.

Which and how many problems are selected is very situational, depending on the time pressure, funds available for contingencies, the firm's experience in launch control, and the venture manager's personal preferences. Many venture managers have been burned on previous launches and have developed biases toward certain events.

Developing Contingency Plans

Once we have reduced the problem list to a size the team can handle, we have to ask: "If any of those events actually happens, is there anything we can do?" For example, even though competitive price cuts and competitive product imitation are on many lists, there is usually nothing the firm can do. The competitor is going to try to hold most of its share, and the developer is usually better off to ignore the competitor's actions and market the new product on its own merits.

For other events, our planned reaction depends on the type of event. Let's discuss two types: a company failure and a negative buyer action. One common company failure is inadequate distribution, particularly at the retail or dealer level. Correcting the problem usually requires buying more shelf space from the retailer. Retailers sell the one thing they have—shelf space—to the highest bidder. If a new product comes up short, the remedy is to raise the bid for shelf space—special promotions, more pull advertising, or a better margin.

A negative buyer reaction is handled in a similar manner. To achieve awareness, the marketers' program calls for particular actions (sales calls, advertising, and so on). If it turns out that awareness is low, we usually do more of the same action—increase sales calls or whatever. If people are not actually trying the new item, we have ways of encouraging trial (such as mailing samples or trade packages).

Designing the Tracking System

We now have a set of possible negative outcomes, for most of which we have contingency plans for correction in standby, ready to go when needed. The next step is to develop a tracking system that will tell us when to implement those contingency plans. The concept of tracking as applied to a missile is applicable to a new product. Just as we must track a missile to find out if it is achieving its planned trajectory, we must track the new product to determine if it is achieving its planned results.

In developing the tracking system for a new product, three steps are involved. First, we must describe the *planned results*. What is the expected path the new product will take? What is reasonable given the competitive situation, the product's features, and the planned marketing efforts? Second, there must be an *inflow of actual data* indicating progress against the plan. This means quick and continuing market research geared to measure the variable being tracked. Third, we have to *project the probable outcome* against the plan. Unless the outcome can be forecasted, we have little basis for triggering remedial action until the outcome is at hand.

The key is speed—learning fast that a problem is coming about, early enough to do something that prevents it or solves it.

NOTES

1. Robert D. Hisrich and Michael P. Peters, *Marketing Decisions for New and Mature Products*, 2d ed. (Macmillan, 1991), pp. 417–420.

2. Glen L. Urban, John R. Hauser, and Nikhilsh Dholakia, *Design and Marketing of New Products*, 2d ed. (Prentice-Hall, 1993).

3. C. Merle Crawford, *New Products Management*, 4th ed. (Irwin, 1994), pp. 306-316.

Part III

Extensions of the Corporate Venturing Process

There are several vital concerns about the corporate venturing process that could not be readily included in Part II. These are: How can and should a company tailor its corporate venturing process to best fit its situation? How can and should a person behave in order to be successful in the corporate venturing process? These questions will be answered in Part III.

Chapter 11

Customizing the Corporate Venturing Process

In order to describe the venturing process in depth and still be concise, we have concentrated on describing the process for one situation only. Specifically, we described the process for a medium-sized (about 1,000 employees) high-tech (e.g., computers) company following a revolutionary product strategy (specifically a diversified product) that was focusing on product development, supported by an integrated market and production process development.

The corporate venturing process can and should be customized for differences in organization size, product type, and product development strategy. Additionally, developing new services is considerably different from developing new goods, and this subject is discussed in detail.

CUSTOMIZING THE VENTURING PROCESS

Customizing Venturing Process for Organization Size

We will discuss how the venturing process should be customized for two situations on either side of our medium-sized model company. We will first discuss some of the problems that small companies (less than 500 people) often encounter and how they can be solved. Then we will do the same for large (greater than 2,000 people) complex companies.

The Venturing Process in Small Intrapreneurial Firms

The hands-on, close, and continuing involvement of the CEO (the intrapreneur) in the venturing process is indicative of the small intrapreneurial firm. To be successful, most small companies are running "lean and mean." A fully dedicated venture team is often a luxury they cannot afford. The CEO often acts as a one-man venture team.

Small intrapreneurial companies have some built-in advantages over their larger rivals when it comes to developing and introducing new products. New products generally go through the development process much faster and for a fraction of the cost. Small companies can compete on the basis of development time much more successfully than large companies.

The active role of the CEO in the venturing process tends to keep everyone focused and motivated and helps cut through the various delays and roadblocks found in large companies. Most of the key participants in the venturing process are too busy to get involved in the kind of political infighting that so often slows down and sometimes derails the new product development process in large companies.

However, there are some disadvantages to being a small company. With limited talent, the small company often subcontracts for critical elements of the process or must depend on outside suppliers for critical technology and expertise. This makes them very dependent on these outside suppliers, over which they have little control, and may result in slipped schedules or faulty designs. Small companies must ensure that their outside suppliers are adequately monitored so as to prevent such problems.

Also, the product champion in a small company is likely to be the CEO. This can present a problem, since it is very difficult for an employee to tell the CEO that the CEO's idea is no good, let alone convince him of that fact. If the CEO is convinced that it is a good idea, it will be difficult to kill the venture.

Many small companies, particularly those with strong intrapreneurs as CEOs, feel they know what the customer needs and wants and that marketing research and testing are a waste of time and money. They need to be convinced that they should invest some resources in market research and testing just to find out for sure whether they are on the right track or not. A little money in the beginning can save a lot of grief later.

Often the small company tends to bypass the preparation of the venture plan because of the high interest of the CEO to get the venture underway. This is a mistake. Even though approval of the venture is almost certain, the venture plan should still be prepared, to provide a road map for the future and to identify possible future problems. The venture plan is the starting point for many things to come, and *no* company can afford to omit it. It does not have to be as long as one for a large venture in a large company, but it should still be prepared.

Often the CEO is so emotionally involved with the new product that he or she does not really listen to any of the negative feedback from internal or external people. This means that many of the small improvements that should be made in the product are never made. Thus, one of the challenges in a small company is to set up a review process that has sufficient independence from the CEO to ensure that the deficiencies in the product are identified and corrected before the product is launched.

The Venturing Process in Large, Complex Companies

Most of the books, seminars, and articles that deal with new product development are oriented toward large, complex, multiproduct, and multidivisional companies. Yet in spite of all this literature and the earnest efforts of many dedicated professionals, it often take three times as long, requires three times more people, and costs three times as much for a large company to bring a new product to market than it does for a small company. We will look at some approaches to change this deplorable situation.

Streamline the venturing process. A large company must *streamline the venturing process* to be successful in new product development. By streamlining the process we mean cutting out all those actions that do not contribute to the development of new product. Cut out all unnecessary paperwork and all unnecessary meetings, and get rid of all unnecessary people. New product development is an exciting and interesting activity that attracts many "wannabe" contributors. However, if they are not really contributing, they should not be taking the time and money of those who are.

Keep the core venture team lean, mean, and very professional. The core team is the small group of people that makes all the venture decisions and drives the venture. It must be kept small and professional so that all decisions can be made competently and rapidly. The members of the virtual team are needed to contribute their expertise, but they should not be in the decision-making loop.

Select a strong leader. As we discussed in Chapter 8, no other single decision has more influence on the chances for success. With the right leader, one that high level management respects and trusts, most of the other steps will fall into place. Odds are high that the person you want is busy on sixty other things, and it may take some effort to break him or her free. However, the return on this effort is very high.

Let the venture team manage the venture. The role of high-level management in product development is one of facilitating, not controlling. Only the members of the core team have the information and experience to make proper decisions—let them make them! High-level management should give the venture team the responsibility and authority to make all decisions regarding the venture. They should resist any attempt to bring decision making back upstairs.

Customizing Venturing Process for Product Types

The basic process of new product development can be applied to a wide variety of product types. In Part II of this book we discussed the new product development process for high-tech products. In this section, we will discuss how the process can be customized for the following types of products: a consumer packaged good, a consumer durable good, and an industrial good. Because of its marked difference and importance the new product development process for services is discussed in a special section at the end of the chapter.

New Product Development Process for Consumer Packaged Goods

A *consumer packaged good* can be defined as follows: It usually sells for less than $20; is eaten, drunk, or applied to the body; comes in a very attractive package; is sold in a supermarket or drugstore; and relies heavily on advertising and in-store position and display. Consumer packaged goods account for a sizable majority of new products that reach the market in the United States each year. Not surprisingly, consumer packaged goods companies usually devote a higher percentage of their resources and more of their best and brightest marketing people to new product introduction than do companies developing other product types.

In spite of the attention on introduction, the success rate for consumer package goods is not appreciably better than other product types. There are two reasons for this:

1. Competition for shelf space in the supermarket, the discount house, the drugstore, and other retail chains grows more intense each year. Stores cannot realistically expand their shelf space to display a new product. Each new product must compete against all other products to win shelf space.

2. All too many new consumer packaged goods offer no tangible benefit and often only the scantiest psychological benefit or convenience over products already on the market. Often what is new is very minor indeed. Many new consumer products merely add one ingredient or provide an established product in a new flavor, new package, or new size.

Packaging and branding is important for consumer package goods. The packaging, including the design and configuration of the package, and the brand name of the product are critical to its success. A well-organized consumer packaged goods product development operation gives equal or greater weight, time, and effort to packaging than to formulating the product itself. In such product categories as cosmetics, it is not uncommon for the cost of the packaging to equal or exceed the cost of the ingredients of the product.

Positioning is important for consumer package goods. A new product can be a mass market item that is given strong advertising and marketing support for volume sales in the mass market. Or, it can be a specialty item, precisely targeted to a market niche of customers who have a specific need. The market niche can be an age group, income group, ethnic group, life style group, or any group that has special, identifiable needs. Precise definition of the niche is essential, as is the sharply targeted advertising.

There is no middle ground in the fiercely competitive world of consumer packaged goods. The *stuck-in-the-middle product* that cannot generate the market muscle needed to compete in the mass market and does not have the unique features or benefits necessary to make it a niche product is doomed to failure.

New Product Development Process for Consumer Durable Goods

While consumer packaged goods are truly consumed, consumer durables are characterized by a long life. Typically, they come on a hanger or have an electric plug attached to them, or you sleep on them, sit on them, walk on them, ride in them, or store things in them. Furniture, clothing, automobiles, home appliances, and electrical and electronic products are major categories of consumer durables.

Critical to the success of new products here is a new design, new technology, adding new features and new applications, and providing new benefits, especially cost reduction based on improvement in the technology. In fashion goods, furniture, china, and tableware, design is often everything. New design can be tested in focus groups and consumer panels to lessen the risk of the new product introduction. New technology and new applications of old technology are critical in such areas as consumer electronics and small electrical goods. We will look at new product development in several major fields: consumer electronics, furniture/furnishings, and fashion merchandise.

Consumer Electronics. More than any other category of consumer durables, consumer electronics is still technology driven. Sometimes the application of an already established technology to another product category can create a new market. For example, a major new product category, the food processor, is basically a new configuration of cutting blades, along with a strong industrial-level motor, attractively packaged and promoted to the cook.

However, styling and design are becoming more important as technology brings these products closer and closer to the practical limits of perfection. As these products approach technical perfection, they start assuming many of the characteristics of a fashion product. They are increasingly sold and differentiated primarily on the basis of styling and pricing rather than technical specifications.

Furniture/Furnishings. Niche marketing is widely practiced in this category. Life-style and demographic changes including second homes, condominiums, and smaller families have created specific new product planning opportunities. Product such as waterbeds appeal to specific life-style groups. Outdoor and patio furniture has grown apace with the rise of the barbecue culture in the Sunbelt states. However, some types of furniture associated with life-styles that are fading away, for example, formal dining rooms, parlors, and so on, are now struggling to maintain their sales volume.

Fashion Merchandise. While fashions change quickly, this industry has been slow to adopt the product planning techniques such as market research utilized in other consumer goods categories. Speed of response time is still essential, and here entrepreneurs still make multimillion-dollar decisions on specific lines and styles based on "gut feelings."

In fashion merchandising, it is critical to be in tune with the dominant life styles and values of the target market. In the 1960s, the miniskirt conquered the fashion world because it expressed the spirit of youthful rebellion and embodied the freedom that was the hallmark of those turbulent years. When designers tried to reintroduce the miniskirt in the late 1980s, it was a total bomb, because the psychology and the mindset of the target market had completely changed.

New Product Development Process for Industrial Goods

Industrial goods are marketed to commercial enterprises, governments, and other nonprofit institutions for resale to other industrial customers or for use in the goods and services that they in turn produce. By contrast, consumer goods are sold to individuals and families for personal consumption. The types of industrial products that businesses and other institutions buy include *heavy equipment*, such as machine tools, trucks, and blast furnaces; *light equipment*, such as typewriters, portable power tools, and measuring instruments; *construction*, such as factories, office buildings, and docks; and *component parts*, such as motors, gears, and pumps.

Traditionally, industrial customers have been categorized as users, OEMs (original-equipment manufacturers), and dealers and distributors. The *user* customer is one who buys a product (such as a turret lathe or a grinding wheel) to use in his business. The *OEM* is one who buys a product to incorporate into what he in turn makes and sells. For example, a television-set manufacturer buys electronics parts to put in the sets he makes. Finally, *dealers and distributors* are those who buy products to resell in essentially the same form to users and OEMs. Steel and chemical distributors fall in this third category.

In the industrial market, relationships between the producer and the customer tend to be closer, more complex, and continuing in nature. Many OEMs, such as automobile manufacturers, seek out and often fund companies to develop components for the new OEM products they are introducing, such as a new automobile model. In areas such as machine tools and buildings, the new product is jointly designed, developed, and produced by the producer and user. In some rare cases, even a distributor will arrange with a company to develop a product for which it has experienced a strong need.

Variations in Venturing Process across Product Types

In this section we will track how the various stages of the venturing process (idea generation, concept evaluation, preliminary design, build and test, and launch) change to match the various types of products (consumer packaged goods, consumer durable goods, industrial goods, and high-tech products).

In idea generation, as the product type shifts from a consumer packaged good to an industrial good to a high-technology product, lead users become more important in coming up with new ideas. Such users are likely to experience greater need and may actually modify existing products to meet those needs. By tapping lead users, new needs and new solutions can be identified early.

As the product types shifts toward industrial goods and high-tech products, the role of technology-push ideas and R&D becomes more important. In fact, the developers of industrial goods and high-tech products must be thinking of enhancement to their core technologies as the means by which to fulfill customer needs. If they do not have future technology to meet future needs, they risk developing products that are obsolete as soon as they reach the market.

Engineering and consumer testing of prototypes is undertaken for all types of products. Test marketing is almost always used for consumer packaged goods. Because of higher costs and smaller markets, test marketing is used less often for durable, industrial, and high-tech products. For these products, much more emphasis is placed on prototype testing and the pre-launch analysis.

In industrial products, the user is very often directly involved in testing. If the product is sufficiently important to their production process, they might become involved in joint development. In high-technology products, especially software, there is the concept of a beta test. In a beta test, the user knows that he/she is working with a product that is still in development. But because the user's needs are so acute, the user is willing to live with some "bugs" and work with the product developer to identify and remove the bugs and suggest new features.

Customizing Venturing Process for Venture Strategies

In this section we will investigate how the new product development process should be customized to best fit the venture strategies discussed in Chapter 2. The nine product venture strategies are listed in Figure 11-1.

Evolutionary Product Venture Strategies

Product Cost Reduction. This venture is undertaken to reduce product cost without changing performance. The need for a cost reduction development is normally determined by marketing's assessment of a product's price competitiveness in current markets and not by inputs from customers or technology. A product cost reduction venture is often scheduled during the mature phase of of a product's life cycle, when it is facing fierce cost competition. Very often, the production process is also changed to further reduce the cost of the product.

In the testing stage, only engineering technical tests need to be conducted, since the only thing we need to determine is that the performance did not change. There will be a concerted effort to ensure that the savings necessary to be price

Figure 11-1
Types of Product Venture Strategies

Evolutionary Strategies	*Revolutionary Strategies*
Cost Reduction (COST)	Differentiation (DIFF)
Repositioning (POS)	Diversification (DIV)
Modification (MOD)	Breakthrough (BRK)
Consolidation (CON)	Platform (PLAT)
Imitation (IMI)	

competitive have been attained. Normally a test market is not scheduled for a product cost reduction, since the product is currently well accepted in the market.

Product Repositioning. Although listed under product development strategies, product repositioning is really more of a market development venture. Existing products are retargeted for a different market. There is essentially no performance change to the product and only minor changes in branding, packaging, and the like. Most of the development effort involves developing new marketing programs for the new market. There is no need for product design and testing effort. However, if there is a significant difference between the old market and the new market, consumer testing of the product and even test marketing may be advisable.

Product Modification. A product modification involves altering one or more features of an existing product. The existing product is then discontinued, and the modified product is marketed in its place. The idea for modifying an existing product can come either from customers' needs or technology push. In most cases it comes as a result of advances in technology since the product was first introduced. A full-blown product design need not be conducted since only a minor change is being made to an existing design. In general, modified products will be manufactured by the same production system as the original product, so that no redesign of the production system is required. Engineering and consumer testing of the product prototype is normally done, but test marketing is usually not scheduled since there is so little difference from the original product.

Product Consolidation. The need for a product consolidation is normally generated by the company's high-level management in response to a strategic need to narrow the product line because of a shrinking market share. Normally in product consolidation, a firm endeavors to develop one product that will replace two or more existing products. Instead of having two or more products targeted for two or more market segments, we now have the consolidated product targeted for the entire market. One of the goals of consolidation is to develop a product that can be produced more efficiently and effectively. A firm that is starting to compete on a cost basis in a broad market will often turn to consolidation to achieve a competitive advantage. Very often a market consolidation and a process consolidation are accomplished in parallel with a product consolidation. Normally the consolidated product undergoes the full-blown design and test stages and may be be subjected to test marketing.

Product Imitation. A product imitation is based on quickly copying another firm's product before the originator can achieve success and dominate the market. The idea for the product imitation comes primarily from a competitor analysis in industries, such as the fashion and design industries, for clothes, furniture, and small appliances. Product imitation requires primarily a good capability in *reverse engineering*, where the imitating firm dismantles and analyzes the originator's product and designs one slightly different and, it hopes, better that does not violate patent law. Reverse engineering requires a rapid and competent engineering force but requires little in the way of creative R&D effort. The launch decision should be based on whether the product imitation is sufficiently better than the original product to warrant introduction into the market. Engineering tests should be conducted on the prototype, but consumer tests of the prototype and test marketing can normally be eliminated. These tests are currently being performed, in essence, by the original product in the actual market.

Revolutionary Product Venture Strategies

Product Differentiation. Differentiated products often result when different versions of a product are developed to meet the needs of several market segments exactly. In order better to satisfy the needs of customers, a market is often divided into several segments, with the needs of each segment defined more accurately. Then differentiated products are developed to satisfy the customers' needs exactly in each segment. The development of a differentiated product will normally result in the parallel development of the associated market segment. For best success the product and market development should be coordinated closely. Normally all the stages of the development process are conducted for a differentiated product, except perhaps the test market step.

Product Diversification. Product diversification involves developing a product so different from existing products that a new product *family* is created. Very often, this new product family is sold in a completely different major market and produced by a completely new production process. A product diversification would require a very complex development effort, for both engineering and marketing, since the development is outside the company's area of engineering and marketing expertise. In many cases diversified products are the result of a very intense R&D effort on the part of the company, coupled with considerable marketing research effort. This type of product development requires the full-blown product development process, with nothing omitted.

Product Breakthrough. Product breakthroughs are inventions that are completely new to the whole world. Developing a breakthrough product has all the complexities of diversified products, with a few new ones. Since the product breakthrough is new to the world, both the developer and the customers are completely unfamiliar with the product. The developer must not only perform the normal development but must also determine how the customer can use the product and convey this information to the customer in a non-intimidating manner. All steps of the new product development process are required, with emphasis on customer product testing. Comprehensive and thorough customer product testing of the breakthrough product is required to enable the developer to learn how the customer can best use the product.

Platform Product. The development effort for a platform product involves the development of extensive advanced technology that will support a whole new family of products. The first, or platform product, is not the most important result of the development effort. The comprehensive body of technology that will support the development of an entire family of products is more important. The initial platform products are almost entirely technology driven. Follow-on derivative products will utilize the basic technology to develop products to satisfy different needs. The full-blown product development process is required for the platform product.

NEW PRODUCT DEVELOPMENT PROCESS FOR SERVICES

The basic principles and process for new product development, discussed previously in this book, are as applicable for intangible services as they are for tangible goods. However, there are several significance differences between goods and services that cause the details of the service development process to be somewhat different. Figure 11-2 provides a list of twenty-one ways that services differ from manufacturing. The first thirteen items on the list are of most concern to service developers. In the following pages, we will discuss how these differences influence the development process for services.

Nature of Services

A service is more difficult to identify and define than a good. This problem is mainly due to the intangible nature of services, but the presence of the customer in the service delivery also complicates the situation. To aid in the definition of a service, the concept of a *service package* is used. The *service package* is defined as the sum total of the goods, services, and experiences provided to the customer. It consists of the following four parts:

1. *Core (explicit) Services*. Core services provide the benefits that are readily

Figure 11-2
Differences between Services and Goods

1.	Services produce intangible output.
2	Services cannot be inventoried, i.e., they are perishable.
3	Services are consumed simultaneously with production.
4	High customer contact continues throughout the service process.
5	Customer often participates in providing service.
6.	Service firms are labor-intensive.
7.	Service firms have no R&D or Engineering departments.
8.	Service facilities are decentralized and located near customers.
9.	Services cannot be patented.
10.	Services can be easily emulated.
11.	Response time is more critical for services.
12.	Quality control is primarily limited to process control.
13.	Economies of scale limited for services.
14.	Services cannot be mass-produced.
15.	Services produce variable, nonstandard output.
16.	Skills are sold directly to the customer.
17.	High personal judgment is required by service provider.
18.	Measures of effectiveness are subjective.
19.	Quality of services is difficult to measure.
20.	Pricing options are more elaborate for services.
21.	Except for information services, services cannot be transported.

appreciated by the customer and comprise the essential features of the service. They are the centerpiece of the service offering and are the basic reason for being in business. Without the core services, the business enterprise would make no sense. Examples of core services are legal advice from a lawyer and health care from a physician.

2. *Facilitating (implicit) Services.* The facilitating services need to support, complement, and *add value* to the core services. These are benefits, often psychological, that the customer may sense only vaguely, but they can be very important. They should not be a hodgepodge of "extras," thrown in without forethought. All the facilitating services should provide "leverage," that is, help build up the value of the total service experience in the customer's eyes. Examples are the friendliness of the server, the feeling of competence the server exudes, and the feelings of privacy and security provided.

3. *Facilitating Goods.* The material purchased by, consumed by, or provided to the customer along with the core service. Examples are food items, legal documents, and medical supplies.

4. *Supporting Facility.* The physical resources that must be in place before a service can be offered. Examples are a lawyer's office, a physician's office, a hospital, and an airplane.

In a primary-care hospital, for example, the core service provided the customer (patient) consists of lodging, food service, nursing care, and administering medical treatments ordered by the physician. Facilitating services would be the friendliness of nurses, the cleanliness of the hospital, and telephone and TV services. Facilitating goods would be the medical supplies, food items, bedding, and special clothing. The supporting facility would include the hospital building plus all the installed special medical equipment, such as X-ray machines.

It is helpful to think of the service strategy, service package, and service delivery system as interrelated in the following way:

SERVICE	SERVICE	SERVICE
STRATEGY ---------------)	PACKAGE ----------------)	DELIVERY SYSTEM
Defines the Business	Defines the Offer	Delivers the Service

The service package should follow logically from the service strategy. It constitutes the basic value delivered. The service package concept provides a framework for thinking systematically about the delivery system. The design of the service delivery system must be such that it will deliver the service package in an effective and efficient manner to satisfy the service strategy

When designing the service package, it is important to design concurrently the service delivery system. In manufacturing, one can design the product and process in sequence. Sequential design is not as good as concurrent design, but it can be done. In services, sequential design of the service and the service delivery system is virtually impossible. In most cases the delivery system is the tangible representation of the intangible service, and you cannot design one without designing the other. *Concurrent* design of the service package (product) and the service delivery system (process) is even more important for services than it is for goods.

The Service Organization for Innovation

By and large, service firms do not have the formal organization and procedures effectively to plan and control their new product development activities. Most service firms do not have an R & D or Engineering department. Of the departments normally involved in new product (goods) development (Marketing, Engineering, and Operations), a service firm only has two (Marketing and Operations). The division of responsibility between these two for generating and designing new services is far from clear, although marketing usually generates the ideas and operations usually implements them. Marketers probably play the greater role in service innovation. Since most service firms follow a evolutionary or conservative innovation strategy, marketing tends to concentrate on service modifications rather than new-to-the-world services.

Service Innovation Strategies

For a manufacturing firm, product innovation is often driven by engineering-based technology research. However, for service firms, most new service ideas are customer or need generated. In service firms, customers interact directly with the service process, and this focus on meeting customer needs drives service innovation and explains why customer needs play such a central role in service innovation.

It is important to recognize that service-sector innovation begins with the client or customer. Service concepts or ''products'' in search of customers are more difficult to turn into successes. To work, service innovation requires empathy and listening closely to what clients or customers are saying, even when they are not clearly articulating their wishes. The most successful innovations occur in response to or in anticipation of customer needs or requirements.

The introduction of new technology, however, does have an ancillary effect on service innovation. For example, the TV has spawned the television entertainment industry, and the VCR has generated a video rental business and created a renewed demand for old movies. Thus, new technology can *facilitate* a new service but does not truly generate it. Someone must still figure out how to use it in such a way that people will purchase it.

Services Are Intangible and Not Patentable. Services are intangible products that cannot be patented because the required drawings cannot be prepared. Thus, patents cannot protect new services from competition. Competitors can copy a new service at will. To secure the benefits of a novel service concept, the firm must expand extremely rapidly and preempt competitors. Franchising has been the vehicle to secure market areas and establish a brand name.

Services Use the Imitation Strategy Extensively. The *imitation strategy* is used much more in services than in manufacturing. Since services cannot be patented, there is no law preventing one company from copying the services of another. In fact, imitation is one of the primary ways of developing new services. Services can be reverse engineered much more rapidly than can goods. By copying a competitor in a different geographical area, a service firm can rapidly launch a proven service in its area without any of the normal development cost and risks. Keeping tabs on competitors in their industry is a very good strategy for service firms.

Response Time Is More Critical for Services. Since services cannot be inventoried, they cannot be delivered from "off the shelf" as goods can. As a result, to be successful, the firm's service delivery system must be designed to deliver services more rapidly than the competition. This is especially true of commonplace or commodity services that are available from a number of service firms. Also, speed in developing new services is important to enable the service firm to enjoy the "first-in-the-market" privileges, since patent protection is not available.

The Services Innovation Process

Overall

Service Iterations Are More Frequent. As iterations of the development process are less expensive in services (no tangible good to change), they are shorter and more frequent. Most service developments proceed rather rapidly to prototype stage because there is less cost involved. This lets customers see the "finished" product more quickly, with less trouble in making the changes they suggest.

Services are Labor intensive. In most service organizations, labor is the important resource that determines the effectiveness of service delivery. People are an important component of any new service. If the service is to have high quality and meet the needs of the customers, the personnel must be adequately trained before launching the new service. People are very versatile components that can be shaped to fit into any system; but training is needed to provide the necessary shaping. Training is a more important part of developing and launching a service than it is in manufacturing.

Quality Control Is Primarily Limited to Process Control. Since services are intangible and are consumed simultaneously with production, quality control by means of acceptance sampling of completed services is not feasible. Thus, we must concentrate on controlling the delivery process. In many cases, this comes down to controlling the actions of people. People can be controlled by direction and training, with the latter normally being the most effective.

Service Idea Generation

Most New Service Ideas Are Need Based. Most of the new service ideas are based on the needs of customers. Changes in buyer behavior often create opportunities for new services. For example, one of the most significant developments has been the growing proportion of working women. This has generated an unprecedented level of need for child day care, special shopping services, and the like. Also, the aging of the population and the trend toward deinstitutionalization has created a strong need for home health care, especially for the elderly.

Competitors. Competitors are another powerful source of new ideas in service businesses. It is not uncommon for innovative service ideas to sweep entire industries. Home equity loans have taken the banking business by storm. ''Super-Saver'' fares put pressure on competing airlines to follow suit. Since services cannot be patented, there is no law preventing one company from copying the services of another. In fact, it one of the primary ways of developing new services.

Technology Facilitates New Services. Technology works somewhat differently in the creation of services than it does in the creation of goods. In new goods development, the technology is incorporated directly into the new good, for example, the pentium processor is incorporated into a new IBM personal computer. In services, the technology is incorporated into either the *facilitating good* or the *service delivery system* that *supports* the service. For example, the improvement in the design of the hardware for the Internet has greatly improved the services that the Internet can provide. The new Internet services are a result of the hardware improvements but do not include them. More sophisticated diagnostic equipment can enable a medical professional or an automobile repair shop to offer new kinds of services or shorten repair time.

Complementary Services. Services tend to be subject to severe fluctuations in demand without the ability to use inventories as buffers. Since many service providers have expensive facilities (airplanes, hotels, resort facilities, etc.), they must find some way to utilize these facilities during periods of low demand. Thus, one approach for idea generation for services is developing concepts for *complementary services* to fully utilize facilities during periods of low demand. Hamburger chains add breakfast items to their menus, while coffee shops add dinners to theirs. Northern resorts serve as ski resorts in the winter and as hiking and camping resorts in the summer. Urban hotels that cater to the business traveler during the week offer ''getaway weekend packages'' to the local populace on the weekends.

Designing Services

Design Method Used for Services. Because of the *intangibility of services*, the normal method of design for tangible goods, that of making drawings, blueprints, and such, cannot be used for services. How can you draw an intangible service, such as a massage or a doctor's examination? You cannot. *The best that can be done is to describe the effect of the service on the customer, in words, and then draw a flow chart of the service delivery system.* Since the service delivery system is tangible, it often becomes the focus of development rather than the service itself.

One of the most sophisticated and promising flow-charting approaches to designing service delivery systems is an approach that yields what Shostack calls a service blueprint.[1] The steps involved in developing a service blueprint are as follows:

1. Identify processes. The first step in creating such a blueprint is mapping the processes that constitute the service. Figure 11-3 maps the operation of a bank lending service. *The line of visibility* separates activities of the front office, where customers interact directly with bank personnel in receiving service, from the back-office processing, which is out of customer view.

2. Isolate fail points. Having diagrammed the processes involved, the designer can now see where the system might go awry. On Figure 11-3, the possible failure points are indicated by a white "F" in a black circle. For example, mistakes are possible in "Initial screening" or "Verify income data." The designer must develop a subprocess that will detect and correct the possible errors. The identification of fail points and the design of fail-safe processes are critical. The consequences of service failures can be greatly reduced by analyzing fail points in the design stage.

3. Establish a time frame. Since all services depend on time, which is usually the major cost determinant, the designer should make every effort to minimize time. Places in the service delivery system where customer waiting could be anticipated are indicated by a white "W" in a black triangle.

In summary, a service blueprint is a precise definition of the service delivery system that allows management to test the service concept on paper before final commitments are made. The blueprint also facilitates problem solving and creative thinking by identifying potential points of failure and highlighting opportunities for reducing service times and enhancing customers' perceptions of service.

High Customer Contact throughout the Service Process. The presence of the customer in the service process requires an attention to facility design that is not found in manufacturing. The fact that automobiles are made in a hot, dirty, noisy factory is of no concern to the eventual buyers because they will first see the product in the pleasant surroundings of the dealer's showroom. The presence of the customer on the service site requires attention to the physical surroundings of the service facility that is not necessary for the factory. As indicated earlier, the *supporting facility* is an important part of the *service package*. The quality of service is enhanced if the service facility is designed from the customer's perspective. Attention to interior decorating, furnishings, layout, noise, and even color can influence the customer's perception of service.

Customer Often Participates in Providing Service. An important consideration

Figure 11-3
Service Blueprint of a Bank Lending Operation

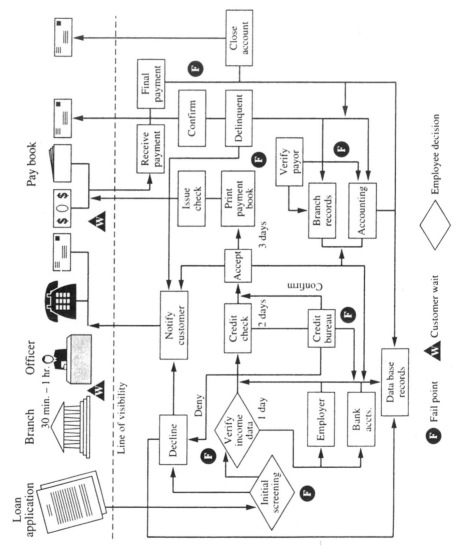

in providing a service is the realization that the customer can play an active part in the process (often called self-service). To obtain customer participation, the customer must receive some value in return for participating. A few examples illustrate how and why customers participate directly in the service delivery system.

- The popularity of *supermarkets* and *discount stores* is predicated on the fact that customers are willing to assume an active role in the retailing process in return for lower prices and faster service.
- The success of *self-service gasoline stations* and *automated bank teller machines* presumes that customers are willing to perform part of the service themselves in return for faster service at less cost.
- In return for the customer accepting a reduced menu, placing the order, and clearing the table after each meal, the *fast food restaurant* provides meals with faster service and lower costs.

Front-Office/Back-Office Operations. A popular design approach to improve the overall efficiency of services is to keep separate from customers those portions of the operations that do not require direct customer contact. For example, in the bank shown in Figure 11-3, only those people shown above the line of visibility (loan officer and teller) need to have contact with the customers. All the others, below the "line of visibility," can perform their jobs more efficiently if they are isolated from the customer. Separation of back-office operations from the front, coupled with modern information technology and international overnight package delivery, makes it possible to locate back-office operations at a considerable distance from the customer and in some instances in other countries.

Building and Testing for Services

Since services are intangible, one cannot really build a service. Instead, one can only build the service delivery system, which is tangible. The development of new goods involves building and testing a prototype prior to full-scale production. However, this testing approach is not possible for services. Service firms cannot really develop a prototype of their service. It is either the full-blown service or nothing. For this reason, services are apt to develop a *pilot* of the service without ever developing a *prototype*. In a pilot the service is in its final form but is offered in a limited location or to a limited market. Currently most new service concepts are proven in the field through pilot testing of the final service rather than laboratory testing of a prototype service.

NOTE

1. G. Lynn Shostack, "Designing Services That Deliver," *Harvard Business Review* 62, no. 1 (January-February 1984).

Chapter 12

Guidelines for Innovators and Intrapreneurs

Survival of the venture in the corporate environment is not easy. Under the best of conditions, the venture is created within a culture that supports and rewards innovation and intrapreneurship. But such an ideal situation is not always encountered. Even in the best-managed firms, would-be innovators face a number of significant obstacles, including the competition for resources. Successful venture managers must know how to use the system to overcome such obstacles and advance their venture.

This chapter is designed to help intrapreneurs achieve greater venturing success in a corporate environment. It shows what they can do to minimize organizational and professional risks and to maximize both the performance of their ventures and their own careers. The probability of venturing success can be improved by understanding and following the principles stated in the following sections.

GUIDELINES FOR INTRAPRENEURING

Guidelines for Interfacing with Parent Organization

As those directly involved in corporate venturing know, a large part of the battle to establish successful ventures depends on managing the internal relationships and the expectations of the sponsoring parent organization. The key problem faced by the venture group and especially by the venture manager is to achieve enough credibility so that they are free to concentrate on managing the venture rather than negotiating constantly with their parent organization.

The need to manage the relationships and expectations of the parent firm arises because every corporate venture is an assault on the status quo. Ventures represent a major deviation from the existing corporate culture and management practices, often pushing both to the limits. Survival in this environment depends on a finely tuned instinct and a different set of rules than those that apply to established businesses.

Be Innovative and Resourceful in Obtaining Approvals

At various stages in the venturing process, the venture manager must obtain approval from the parent organization. The follow subsections offer some ideas obtained from experienced venture managers for obtaining approval for various aspects of the venture.

Ask for the Smallest Possible Decision. The venture manager should strive to keep the magnitude of decisions required by higher authority as small as possible consistent with achieving the venture's objectives. In keeping with the need to establish credibility, the venture manager must concentrate on achieving a first small step that shows the value of the idea rather than on seeking support for the total venture at the outset. Even getting approval for the first step can be a major hurdle in some firms. The process usually begins with proposing a new-venture idea and obtaining funds or time for concept testing. A common procedure is for the idea originator to write up the idea and present it through proper channels for approval and funding.

Don't Ask for Permission. An uncommon, but by no means unknown, procedure is to bootleg the first step—to find a way of accomplishing it without obtaining approval. After having successfully completed the first step, obtaining permission for the second step is much easier.

Use Customers. Customers can often be the venture manager's most effective allies in the effort to secure approval, especially for testing new ideas. An interested prospective customer can demonstrate the need for an innovation to reluctant management and create pressure for rapid approval of the test. Customers often have more credibility than do venture managers.

Use Suppliers. Suppliers can also be enlisted as allies in the process of testing an idea.

Find and Use Allies

In developing a new venture, it is critically important to find allies within the organization. Such allies should include (1) people with knowledge and skills who can contribute to the program; (2) people with influence who will support the program; and (3) an executive champion who can act as a buffer, an adviser, and a guide through the corporate bureaucracy. At DuPont, for example, innovators are encouraged to get assistance from people outside their immediate area of activity. At 3M, innovators are encouraged to seek sponsorship anywhere in the firm they can find it. Having an executive sponsor or champion is an important success factor in venturing.

Form Coalitions

In large organizations, intrapreneurs need coalitions of support to continue their work. This support is more than putting together an intrapreneurial team. Coalition building involves finding sponsors and receiving blessings (either active support or benign neglect) from superiors. Even though there may be a brilliant creative concept, with someone with vision pushing it, it still has to be sold to other people in the organization in order to get it implemented.

What makes venture managers effective in organizations is their ability to develop a whole set of backers and supporters for innovative activities, which helps lend the power necessary to achieve these activities. In this sense intrapreneurs inside a corporation are just like entrepreneurs outside: They have to find bankers, people who will provide the funds; they have to find information sources; and they have to find legitimacy and support, people who will champion the project to other powerholders.

Persuade Management to Relax Policies and Procedures

The culture, policies, and procedures of the parent firm—which often appear to be irrelevant, arbitrary, and a bunch of bureaucratic nonsense to those trying to get a venture off the ground—are nothing more than the adaptive mechanisms that the parent found effective as its business developed. The venture manager must understand the life-cycle stage of the parent business and, with the help of the executive champion, use that information to convince high-level management that current practices of a large corporation in the late stages of its life cycle are not appropriate for a small early-stage venture. Policies and procedures must be appropriate for the stage of the venture's life cycle. It is easier to convince senior management if the argument is presented in terms of differences in life cycle rather than as an attack on bureaucracy and bureaucrats.

Guidelines for Developing an Intrapreneurial Management Style

Undercommit and Overperform

The greatest need and the greatest deficiency of new-venture managers is credibility. To cope with the rapidly changing situation in the venture, venture managers need far greater freedom in decision-making than traditional managers. Yet high-level managers are reluctant to grant such freedom to someone whose credibility has not been established and who does not fit the corporate mold.

The best way to earn credibility is to have a track record of meeting commitments. In building this credibility, it is essential for venture managers to understand that nobody cares how well they do in the absolute sense—only how close they come to meeting their commitments. This is a truth that applies to many situations in addition to venture management. Senior management and others really do not know what a venture (or some other effort) *should* be able to do. They only know what the venture (or some other effort) said they *would* do. Therefore, actual performance is tested against commitments rather than some absolute criteria.

Because meeting commitments is more important than absolute performance, a fundamental rule for venture managers is to undercommit and overperform.[1] This will enable them to develop a track record of consistently meeting commitments, which will build credibility. This rule is particularly applicable when it comes to predicting the level of sales to be achieved by a given time, which tends to be the most unreliable prediction in a plan. Thus, it is advisable for venture managers to predict the lowest sales level at which the plan will be accepted, even if that level is lower than private expectations.

For most ventures, the recommended strategy of undercommitting and overperforming is easier said than done. If you state your venture's goals and values too conservatively, you run the risk of losing the funding battle with ventures that state their goals and values more optimistically. Precisely how far to undercommit must be weighed in the context of each situation: What will it take to get the venture approved? What level of performance can actually be achieved?

Coping with Unanticipated Problems

Any new product or service will be plagued with a variety of unanticipated startup problems.[2] Many of these problems cannot be predicted, no matter how well-planned the venture or how careful the testing program. Really, what is critical is the response. Two typical responses are fatal to the long-run success of a new venture and venture manager. The first is to presume that someone is to blame and then proceed to seek out the culprit. This temptation is strongest when an unforeseen problem is delaying delivery of one of the first orders, raising cost way above estimates and threatening the very reputation of the fledgling venture's performance. Second, in their haste to get early sales and installations, venture managers often seek to ignore, hide, or gloss over early difficulties. Often the rationalization is that every new product is defective and that the difficulties can be solved by retrofitting later, either on the customer's premises or at the end of the line. Such tactics discourage early customers, demoralize staff, and accustom the entire new venture to less-than-perfect quality and poor standards.

The development period is expected to identify flaws in materials, methods, design, and even the concept itself. If not solved aggressively at this stage, these problems will haunt and potentially destroy the credibility of a new venture at a later stage. *Successful venturing involves being sensitive to, tracking down, and solving every unanticipated problem in an aggressive style and avoids seeking to punish culprits or rushing to production before ready.*

Avoid Premature Publicity

Senior management is often tempted to publicize the expected outcomes of a venture long before anything has really been accomplished. Resist this temptation with all your strength. It can result in nothing but harm. Celebration should be postponed until there are real outcomes to crow about. First, members of the parent organization become jealous of the publicity and the exalted status of the venture team, which makes cooperation with them even more difficult. Second, expectations rise. Since these expectations are often not met, this often results in a period of deflation and demoralization.

Premature publicity also aids competitors, by giving them more time and information to counterattack. Granted, there are exceptions, particularly in high-tech ventures, when early publicity can be used deliberately to induce potential customers to postpone buying a competitor's product. Although this type of early-stage publicity may be a strategic necessity, failure to fulfill such promises can have a high reputation cost.

Share Credit

The development of something new unleashes people's creative energy. It is exhilarating, thereby stimulating personnel in a way that routine work cannot do. Giving people the opportunity for innovation and recognizing them for it fulfills both organizational and individual needs. Instead of simply taking all the credit themselves, venture managers should ensure that everyone who worked on or with the venture team gets rewarded. In the long run this will pay big dividends, not only for the individuals but also for the venture manager and the parent organization.

Control Time Expectations

When people hear about a new venture, a clock begins running in their minds. After a certain length of time they run out of patience if they do not see results. When their time is up, it does not matter whether you are ahead, behind, or on schedule—your time is up.[3] Following are three suggestions for controlling these time expectations: First, do not call it a venture until all the risky R & D is completed and you are within striking distance of the market. Second, keep your venture quiet; the clock does not start until people hear about it. Also, the more they hear, the faster their clock runs. Third, if your business uses the product family approach, try to get one member of the family completed quickly and profitably. The existence of a winning product gives hope and resets the clock, even if the total business is not yet making money.

Guidelines for Managing the Venture Team

Choosing Team Members

As you develop your venture plan and identify the factors that mean success or failure for your venture, you will learn what skills are indispensable. Your major selection task is to find those people whose skills complement your own and those of others already on the team, *and who have the right values, beliefs, and attitudes* for intrapreneuring. Team members should be intrapreneurs in their own right. They too must take risks and suffer the indignities of a commitment to a sometimes unpopular cause.

One intrapreneur used an unorthodox but effective method for selecting members of his venture team. He made four lists. First, he went to personnel and obtained a list of people who were "good engineers, but," with the *but* implying some kind of troublemaking. Second, he went to the model shop and asked the machinists which engineers knew what they were doing in a hands-on way. Third, he went to the parking lot and copied the license plates of all motorcycles, pickup trucks, and sports cars. He then referred to the company's roster of license numbers to get the names of the owners. The fourth list consisted of those engineers who skydived, rock climbed, or hang glided. When one name appeared on two or more lists, he knew he had a serious maverick and a person of courage and thus a good candidate for intrapreneuring.

Freeing People to Join Venture Team

One of the most difficult problems in forming a venture team is the resistance of some managers to letting people join the venture team. A division may fight your attempt to hire their people. The intrapreneur rarely has the clout to take on a division in the parent organization. This is one time your sponsor or executive champion is sorely needed. Freeing people for a venture team is an issue on which corporations must change. If they want ventures to succeed, they must let people join venture teams.

Building an Intrapreneurial Team Culture

Very few ventures of any significance are implemented by one person alone. Other people's effort makes it happen—whether they are assistants, subordinates, staff, a special project team, or a task force of peers assembled just for this effort. Regardless of who the people are, it is critical they feel like a *team* in order to make any new idea work. Participative management and full involvement turn out to be critical in the team effort required for a venture.

To be most effective a venture team must develop an intrapreneurial team culture in addition to using good management practices. Development of an intrapreneurial team culture requires performance of the following tasks:

- Provide leadership that produces a can-do, opportunity-seeking, egalitarian venture culture—leadership that is involved, not distant; that creates clarity and focus; and, most important, that offers a vision of what the venture can become.
- Concentrate on people—their selection, training, empowerment, and, as necessary, replacement.
- Delegate whole tasks, not individual actions; manage managers, not their work.

- Ensure evaluation is based on performance, not on behavior, unless behavior is destructive to the culture being sought.

Recognize and Adapt to the Venture's Life-Cycle Management Needs

As the venture progresses through its life cycle, the leadership requirements for the venture change.[4] At the start of the venture, a person with a strong vision and the energy and persistence to make that vision a reality against seemingly overwhelming odds is needed. As the venture progresses through technical development, most ventures require a manager who is at home with technical details and is capable of coordinating a number of engineers in a massive technical design, build, and testing effort. In the launch stage, a person with a good appreciation and knowledge of both manufacturing and marketing is needed. Often, good technical managers are not good at managing "making and selling." Also, the need for administration grows as the venture grows. If this need is not anticipated and met, many problems will result.

Understanding the venture life cycle and its implications is crucial for the intrapreneur. Unless the venture manager acts to supply the needed management skills at each stage, higher-level management may have to intervene. This does not mean that all skills have to reside in one person. Rather, the venture manager must be aware of his or her strengths and weaknesses and must take the initiative in building a team with the necessary combination of knowledge and skills. Self-knowledge and self-honesty are critical prerequisites for achieving the right combination.

THE FOUNDATIONS OF INTRAPRENEURIAL POLITICS

Introduction

Political behavior is the general way by which people attempt to obtain and use power in social settings. Put simply, the goal of such behavior is to get one's own way about things. *Organizational politics* can be defined as the activities that people in formal organizations perform to acquire, enhance, and use *power* to obtain their preferred outcomes in a situation where there is uncertainty or disagreement. *Intrapreneurial politics* is a special case of organizational politics that involves using political behavior in initiating, developing, and launching a new venture within a business organization.

Some managers view both power and politics with suspicion. They associate politics with shady behind-the-scenes dealing and back stabbing. Yet both politics and power are honest tools that people can use to influence others. Both can and should be used ethically for perfectly legitimate ends; that is the approach we emphasize here. Since it is difficult to imagine an organization that is free of political behavior, it makes more sense for intrapreneurs to focus on how to use politics to promote their ventures rather than ignoring or trying to eliminate politics.

Ignoring politics is tantamount to passively accepting its results. Many venture managers have formulated venture plans that were *technically* sound but have had trouble implementing them because they failed to understand the political requirements for starting a venture. Given the small size of the venture relative to the parent and its absolute dependence on the firm's resources, venture plans must be *politically* correct as well as technically correct.

The harsh reality is that all organizations are inherently political, with individuals acting in their own interests. To implement a venture plan, the venture manager must often attempt to influence other people, particularly the key stakeholders on whom the venture depends. Failure to identify these stakeholders and to influence their behavior can drastically slow the venture's progress, if not halt it entirely.

In the following pages, we will first set forth the fundamental principles of using power in an innovative organization. We will then provide a general approach for *intrapreneuring with power*, followed by some specific techniques for using power in the pursuit of the venture's objectives.

Power: The Basis of Organizational Politics

Organizational politics cannot exist without the presence and exercise of power. *Power* is the potential ability of person or group A to influence the behavior of person or group B so that B does something he or she would not otherwise do. This definition implies (1) that power is a *potential* that need not be actualized to be effective, (2) a *dependency* relationship, and (3) the assumption that B has some *discretion* over his or her own behavior.

It is important to note that power is a potential that need not be used. One can have power but not impose it upon anyone. Also, it is important to note that power is a function of *dependence*. The greater B's dependence on A, the greater is A's power over B. Dependence, in turn, is based on the alternatives that B perceives and the importance that B places on the alternatives that A controls. A person can have power over you only if he or she controls something you desire.

Bases and Sources of Power

Realizing that we need power in order to influence other people, from where and how do we acquire power? We will answer this question by describing the *bases of power* and the *sources of power*. **Bases of power** refers to what the powerholder has that gives him or her power. Your bases are what you control that enables you to influence the behavior of others. There are five power bases: coercive, reward, expert, legitimate, and referent. **Sources of power** tell where the powerholder gets his or her power base. There are six sources of power: the

controlling information, critical supplies, or anything that others want, they become dependent on you.

Dependency is increased when the resource you control is *important, scarce,* and *nonsubstitutable,* as discussed in the following paragraphs.

Importance. If nobody wants what you have, it is not going to create dependency. To create dependency, the thing(s) you control must be perceived as being important. Apple Computer, which is heavily technologically oriented, is highly dependent on its engineers, who comprise the most powerful group. However, at Procter & Gamble, marketing is the name of the game, and marketers are the most powerful group.

Scarcity. If something is plentiful, possession of it will not increase your power. A resource needs to be perceived as scarce to create dependency. This can help to explain how low-ranking members in an organization who have important knowledge not available to high-ranking members gain power over their superiors. Possession of a scarce resource—in this case, important knowledge—makes the high-ranking member dependent on the low-ranking member.

Nonsubstitutability. The fewer the viable substitutes that a resource has, the more power your control over that resource provides. If another person has no alternative resources, he is completely dependent on you; and you therefore wield considerable power over him.

Summary

The foundations of understanding power begins by identifying where your power comes from (sources) and what methods (bases) you have available to exert influence. As *sources* of power, individuals can use their position in the structure, their personal characteristics, their knowledge and mental skills, and their resource and information control or can take advantage of their reputation. Control of one or more of these sources allows the powerholder to influence others using one or more of the following *methods*: legitimate, reward, coercion, expert, or referent. The strength of the power exerted by person A over person B is determined by the dependency of person B on person A; the greater the dependency, the greater the potential power.

EFFECTIVE USE OF POWER IN INTRAPRENEURING

In the preceding section we provided a brief summary of the foundations of power and influence. In this section, we will discuss how to use power effectively. We will first discuss the general approach or strategy for using power in intrapreneuring, followed by some specific techniques and the political solutions to several specific problems.

General Approach for Intrapreneuring with Power

What does it mean, to intrapreneur with power? In essence it means to use power effectively in the intrapreneuring process.[7] We will attempt to clarify the meaning of *intrapreneuring with power* by explaining the overall process in five steps:

1. Decide what your venture's vision and objectives are. What are you trying to achieve?
2. Diagnose the venture's environment (especially the parent organization) to determine which individuals and groups are influential and important in achieving your goal.
3. What are their points of view likely to be? How will they feel about what you are trying to do? What are their sources of power and influence? What responses can you expect from them?
4. What are your sources of power and influence? What sources of power can you develop to gain more control over the situation? With your sources of power, which strategies and tactics for using power seem most appropriate?
5. Considering the above, formulate a political strategy and courses of action to achieve the vision and objectives of your venture.

The *first* step is to clarify your vision and objectives. This clarification step serves two purposes: First, it provides a basis for identifying who, inside and outside the firm, will be affected if the venture accomplishes its stated objectives. These people will almost certainly want either to support the venture or to obstruct its progress. Second, it enables the venture manager to identify what kind of help is needed for the venture to succeed.

The *second* step involves systematically identifying all the people, groups, or organizations on whom the venture's outcome depends. These parties include:

- the major internal units that would be affected by the venture's success (for example, departments competing for the resources needed by the venture)
- the venture's prospective customers, distributors, and suppliers and their competitors
- such groups as shareholders, employees, and unions (These groups should be retained only if they are relevant to the outcome.)

We need to recognize that, in almost every organization, there are varying interests. This suggests that one of the first things we need to do is to diagnose the political landscape and figure out what the relevant interests are and what important political subdivisions characterize the organization. It is essential that we do not assume that everyone necessarily is going to be our friend or agree with us—or even that preferences are uniformly distributed. There are clusters of interest within an organization, and we need to understand where these are and to whom they belong.

In the *third* step, we must figure out what point of view these various individuals and subunits have on issues of concern to us. As a starting point we should identify the venture's opponents and allies. The opponents are those groups that will be, or we think will be, adversely affected if the venture succeeds. The analysis should turn up two or three key internal parties who are likely to obstruct the venture's progress. It should also identify two or three key external parties that have a vested interest in the venture's failure. We pinpoint their strengths and weaknesses.

Also, the venture manager should identify key allies inside and outside the firm. All parties that would benefit from the venture's success should be identified. Even if they have not yet become allies, they are potential allies. The allies are the players whose support is most critically needed to promote the venture's progress. Particular attention should be paid to those who can help the venture meet its immediate objectives. With limited resources, the venture manager must rely on the resources of allies whenever they are available.

It also means understanding why they have the perspective that they do. It is all too easy to assume that those with a different perspective are somehow not as smart as we are, not as well informed, or not as perceptive. If we make this assumption, we are likely to do several things, each of which is disastrous. First, we may act contemptuously toward those who disagree with us—after all, if they are not as competent or as insightful as we are, why should we take them seriously? It is rarely difficult to get along with those who resemble us in character and opinions. The real secret of success in organizations is the ability to get those who differ from us and whom we do not necessarily like to do what needs to be done. Second, if we think people are misinformed, we are likely to try to ''inform'' them or try to convince them with facts and analysis. Sometimes this will work, but often it will not, for their disagreement may be based not on a lack of information but on a different perspective on what our information means.

In the *fourth* step we understand that intrapreneuring with power means that to get things done, we need power—more power than those have whose opposition we must overcome. Thus, it is imperative to understand where our power comes from and how our sources of power can be further developed. The previous section on the foundations of intrapreneurial politics provided a beginning, but only a beginning, to what is a very important and fascinating subject. To effectively intrapreneur with power, we need to go beyond this beginning.

We are sometimes reluctant to think very purposefully or strategically about acquiring and using power. We are prone to believe that if we do our best, work hard, are nice, and so forth, things will work out for the best. We don't mean to imply that one should not, in general, work hard, try to make good decisions, and be nice, but these and similar platitudes are often not very useful in getting things done in our organizations. We need to understand power and try to get it. We must be willing to do things to build our sources of power, or else we will be less effective than we might wish to be. The building of reputational power is one of the more important and difficult tasks for an inexperienced venture manager.

The *fifth* and last step is to formulate a political strategy and courses of action for achieving the vision and the objectives of the venture. Since the goals of the venture manager and his or her allies may not be perfectly congruent, one of the first steps is to negotiate agreements with all allies that they will be enthusiastic about implementing. The manager should attempt to structure "win-win" agreements—agreements that will benefit all parties.

We must understand the strategy and tactics through which power is developed and used in organizations. This includes the importance of timing, framing the problem, controlling the agenda, the social psychology of commitment, and other forms of interpersonal influence. These topics are covered very briefly in the next section. If nothing else, such an understanding will help us become astute observers of the behavior of others. The more we understand power and its manifestations, the better will be our clinical skills. More fundamentally, we need to understand the strategies and tactics of using power so that we can consider the range of approaches available to us and can use what is likely to be effective.

Again, as in the case of building sources of power, we often try not to think about these things, and we avoid being strategic or purposeful about employing our power. This is a mistake. Although we may have various qualms, there will be others who do not. Knowledge without power is of remarkably little use. Power, without the skill to employ it effectively, is likely to be wasted. *Intrapreneuring with power means more than just knowing the ideas discussed here. It means being willing to do something with that knowledge. It requires political savvy to get things done—and the willingness to force the issue.*

Specific Techniques for Acquiring and Using Power

In this section we will discuss some specific techniques for acquiring and using power that will supplement the general approach provided in the preceding section.

Techniques for Acquiring Power

Creating First Impressions. Because reputational power is affected by first impressions, it is important to develop a good track record early. If you get off to a poor start, it may be necessary to switch to a different unit within the organization or even to a different organization in order to repair your reputation and get your career moving again. Those who maintain power and influence over a protracted period of time do so because they are conscious of how power, particularly reputational power, is developed and what its sources are. They work to acquire and maintain these sources through planned effort.

Avoiding Fights You Cannot Win. Because of the importance of reputation as a source of power, one should avoid at all costs those issues on which you would lose—even if you are absolutely certain that you are right. Being on the losing side of issues, particularly if it happens repeatedly, gives one the reputation of being a loser. Such a reputation is a serious drain on your power and influence. One should avoid an issue until you have enough time to marshall the allies and support needed to win the fight. Avoiding an issue is not a sign of weakness—it is a sign of smart politics.

Getting People Committed. If people become committed to a task or project, they will pursue that project without further external influence. People will become committed to a project when they choose it voluntarily with little or no external pressure and when their actions are visible and public so that they cannot deny being responsible for them. Thus if we can get a person to undertake any action associated with a project, no matter how small, that person is apt to become committed to the entire project. For example, an automobile salesperson will try to get you to test-drive a car. Once you have made the effort to come to the dealer and drive a car, you are less likely to leave without buying.

Techniques for Influencing the Issue

Using Outside Experts. The opinions of outside experts and consultants carry considerable weight in organizations, and many consultants can be swayed by political interests. Consultants know who is paying them, and even perfectly honest consultants are likely to give opinions consistent with those of their employer. Hiring an outside consultant can be a clever political move for the person who does the hiring. The internal manipulation of numbers and facts to support one's position can be quite damning if you are caught. A better strategy is to employ an outside expert to produce the numbers and answers you need. Outside experts are less likely to be caught; and if they are, you can claim they did it on their own.

Framing the Problem. In much the same way that pictures are framed, questions and problems are framed. The context in which they are viewed and discussed often determines what gets done. Establishing the framework within which issues will be viewed and decided is often tantamount to determining the result. Because the framing of an issue can decide its outcome, it is important to set the terms of the discussion early in the process. The ability to write intelligent memoranda that establish the framework for discussion will enable you to unobtrusively guide future discussions to a conclusion favorable to your viewpoint.

Controlling the Agenda. A person may not be able to persuade a group to reject a particular idea, but he or she may be able to keep the group from ever considering the idea. The person who controls a meeting's agenda, for instance, may consistently put a particular idea last on the agenda and then take up time so that the meeting adjourns before ever considering the item. In Congress, the leaders who control procedural matters hold tremendous power because they can decide whether a bill goes before Congress or not.

Agendas represent a sequence of decisions. These decisions, once taken, may produce behavioral commitments that affect how subsequent decisions are made. Agendas can be used to build commitments to a course of action that might otherwise be impossible to obtain. Because of the committing effects of a sequence of choices, the order of presentation becomes an important tactical decision.

Controlling Decision Parameters. Someone who cannot control an actual decision can, with enough cleverness and forethought, control the criteria on which the decision is based. Suppose a manager wants to hire a friend's son who has an excellent education but little experience. The manager participates in deciding which qualities the job candidate should have and subtly persuades the others that the job requires an intimate knowledge of the latest theories and research. The hiring committee then chooses the manager's favorite on the basis of his education without the manager even being a member of the hiring committee.

Controlling Lines of Communication. Some people create or exploit situations to control lines of communication, particularly access to others in the organization. Secretaries frequently control access to their bosses. A secretary may put visitors in contact with the boss, send them away, delay the contact by delaying the return of phone calls, and so forth. They can use their position to achieve their own ends through political behavior.

Techniques of Timing

Moving First. There are numerous advantages to acting first. By staking out a position, by taking some action that will be difficult to undo, we can compel those who come later to accommodate themselves to our position. Once a project is started, for instance, it is very difficult to stop it. When it is difficult to undo what you have accomplished, your actions serve as a base for further negotiations. You may set both the terms of the debate and the framework for subsequent action. Also, being first often provides the advantage of surprise and the possibility of finding your opponent unprepared.

Delaying. One of the best ways to stop something is to delay it, and a very successful way of delaying something is to call for further study. Delay works for several reasons. First, the proponents of an initiative may simply tire of the effort, particularly if they see it going nowhere. Second, it is possible that backers of a project may no longer be around, if the delay is sufficiently long. Third, delay is effective because decisions sometimes have deadlines associated with them, and a delay may result in rejection.

Using Deadlines. Deadlines are an excellent means of getting things accomplished. They convey a sense of urgency and importance and provide useful countermeasures to the strategy of interminable delay. Deadlines always favor the side that has the momentum or edge. If you are ahead, propose a deadline so that you can win before the tide changes. If a new plan is proposed near a deadline, it cannot receive as much scrutiny and attention as if it had been proposed earlier. Proposals made near the deadline are more likely to pass than if they had been proposed earlier.

Selecting Propitious Moment. Perhaps the scarcest resource in organizations is attention. Time spent attending to one issue is time not devoted to other concerns. Thus, finding the right time to advance one's idea is critical. A good idea at the wrong time will be ignored and shunted aside. On the other hand, an idea for a new product, which would otherwise have languished, may be received eagerly if the time is right, the competition keen, and attention focused on promising new products. This is one reason that persistence so often pays off.

Political Solutions to Major Intrapreneuring Problems

There are two serious situations specific to venture management that can benefit from political solutions. First, venture managers have *very little power* in the parent organization, and they must learn well how to use what they have and also learn how to obtain additional power. Second, venture managers are often *desperately short of resources*, yet they must compete for them internally against powerful, established elements of the parent organization that resent the venture's intrusion onto their resource turf.

Scarcity of Power

Symptoms and Causes of the Power Scarcity Problem. A new venture manager has very little power in the parent organization. Although the members of the venture team recognize the manager's authority, or legitimate power, to direct them, the venture manager has no legitimate power over members of the parent organization nor any coercive, reward, or referent power over members of the parent organization. The only power the venture manager possesses is expert power, which pertains only to the technical aspects of the venture and not to funding or other nontechnical resources. To influence members of the parent organization, the manager must learn to use expert power wisely and endeavor to acquire additional power.

Possible Solutions for the Power Scarcity Problem. To solve the power scarcity problem, the intrapreneur can use the general techniques for acquiring and using power discussed previously. In addition, a number of techniques useful unique to the venturing situation are described in the following paragraphs.

Find a Powerful Executive Champion. An executive champion is a high-level executive in the parent company who acts as a protector and modifier of rules and policies and who helps the venture obtain the needed resources. The executive champion should be an aggressive person who is well respected by all members of the high-level management team and who knows the way through and around the company bureaucracy. Having a forceful and capable executive champion is an important success factor, particularly in the early stages of venturing. One way of approaching a senior manager to become your executive champion is to go to him or her for advice. After giving advice, the senior manager may become so involved that he or she will agree to be your executive champion.

Giving and Receiving Help. Solving problems for someone is an effective way to develop social assets such as liking, gratitude, or obligation that can be used to develop power and influence. Surprisingly, asking for help can generate power just as effectively. People often develop an affinity and a high sense of responsibility for those they assist. Venture managers who seek and follow advice are frequently able to elicit other types of support as well. Individuals who have given advice may also provide endorsements, recommendations, or even funding.

Giving and Receiving Information. Information is valuable currency in a high-tech business. By sharing information that is important to others, the venture manager may be able to build up a credit of obligation or affinities that can be cashed in at a future date.

Giving and Receiving Favors. We can generalize the above strategies and say that any time you exchange favors with another person or group, you will generate a base for influence. Favors can be interpreted broadly to include assistance, information, gifts, invitations, or anything you and the other person value. The idea is to capitalize on the societal norm of reciprocity, which says that we are *morally obligated* to repay favors even though there was no specific agreement for repayment at the time of receipt.

Giving People an Opportunity to Demonstrate Competence. People enjoy a chance to show their skills, flex their muscles, and display their talents. Creating or finding opportunities for others to shine and look competent in public can engender considerable social goodwill.

Scarcity of Resources

Symptoms and Causes of the Resource Scarcity Problem. Any new corporate venture requires an adequate supply of resources, including funds, people, materials, and often access to capacity in the organization's production and service systems. Yet the venture manager generally faces severe constraints in the amount of resources available for the venture. More often than not, the venture manager is seen as an internal competitor attempting to invade the resource turf of the firm's established and powerful departments.

Possible Solutions for the Resource Scarcity Problem. Since venture managers have limited power and funds, they must couple what little power they have with a lot of ingenuity to obtain the necessary resources for their venture. The basic mechanism that venture managers can employ is to co-opt resources that are currently being underutilized. Why should any owner of an underutilized resource willingly give it up, you might ask? The answer lies in the extent to which venture managers can draw on the power they have generated through the power-building processes described in the preceding section. These activities create a reservoir of goodwill, liking, trust, gratitude, and obligations that are often just as valuable as currency to the venture manager—and sometimes more valuable.

There are four main classes of co-optation strategies for taking advantage of underutilized resources: borrowing, pandering, begging, and scavenging. Each of these strategies has distinctive characteristics related to permanence of ownership of the resource and the resource's perceived value in the eyes of the original owner.

Borrowing. Borrowing strategies are employed temporarily or periodically to obtain the use of assets or other resources, on the premise they will eventually be returned. In a "resourceful" example of borrowing, a manager charged expenses for the venture to the accounts of the firm's other divisions. Knowing that this action would not be detected for about a year, he expected he would then have the funds to repay the "borrowed" funds.

Pandering. Pandering involves catering to or exploiting the weaknesses or special interests of others. For example, an intrapreneur needed the assistance of the top physicist in the firm. With no money, the intrapreneur told the physicist that if he would help, his name would be put on the patent resulting from the venture. The physicist agreed to help since the patent represented a valuable and prestigious reward for him. By catering to the physicist's special interests, the intrapreneur obtained the physicist's time by means of a patent he did not yet have and which did not cost a cent.

Begging. Begging or "tin-cupping" strategies are employed to secure resources by appealing to the owner's goodwill. In this way, venture managers gain the use of resources without needing to return them, despite the fact that the owner recognizes the value of the assets.

Scavenging. Scavenging strategies extract usage from resources that others do not intend to use and might actually welcome giving away. This approach involves learning about unused or underused resources and putting such resources to use while relieving the original owner of the burden of getting rid of them.

NOTES

1. Zenas Block and Ian C. MacMillan, *Corporate Venturing* (Harvard Business School Press, 1995), pp. 259–262.

2. Robert A. Burgelman and Leonard R. Sayles, *Inside Corporate Innovation* (Free Press, 1986), pp. 156–157.

3. Gifford Pinchot III, *Intrapreneuring* (Harper and Row, 1985), p. 190.

4. Zenas Block and Ian C. MacMillan, *Corporate Venturing* (Harvard Business School Press, 1995), pp. 274–277.

5. John R. P. French and Bertram Raven, "The Bases of Social Power," in Darwin Cartwright (ed.), *Studies in Social Power* (University of Michigan Press, 1959), pp. 150-167.

6. Stephen P. Robbins, *Organizational Behavior*, 6th ed. (Prentice-Hall, 1993), pp. 413–416.

7. Adapted from Jeffrey Pfeffer, *Managing with Power* (Harvard Business School Press, 1992), to fit the special situation of intrapreneurs.

Appendix

Integrated Venture Map (IVM)

The **Integrated Venture Map** (IVM) enables us to put all our information concerning current and past ventures into a common format to facilitate assessment. The IVM is not only useful for assessing current and past ventures but is also extremely useful in developing the venture strategy and planning new ventures. The IVM can best be understood by going through an example, that of the Cagey Computer Corporation, shown in Figure A-1.

The initial entries, shown in the first column of the IVM, provide the status of products, markets, and processes at the beginning of the map. As shown in the product section of Figure A-1, the Cagey Computer Corporation has a product line consisting of two product families: one composed of three computers (C1, C2, and C3) and the other composed of three printers (P1, P2, and P3). Looking at the market section, we see Cagey is marketing its products in two markets: a Consumer (C) market and an Industrial (I) market. As shown by the initial entries in the IVM in 1990, they are marketing products c1, c2, p1, and p2 in the Consumer (C) market and products c3 and p3 in the Industrial (I) market. Looking at the process section, we can see they are producing the computers (c1, c2, and c3) in their Boston (B) plant and the printers (p1, p2, and p3) in their Hartford (H) plant.

After the initial entries in each area (each horizontal line), there will be no further entries *until there is a change*. Products, markets, or processes that undergo change and cause new entries are indicated by underlined bold italics on the IVM. Development efforts are indicated by dotted lines, with the type of development denoted by three-letter abbreviations, which were explained in Figure 2-1 and the ensuing discussion. For example, on line 5 in column 1991, entry (P1—COST→*P11*) indicates that product P1 underwent a *cost reduction* type of development and was replaced by the lower-priced product P11. To

Figure A-1
Integrated Venture Map for the Cagey Computer Corporation

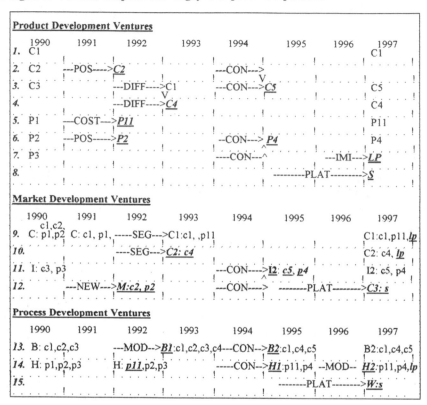

facilitate locating entries on the map, we will provide the year and line in braces after the entry, for example (P1—COST→*P11*) {91–5}.

In 1991, Cagey undertook two product development actions. First, it decided to *modify* its lowest-price printer (P1) to make it faster and more cost competitive. This action is noted on the IVM by (P1—COST→*P11*) {91–5}. Since this was not a major modification, it did not require any concurrent market or process development. Second, the company decided to *reposition* C2 and P2 to the military market to compete for a large number of computers the military was planning to buy. This is indicated by (—POS→*C2*) {91–2} and (—POS→*P2*) {91–6}. From a product development standpoint, the effort was minimal, since the equipment already satisfied most of the military specifications. However, for marketing this meant developing a new market (—NEW→*M*) {91–12}. Marketing to the military is unlike marketing to any other market. The dotted line indicates a causal or time relationship between two or more developments in different areas. In this case the line indicates that the repositioning of products C2 and P2 caused the development of market M.

In 1992, Cagey undertook two closely related developments. First, the company conducted a market *segmentation* development to divide its consumer market (C) into two separate markets: the *domestic* consumer market, C1, and the *foreign* consumer market, C2 (—SEG→*C1*) {92–9} and (—SEG→*C2*) {92–10}. At the same time it conducted a product *differentiation* development of its C1 computer to develop the C4 computer, which was especially configured for the foreign market (—DIFF→*C4*) {92–4}. The C4 computer was enough different that it required a process *modification* development for the Boston (B) plant (—MOD→*B1*) {92–13}.

In 1993 there were no development efforts. The entries in the market and process areas are bringing the IVM up to date regarding what products are assigned to which markets and which processes. However, 1993 was not a very good year for Cagey. It completely missed the boat on the military market and was rapidly losing market share in all other markets, except the foreign market.

In 1994, Cagey decided to downsize and retrench. This required *consolidating* developments in all three areas. In the product area, a consolidation development effort was initiated to replace computers C2 and C3 with computer C5 (—CON→*C5*) {94–2&3} and to replace printers P2 and P3 with printer P4 (—CON→*P4*) {94–6&7}. In the market area, a consolidation development effort was initiated to retreat from the military market and form one industrial market (—CON→*I2*) {94–11}. In the process area, both plants underwent a *consolidation* development reducing the size and variety of their processes and improving their efficiency (—CON→*B1*) and (—CON→*H1*) {94–13&14}.

In 1995, Cagey made a bold but risky move by electing to go into the software business. This was initiated and made possible by its new CEO, who came from Microsoft and brought a number of software engineers with her. They rented a facility in Worcester to be the nucleus for current and future software work (—PLAT→*W*) {95–15} and started a *platform* software development effort (—PLAT→*S*) {95–8} to develop the Ultimate Web Browser as its first product. However, this was to be only the first in a long string of Internet software products. Since marketing software is completely different from marketing computer equipment, a *platform* marketing development was also initiated (—PLAT→*C3*) {95–12}. Note the longer development times for these *platform* development efforts.

In 1996, Cagey decided to get into the laser printer business. It did this not by an original development effort but by reverse engineering laser printers from Hewlett-Packard, Canon, and others. This is indicated by (—IMI→*LP*) {96–7}. Note the short development time for an *imitation* development. No market development was needed, but a modification was needed at the Hartford plant to manufacture it (—MOD→*H2*) {96–14}.

In 1997, for demonstration purposes, we entered the final status of the products, markets, and processes in each area. If this were a real continuing IVM, these status entries would not be made, and only change entries would be made.

The example that we just completed doesn't adequately demonstrate the power of the IVM. Reducing the size of the IVM to fit the page of a book requires crowding a lot of information into a small space. Having to use abbreviations and other shorthand devices makes it more difficult to read and understand. Also, we had Cagey Computer do a lot of radically different things in a short time frame, just to demonstrate the IVM. With these artificialities removed, the IVM becomes a much more usable tool. Being able to use the actual names of the products, markets, and processes would make the IVM much easier to read and use.

The main benefit of the IVM comes from having engineering, marketing, and production talking in the same language and using the same map to facilitate planning integrated development ventures. The map tells not only where you have been but where you are going.

Selected Bibliography

GENERAL CORPORATE CULTURE

Belasco, James A., and Ralph C. Stayer. *Flight of the Buffalo*. Warner Books, 1993.
Deal, Terence E., and Allan A. Kennedy. *Corporate Cultures*. Addison-Wesley, 1982.
Garfield, Charles. *Second to None*. Irwin, 1992.
Higgins, James M. *Innovate or Evaporate*. Management Publishing, 1995.
O'Toole, James. *Vanguard Management*. Doubleday, 1985.
Ouchi, William G. *Theory Z*. Avon Books, 1981.
Pascale, Richard T., and A. G. Athos. *The Art of Japanese Management*. Warner, 1981.
Schein, Edgar H. *Organizational Culture and Leadership*, 2d ed. Jossey-Bass, 1992.
Trice, H. M., and J. M. Beyer. *The Cultures of Work Organizations*. Prentice-Hall, 1993.

CONTENT OF AN INNOVATIVE CULTURE

Berger, Brigette. *Culture of Entrepreneurship*. ICS Press, 1991.
Collins, James C., and Jerry I. Porras. *Built to Last*. HarperBusiness, 1994.
Kotter, John P., and James L. Heskett. *Corporate Culture and Performance*. Free Press, 1992.
Kunda, Gideon. *Engineering Culture*. Temple University Press, 1992.
Naisbitt, John. *Megatrends: Ten New Directions Transforming Our Lives*. Warner Books, 1982.
Naisbitt, John, and Patricia Aburdene. *Megatrends 2000*. William Morrow, 1990.
Naisbitt, John, and Patricia Aburdene. *Reinventing the Corporation*. Warner Books, 1985.
Peters, Tom. *Liberation Management*. Knopf, 1992.
Peters, Tom. *Thriving on Chaos: Handbook for a Management Revolution*. Knopf, 1987.
Peters, Tom. *The Tom Peters Seminar*. Vintage, 1994.
Peters, Tom, and Nancy Austin. *A Passion for Excellence*. Random House, 1985.
Peters, Tom, and Robert H. Waterman, Jr. *In Search of Excellence*. Harper and Row, 1982.

Schneider, Benjamin (ed.). *Organizational Climate and Culture*. Jossey-Bass, 1990.
Schneider, William E. *The Reengineering Alternative*. Irwin, 1994.
Toffler, Alvin, and Heidi Toffler. *Powershift*. Bantam Books, 1990.
Waterman, Robert H. *What America Does Right*. Norton, 1994.

STRATEGIC AND CULTURAL LEADERSHIP

Block, Peter. *The Empowered Manager*. Jossey-Bass, 1987.
Block, Peter. *Stewardship*. Berret-Koehler, 1996.
Conger, Jay A. *The Charismatic Leader*. Jossey-Bass, 1991.
Jones, Patricia, and Larry Kahaner. *Say It and Live It*. Currency Doubleday, 1995.
Kouzes, James M., and B. Z. Posner. *The Leadership Challenge*, 2d ed. Jossey-Bass, 1995.
Kozmetsky, George. *Transformational Management*. Ballinger, 1985.
Leavitt, Harold J. *Corporate Pathfinders*. Penguin, 1986.
Nanus, Burt. *Visionary Leadership*. Jossey-Bass, 1992.
Wall, Bob, Robert S. Slocum, and Mark R. Sobol. *The Visionary Leader*. Prima, 1992.
Wilkins, Alan L. *Developing Corporate Character: How to Successfully Change an Organization without Destroying It*. Jossey-Bass, 1989.

ORGANIZING FOR INNOVATION

Ackoff, Russel L. *The Democratic Corporation*. Oxford University Press, 1994.
Crawford, Richard. *In the Era of Human Capital*. HarperBusiness, 1991.
Davidow, William H., and M. S. Malone. *The Virtual Corporation*. HarperBusiness, 1992.
Handy, Charles. *The Age of Unreason*. Harvard Business School Press, 1989.
Handy, Charles. *Understanding Organizations*. Harvard Business School Press, 1993.
Handy, Charles. *The Age of Paradox*. Harvard Business School Press, 1995.
Lipnack, Jesson L., and Jeffrey Stam. *The Age of the Network*. Omneo, 1994.
McLagan, Patricia, and Christo Nel. *The Age of Participation*. Berrett-Koehler, 1995.
O'Toole, James. *Leading Change*. Ballantine Books, 1996.
Quinn, James Brian. *Intelligent Enterprise*. Free Press, 1992.
Savage, Charles M. *Fifth Generation Management*. Digital Press, 1990.
Senge, Peter M. *The Fifth Discipline*. Doubleday Currency, 1990.
Tapscott, Don, and Art Cast. *Paradigm Shift*. McGraw-Hill, 1993.

EMPLOYEE MANAGEMENT AND TEAMWORK

Belcher, John G. *Productivity Plus*. Gulf Publishing, 1987.
Boyett, Joseph H., and Henry P. Conn. *Workplace 2000*. Plume, 1991.
Carr, Clay. *The Competitive Power of Constant Creativity*. AmaCom, 1994.
Case, John. *Open-Book Management*. HarperBusiness, 1995.
DuBrin, Andrew J. *Reengineering Survival Guide*. Thompson Executive Press, 1996.
Gretz, Karl F., and Steven R. Drozdeck. *Empowering Innovative People*. Probus Publishers, 1994.
Lawler, Edward E., III. *High-Involvement Management*. Jossey-Bass, 1986.

Manz, Charles C., and Henry P. Sims. *Business without Bosses*. Wiley, 1993.
McLagan, Patricia, and Christo Nel. *The Age of Participation*. Berrett-Koehler, 1995.
Schrage, Michael. *No More Teams*. Currency Doubleday, 1995.

IMPLEMENTING CULTURAL CHANGE AND IMPROVEMENT

Deevy, Edward. *Creating the Resilient Organization*. Prentice-Hall, 1995.
Drennan, David. *Transforming Company Culture*. McGraw-Hill, 1992.
Hampden-Turner, Charles. *Creating Corporate Culture*. Addison-Wesley, 1992.
Kilmann, Ralph H., Mary J. Saxton, and Roy Serpa (eds.). *Gaining Control of the Corporate Culture*. Jossey-Bass, 1985.
Lessem, Ronnie. *Managing Corporate Culture*. Gower, 1990.
Pritchett, Price. *Culture Shift*. Pritchett and Associates, 1993.
Wilkins, Alan L. *Developing Corporate Character: How to Successfully Change an Organization without Destroying It*. Jossey-Bass, 1989.

TOTAL QUALITY MANAGEMENT

Bounds, Greg, Lyle Yorks, Mel Adams, and Gipsie Ranney. *Beyond Total Quality Management: Toward the Emerging Paradigm*. McGraw-Hill, 1994.
Dean, James W., and James R. Evans. *Total Quality*. West, 1994.
Goetsch, David L., and Stanley Davis. *Introduction to Total Quality*. Macmillan, 1994.
Harrington, H. James. *Total Improvement Management*. McGraw-Hill, 1995.
Hutton, David W. *The Change Agent's Handbook*. ASQC, 1994.
Joiner, Brian L. *Fourth Generation Management*. McGraw-Hill, 1994.
Wilkins, Robert H. *The Quality Empowered Business*. Prentice-Hall, 1994.

QUALITY FUNCTION DEPLOYMENT (QFD)

Akao, Yoji. *Integrating Customer Requirements into Product Design*. Productivity Press, 1990.
Barnard, William, and Douglas Daetz. *Building Competitive Advantage Using QFD: A Comprehensive Guide for Leaders*. Oliver Wight Publications, 1994.
Barnard, William, and Thomas F. Wallace. *The Innovation Edge: Creating Strategic Breakthroughs Using the Voice of the Customer*. Oliver Wight Publications, 1994.
Bossart, James. *Quality Function Deployment: A Practitioner's Approach*. ASQC Press, 1991.
King, Bob. *Better Designs in Half the Time—Implement QFD in America*. Goal/QPC, 1987.

REENGINEERING AND PROCESS MANAGEMENT

Burton, Terence T., and John W. Moran. *The Future Focused Organization*. Prentice-Hall PTR, 1995.
Dimancescu, Dan. *The Seamless Enterprise*. Omneo, 1992.

Hammer, Michael, and James Champy. *Reengineering the Corporation*. HarperBusiness, 1993.

Hammer, Michael, and Steven A. Stanton. *The Reengineering Revolution*. Harper-Business, 1995.

Hunt, V. Daniel. *Process Mapping*. Wiley, 1996.

Hunt, V. Daniel. *Reengineering*. Omneo, 1993.

Nolan, Richard L., D. B. Stoddard, T. H. Davenport, and S. Jarvenpaa. *Reengineering the Organization*. Harvard Business School Publishing, 1995.

Nonaka, Ikujio, and Hirotaka Takeuchi. *The Knowledge-Creating Company*. Oxford University Press, 1995.

DESIGN FOR MANUFACTURABILITY (DFM)

Boothroyd, Geoffrey. *Assembly and Product Design*. Marcel Dekker, 1992.

Boothroyd, Geoffrey, and Peter Dewhurst. *Product Design for Assembly*. Wakefield, RI: Boothroyd Dewhurst, Inc., 1989.

Boothroyd, Geoffrey, Peter Dewhurst, and Winston A. Knight. *Product Design for Manufacturing*. Marcel Dekker, 1994.

Bralla, James G. (ed.). *Handbook of Product Design for Manufacturing: A Practical Guide to Low-Cost Production*. McGraw-Hill, 1986.

Cubberly, William H., and Ramon Bakerjian. *Tools and Manufacturing Engineers Handbook*. Society of Manufacturing Engineers, 1989.

Trucks, H. E. *Designing for Economical Production*. 2d ed. Society of Manufacturing Engineers, 1987.

TECHNOLOGICAL INNOVATION

Burgelman, Robert A., and L. R. Sayles. *Inside Corporate Innovation*. Free Press, 1986.

Clark, Peter, and Neil Stanton. *Innovation in Technology and Organization*. Routledge, 1989.

Drucker, Peter F. *Innovation and Entrepreneurship*. Harper and Row, 1985.

Ettlie, John E. *Taking Charge of Manufacturing*. Jossey-Bass, 1988.

Foster, Richard. *Innovation: The Attacker's Advantage*. Summit Books, 1986.

Freedman, George. *The Pursuit of Innovation*. AmaCom, 1988.

Gattiker, Urs E. *Technology Management in Organizations*. Sage, 1990.

Goodman, Richard A., and Michael W. Lawless. *Technology and Strategy*. Oxford University Press, 1994.

Henry, Jane, and David Walker (eds.). *Managing Innovation*. Sage, 1991.

Hill, Christopher T., and James M. Utterback. *Technological Innovation for a Dynamic Economy*. Pergamon Press, 1979.

Humphrey, Watts S. *Managing for Innovation*. Prentice-Hall, 1987.

Jelenek, Mariann, and Claudia B. Schoonhoven. *Innovation Marathon*. Blackwell, 1990.

Jewkes, John, David Sawers, and Richard Stillerman. *The Sources of Invention*. 2d ed. Norton, 1969.

Leonard-Barton, Dorothy. *Wellsprings of Knowledge*. Harvard Business School Press, 1995.

O'Neil, Gerard K. *The Technology Edge*. Simon and Schuster, 1983.

Roberts, Edward B. *The Dynamics of Research and Development*. Harper and Row, 1964.

Roman, Daniel D. *Science, Technology, and Innovation*. Grid, 1980.
Rothwell, Roy, and Walter Zegveld. *Reindustrialization and Technology*. Sharpe, 1985.
Tushman, Michael L., and William L. Moore (eds.). *Readings in the Management of Innovation*. HarperBusiness, 1988.
Utterback, James M. *Mastering the Dynamics of Innovation*. Harvard Business School Press, 1994.
von Hippel, Eric. *The Sources of Innovation*. Oxford University Press, 1988.
Wild, Ray (ed.). *Technology and Management*. Nichols Publishing, 1990.

PRODUCT INNOVATION STRATEGIES

Blaich, Robert, and Janet Blaich. *Product Design and Corporate Strategy*. McGraw-Hill, 1993.
Keen, Peter G. W. *Competing in Time*. Ballinger, 1988.
McGrath, Michael E. *Product Strategy for High Technology Companies*. Irwin, 1995.
O'Hare, Mark. *Innovate! Strategies for Gaining Competitive Advantage*. Blackwell, 1988.
Robert, Michel. *Product Innovation Strategy Pure and Simple*. McGraw-Hill, 1995.
Rouse, William B. *Strategies for Innovation*. Wiley, 1992.
Wheelwright, Steven C., and Kim B. Clark. *Leading Product Development*. Free Press, 1995.
Zangwill, W. *Lightning Strategies for Innovation: How the World's Best Firms Create New Products*. Society of Manufacturing Engineers, 1993.

NEW PRODUCT DEVELOPMENT

Bowen, H. Kent, Kim B. Clark, Charles A. Holloway, and Steven C. Wheelwright (eds.). *The Perpetual Enterprise Machine*. Oxford University Press, 1994.
Buggie, Frederick D. *New Product Development Strategies*. AmaCom, 1981.
Clark, Kim B., and Steven C. Wheelwright. *Managing New Product and Process Development*. Free Press, 1993.
Dimancescu, Dan, and Kemp Dwenger. *World Class New Product Development*. AmaCom, 1996.
Erhorn, Craig, and John Stark. *Competing by Design*. Omneo, 1994.
Gevirts, Charles D. *Developing New Products with TQM*. McGraw-Hill, 1994.
Kmetovicz, Ronald E. *New Product Development: Design and Analysis*. Wiley, 1992.
Kuczmarski, Thomas D. *Managing New Products*. 2d ed. Prentice-Hall, 1990.
Martin, Michael. *Managing Innovation and Entrepreneurship in Technology Based Firms*. Wiley, 1993.
McGrath, Michael E., M. T. Anthony, and A. R. Shapiro. *Product Development: Success through Product and Cycle Time Excellence*. Butterworth-Heinemann, 1992.
Patterson, Marvin L. *Accelerating Innovation*. Van Nostrand Reinhold, 1993.
Roberts, Michel, and Alan Weiss. *The Innovation Formula*. Harper and Row, 1988.
Rosenthal, S. R. *Effective Product Design and Development*. Business One Irwin, 1992.
Shostack, G. Lynn, "Designing Services That Deliver." *Harvard Business Review* 62, no. 1 (January-February 1984).
Slade, Bernard N. *Compressing the Product Development Cycle from Research to Marketplace*. AmaCom, 1993.

Smith, Preston G., and Donald G. Reinertsen. *Developing Products in Half the Time.* Van Nostrand Reinhold, 1995.
Souder, William E. *Managing New Product Innovations.* Lexington Books, 1987.
Sowrey, Trevor. *The Generation of Ideas for New Products.* London: Logan Press, 1987.
Thomas, Robert J. *New Product Development.* Wiley, 1993.
Ulrich, Karl T., and S. D. Eppinger. *Product Design and Development.* McGraw-Hill, 1995.
Wheelwright, Steven C., and Kim B. Clark. *Revolutionizing Product Development.* Free Press, 1992.
Wilson, Clement C., Michael E. Kennedy, and Carmen J. Trammell. *Superior Product Development.* Blackwell, 1996.

PRODUCT MANAGEMENT

Crawford, C. Merle. *New Products Management.* 3d ed. Irwin, 1990.
Gruenwald, George. *New Product Development.* 2d ed. NTC Business Books, 1992.
Hisrich, Robert D. and Michael P. Peters. *Marketing Decisions for New and Mature Products.* Macmillan, 1991.
Lehman, Donald R., and Russell S. Winer. *Product Management.* Irwin, 1994.
Scheuing, Everhard. *New Product Management.* Merrill, 1989.
Urban, Glen L., John R. Hauser, and Nikhilsh Dholakia. *Design and Marketing of New Products*, 2d ed. Prentice-Hall, 1993.

CORPORATE VENTURING AND INTRAPRENEURSHIP

Block, Zenas, and Ian C. MacMillan. *Corporate Venturing.* Harvard Business School Press, 1995.
Brandt, Steven C. *Entrepreneuring in Established Companies.* Dow-Jones Irwin, 1986.
Cornwall, Jeffrey R., and Baron Perlman. *Organizational Entrepreneurship.* Irwin, 1990.
Jennings, Reg, Charles Cox, and Cary L. Cooper. *Business Elites: The Psychology of Entrepreneurs and Intrapreneurs.* Routledge, 1994.
Lynn, Gary S., and Norman M. Lynn. *Innopreneurship.* Probus, 1992.
Pfeffer, Jeffrey. *Managing with Power.* Harvard Business School Press, 1992.
Pinchot, Gifford III. *Intrapreneuring.* Harper and Row, 1985.

Index

About the Author

HOWARD W. ODEN is Associate Professor of Management at Nichols College. He served 25 years as a Naval Officer, the first fifteen years in submarines and the last ten as a manager of new product development. Since retiring as a Captain in 1977, he has taught and consulted in product development and operations management and earned a doctorate in business administration. He has written over 40 technical papers and the book *Handbook of Material and Capacity Planning (1993)*.